Stalinist Restructuring in Estonia

TARTU HISTORICAL STUDIES

Edited by
Eero Medijainen and Olaf Mertelsmann

VOLUME 7

Zu Qualitätssicherung und Peer Review der vorliegenden Publikation

Die Qualität der in dieser Reihe erscheinenden Arbeiten wird vor der Publikation durch beide Herausgeber der Reihe geprüft.

Notes on the quality assurance and peer review of this publication

Prior to publication, the quality of the work published in this series is reviewed by both editors of the series.

Olaf Mertelsmann

Stalinist Restructuring in Estonia

From Market to Command Economy

PETER LANG

Berlin - Bruxelles - Chennai - Lausanne - New York - Oxford

Bibliographic Information published by the DeutscheNationalbibliothek
The Deutsche Nationalbibliothek lists this publication in the DeutscheNationalbibliografie; detailed bibliographic data is available in the internet at http://dnb.d-nb.de.

Library of Congress Cataloging-in-Publication Data
A CIP catalog record for this book has been applied for at the Library of Congress.

Förderung durch: The University of Tartu Foundation through the Contemporary History Scholarship; Base Funding by the University of Tartu (PHVAJ17907); Project PRG364 "Reshaping Estonian Energy, Mobility and Telecommunications Systems on the Verge of the Second Deep Transition."
Überarbeitete und aktualisierte Übersetzung von: Olaf Mertelsmann: Der stalinistische Umbau in Estland. Von der Markt- zur Kommandowirtschaft, Hamburg: Verlag Dr. Kovač, 2006.

ISSN 2191-0480

ISBN 978-3-631-91916-3 (Print)
E-ISBN 978-3-631-91917-0 (E-PDF)
E-ISBN 978-3-631-91918-7 (E-PDF)
DOI 10.3726/b21838

Published by Peter Lang GmbH, Berlin, Germany

info@peterlang.com - www.peterlang.com

Table of Contents

List of Abbreviations

CC	Central Committee
CPSU	Communist Party of the Soviet Union
ECP	Estonian Communist Party
ERAF	Branch of Estonian State Archives—Eesti Riigiarhiivi Filiaal
ERA	Estonian State Archives—Eesti Riigiarhiiv
ERM-KV	Estonian National Museum: Archive of the Replies of the Correspondents of the Museum—Eesti Rahva Muuseum—Korrespondentide vastuste arhiiv.
ESSR	Estonian Soviet Socialist Republic
GARF	State Archives of the Russian Federation—Gosudarstvennyi arkhiv Rossiiskoi Federatsii
GDP	Gross Domestic Product
GmbH	Limited Liability Company—Gesellschaft mit beschränkter Haftung
GNP	Gross National Product
Gosplan	State Planning Committee—Gosudarstvennyi komitet po planirovaniiu
KM-EKLA	Estonian Literary Museum: Estonian Archive of Cultural History—Eesti Kirjandusmuuseum—Eesti Kultuurilooline Arhiiv
MTS	Machine-Tractor Station
NKVD	People's Commissariat of Internal Affairs
Orgnabor	Organized Recruitment of Labor
RA	Estonian National Archives—Rahvusarhiiv
RGAE	Russian State Archive of Economics—Rossiiskii gosudarstvennyi arkhiv ekonomiki
RGASPI	Russian State Archive of Socio-Political History—Rossiiskii gosudarstvennyi arkhiv sotsial'no-politicheskoi istorii
SA	Sturmabteilung
SD	Security Service of the Reichsführer-SS—Sicherheitsdienst des Reichsführers-SS
USSR	Union of Soviet Socialist Republics
VKP(b)	All-Russian Communist Party (Bolsheviks)

List of Tables

Preface

For more than a decade, I was involved with a large research project called "The Sovietization of Estonian Society 1940–1956." After studying a wealth of archival documents related to economic history—a topic not well represented in research on Soviet history in the last two decades—I decided to publish a monograph on the economic side of Sovietization and prepare a social history afterwards. A German edition of this book appeared in 2006.[1] The reviews and responses by colleagues encouraged me to update the text based on new literature and additional sources from Russian and Estonian archives and to translate the monograph into English.[2] There are few works on postwar Soviet economic history based on archival research, so I hope this research has contributed something to the field.

My long-standing research on the Soviet period of Estonia's history has been supported at different times by the German Academic Research Office, the German Research Foundation, the Estonian Science Foundation, the Estonian Research Council, Base Funding by the University of Tartu, a Contemporary History Scholarship by the University of Tartu Foundation and by the projects "Globalizing Europe Economic History Network," headed by Stefano Battilosi (European Science Foundation), "Estonia in the Era of the Cold War," led by Tõnu Tannberg, "Baltic Regionalism," headed by Eero Medijainen, "Reshaping Estonian Energy, Mobility and Telecommunications Systems on the Verge of the Second Deep Transition," led by Margit Keller and the project "Baltic100". I was able to benefit from an Adam Smith Fellowship at the University of Glasgow, regular invitations to the University of Umeå, and work done at the former Center for the Study of Soviet History at the University of Tartu.

I have to thank many colleagues for advice, critiques, or support during my long encounter with Soviet history, especially Rutt Hinrikus, Eero Medijainen, Aadu Must, Aigi Rahi-Tamm, Tõnu Tannberg, and Jaak Valge in Tartu, Karsten Brüggemann and Martin Klesment in Tallinn, Riitta Hjerppe in Helsinki, Irēna

1 Olaf Mertelsmann, *Der stalinistische Umbau in Estland: Von der Markt- zur Kommandowirtschaft* (Hamburg, 2006).

2 This research was supported by the University of Tartu Foundation through the Contemporary History Scholarship, Base Funding by the University of Tartu (PHVAJ17907) and the project PRG364 "Reshaping Estonian Energy, Mobility and Telecommunications Systems on the Verge of the Second Deep Transition."

Saleniece in Daugavpils, Elena Zubkova in Moscow, Hans Jörgensen in Umeå, Norbert Angermann in Hamburg, David Feest in Lüneburg, David J. Smith and Geoffrey Swain in Glasgow, and S. G. Wheatcroft in Melbourne. Starting in 2019, the team from our "Second Deep Transition" project inspired me to rethink part of my argumentation; many thanks go especially to Erki Tammiksaar and Laur Kanger. In addition, I wish to thank the competent librarians and archivists of the Estonian National Archives, the Estonian National Museum, the Estonian Literary Museum, the State Archives of the Russian Federation, the Russian State Archive of Social-Political History, the Russian State Archive of Economics, and the university libraries in Tartu, Hamburg, Glasgow, Umeå, and Urbana-Champaign. Of course, all errors and misunderstandings are my responsibility. Chris Springer did the copyediting. The transliteration of Russian is according to the Library of Congress style, and I referred to archival documents according to the Estonian or, respectively, Russian standards.

My greatest thanks go to my family. My wife Marju and my sons Oliver Mihkel, Otto-Mart, and Ole Madis once again showed great patience as the father of the family was busy working on his next book.

Olaf Mertelsmann
Tartu, February 2024

Introduction

Research on the post-socialist transformation in Eastern Europe and the difficulties of introducing a functioning market economy has produced a wave of literature filling entire bookshelves.[3] Discussion will continue, albeit on a smaller scale than in the 1990s, about the best method of establishing a modern and efficient institutional setting for a successful capitalist economy. The very different path from a market to a socialist command economy has not been researched often, despite the fact that so many sources are available nowadays. Serious studies are available, for example, concerning the Soviet Union[4] (the first socialist state) and the German Democratic Republic.[5] In addition, we need to differentiate between territories incorporated into the Soviet Union and countries that preserved their independence as people's democracies; however, in both cases a command economy was established. Still, it should not be forgotten that each country in the Soviet bloc pursued a slightly different path to socialism.

This book presents a case study of the development of one small country during the introduction of the Soviet command economy. Estonia, like Latvia and Lithuania, was occupied by the Soviet Union in June 1940 and annexed six weeks later. Not until 1991 was it able to restore its independence. There were many parallels with, but also differences from, the Sovietization of Eastern Central Europe after World War II. The best comparison is the experience of the Polish

---

3 As an introduction: Anders Åslund, *Building Capitalism: The Transformation of the Former Soviet Bloc* (Cambridge, 2002); Anders Åslund, *How Capitalism Was Built: The Transformation of Central and Eastern Europe, Russia, and Central Asia* (Cambridge, 2007).

4 For example, E.H. Carr and R.W. Davies, *Foundations of a Planned Economy, 1926–1929*, vol. 1 (London, 1969); R.W. Davies (ed.), *From Tsarism to the New Economic Policy: Continuity and Change in the Economy of the USSR* (London, 1990); R.W. Davies, Mark Harrison, and S.G. Wheatcroft (eds.), *The Economic Transformation of the Soviet Union, 1913–1945* (Cambridge, 1994).

5 Joerg Roesler, *Die Herausbildung der sozialistischen Planwirtschaft in der DDR* (Berlin, 1978); Wolfgang Zank, *Wirtschaft und Arbeit in Ostdeutschland 1945–1949: Probleme des Wiederaufbaus in der Sowjetischen Besatzungszone Deutschlands* (Munich, 1987); Albrecht Ritschl, *Quantitative Wirtschaftsgeschichte der DDR* (Berlin, 1995); Dierk Hoffmann, *Aufbau und Krise der Planwirtschaft: Die Arbeitskräftelenkung in der SBZ/DDR 1945 bis 1963* (Munich, 2002); André Steiner, *Von Plan zu Plan: Eine Wirtschaftsgeschichte der DDR* (Munich, 2004).

and Romanian territories occupied by the USSR in 1939 and 1940. In practice, eastern Poland in particular served as a model for Estonia's Sovietization. Unlike in Soviet Russia or the early Soviet Union, the economic restructuring in those territories happened right from the beginning under the conditions of Stalinism. World War II and its consequences also left a strong impact.

Soviet economic history until the outbreak of the war is a well-researched field, but there are very few archive-based studies on the postwar period. We know even less about the economic history of individual Soviet republics. A case study is able to shed light on particular aspects of 1940s and 1950s Soviet economic history from the perspective of one Soviet republic.

Concerning the Sovietization of Central Eastern Europe and the newly acquired territories of the USSR, while politics, state terror, and repression have been researched and will remain a central topic,[6] economics has somehow been largely overlooked. But had there been no extensive nationalization of the economy, collectivization of agriculture (with the exception of Poland), or command economy with a central apparatus for economic planning, the communists' long-term security in power and the long-lasting restructuring of society would have been much less likely. Economic policy provided the regime with the material resources needed to realize its goals. Moreover, economics undermined the position of the former elites.

From today's perspective, the socialist command economy looks like a historic dead end, especially after the collapse of the socialist bloc in 1989 and of the Soviet Union in 1991. It did not always look that way. Before the collapse of socialism and the opening of archives, there was a strong tendency to believe the official representation of facts and to overestimate the economic strength of those states. Of course, this was partly influenced by the Western Cold War strategy to exaggerate the strength of the "enemy." Often, the socialist command economy was even considered an alternative path to a modern industrial society.

---

6 For example, Ernst Birke and Rudolf Neumann (eds.), *Die Sowjetisierung Ost-Mitteleuropas, 1945–1957: Untersuchungen zu ihrem Ablauf in den einzelnen Ländern*, vol. 1 (Frankfurt and Berlin, 1959); Jan T. Gross, *Revolution from Abroad: The Soviet Conquest of Poland's Western Ukraine and Western Belorussia* (Princeton, 1988); Hans Lemberg (ed.), *Sowjetisches Modell und nationale Prägung* (Marburg, 1991); Michael Lemke (ed.), *Sowjetisierung oder Eigenständigkeit in der SBZ/DDR (1945–1953)* (Cologne, 1999); Balázs Apor, Péter Apor, and E.A. Rees (eds.), *The Sovietization of Eastern Europe: New Perspectives on the Postwar Period* (Washington, DC, 2008).

State of Research and Historiography

Aspects of the economic reconstruction of Estonia were already dealt with in the press and in initial academic studies in Estonia during the Stalinist era. But those academic studies should be treated with almost the same caution as those Soviet sources published for a general audience, because they had to present a success story. Admittedly, though, it is sometimes possible to find the same data in newspaper articles as one finds in archival sources. After de-Stalinization began and as censorship eased, the first statistical overviews and research were published. Soviet Estonian and Soviet statistical publications, with all their flaws and problems, provide a rich collection of data[7] offering some insights into the process of economic reconstruction. Often that information was identical to the figures in the archives. In the early 1960s, a number of thematic studies on the economic history and of the industrialization of this Soviet republic appeared.[8] On the one hand, these works were limited by censorship and ideology, and they had to describe the situation in a positive light. On the other hand, they can be used in part even today, because the authors had taken part in the process and/or had access to relevant archival documents.

For the 40th anniversary of the Estonian SSR in 1980, two overviews appeared on the first Soviet year, and they also covered some economic aspects.[9] By that time, ideological restrictions were already easing, and works from this period can even be mined for valuable information today, as demonstrated by a history of collectivization and a history of Estonian workers.[10] The authors had to respect

---

7 *Eesti NSV Rahvamajandus* (Tallinn, 1957); *25 aastat Nõukogude Eesti* (Tallinn, 1965); *Estonskaia SSR za gody sovetskoi vlasti* (Tallinn, 1967); *Narodnoe khoziaistvo SSSR v 1956 godu* (Moscow, 1957); TsSU SSSR (ed.), *Narodnoe khoziaistvo SSSR 1922–1972 gg.* (Moscow, 1972); *Narodnoe khoziaistvo SSSR za 60 let* (Moscow, 1977).

8 Eduard Brandt, *Estonskaia SSR: Razvitie ekonomiki* (Tallinn, 1960); E. Leede, *Bor'ba partiinich organizatsii Estonskoj SSR za povyshenie proizvodeltel'nosti truda v promyshlennosti v gody chetvertoi piatiletki* (Tallinn, 1962); *Nõukogude Eesti majandus 1940–1960* (Tallinn, 1960); Arnold Veimer, *Kompleksnoe razvitie i spetsializatsija promyshlennosti Estonskogo Ekonomicheskogo Administrativnogo Raiona* (Tallinn, 1961).

9 Olaf Kuuli, *Revolutsioon Eestis 1940* (Tallinn, 1980); Vilmar Ruus, *Sotsialistlikud ümberkorraldused Eestis 1940–1941* (Tallinn, 1980).

10 Evald Laasi, *Eesti kommunistlik partei ellu viimas V. I. Lenini kooperatsiooni plaani 1944–1950* (Tallinn, 1980); M. Rubin, "Varumishinnad ja kolhooside rahalised sissetulekud Eesti NSV-s aastail 1950–1960," *Eesti NSV Teaduste Akadeemia Toimetised: Ühiskonnateadused* 30 (1981), pp. 350–361; Raimo Pullat (ed.), *Istoriia rabochego klassa Sovetskoi Estonii* (Tallinn, 1985).

the existing view on history; still, they were able to contribute important information. Due to the political liberalization at the end of the 1980s, it became possible for the first time in the Estonian SSR to publish research that did not have to pay tribute to ideology and that met today's standards on contemporary history. A good example is an article on the situation of Soviet Estonian workers from 1940 to 1960.[11] The works of Soviet Estonian authors should not be ignored; they had direct knowledge of their subject and access to the archives, although their published works were subject to censorship and ideological pressure.

Estonian authors in exile found themselves in different circumstances. Initially, they were often eyewitnesses; therefore, some of the works are tendentious or apologetic. They could not use the archives but had to work with published literature and information transmitted by word of mouth or letters from the homeland. In any case, the most important works contain numerous insights, even those from the times when Soviet Estonian publications were a bit too uncritical. Even today, Alexander Kaelas's 1958 monograph remains an important publication.[12] Many articles on economic questions can be found in the 10-volume series *The Estonian State and the Estonian People in World War II*[13] and the six-volume series *Estonia's Years of Fate.*[14] A number of papers in specialized journals dealt with aspects of economic history.[15] A case study on the Estonian SSR summed up the state of research then.[16] The most important work of exile

---

11 Kulno Kala and Raul Juursoo, "Nõukogude Eesti tööklisklass 1940–1960," *Eesti NSV Teaduste Akadeemia Toimetised: Ühiskonnateadused* 38 (1989), pp. 131–140, 249–259.

12 Aleksander Kaelas, *Das sowjetisch besetzte Estland* (Stockholm, 1958).

13 *Eesti riik ja rahvas teises maailmasõjas*, 10 vols. (Stockholm, 1954–1962).

14 Richard Maasing et al. (eds.), *Eesti saatusaastad, 1945–1960*, 6 vols. (Stockholm, 1963–1972).

15 Elmar Järvesoo, "Die Wirtschaft Estlands und deren strukturelle Veränderungen," *Acta Baltica* 9 (1969), pp. 9–45; Elmar Järvesoo, "Privatunternehmen in der sowjetestnischen Landwirtschaft," *Acta Baltica* 14 (1976), pp. 124–146; Alexander Kütt, "Die Wirtschaft Sowjetestlands," *Acta Baltica* 2 (1962), pp. 107–128; Arnold Purre, "Estlands Industrie unter sowjetischer Herrschaft," *Acta Baltica* 9 (1969), pp. 47–80; Rein Taagepera, "Soviet Collectivization of Estonian Agriculture: The Deportation Phase," *Soviet Studies* 32 (1980), pp. 379–397; Rein Taagepera, "Soviet Collectivization of Estonian Agriculture: The Taxation Phase," *Journal of Baltic Studies* 10 (1979), pp. 263–282.

16 Tõnu Parming and Elmar Järvesoo (ed.), *A Case Study of a Soviet Republic: The Estonian SSR* (Boulder CO, 1978).

research is definitely the history of the Baltic states under Soviet domination by Romuald Misiunas and Rein Taagepera, a key work on the topic.[17]

After Estonia re-established its independence, political history, resistance to the Soviets, and the mass repressions in the 1940s and 1950s understandably became the main focus of Estonian research, although access to archives was now unrestricted.[18] Most of the works were published in Estonian, but several volumes were intended for an international audience.[19] Important

---

17 Romuald Misiunas and Rein Taagepera, *The Baltic States: Years of Dependence 1940–1990* (London, 1993).

18 The most important works: Jüri Ant, *Eesti 1939–1941: Rahvast, valitsemist, saatusest* (Tallinn, 1999); Juhan Kahk (ed.), *World War II and Soviet Occupation in Estonia: A Damages Report* (Tallinn, 1991); Olaf Kuuli, *Sotsialistid ja kommunistid Eestis 1917–1991* (Tallinn, 1999); Mart Laar, *War in the Woods: Estonia's Struggle for Survival* (Washington, DC, 1992); Mart Laar, "Eesti ja kommunism," in Stéphane Courtois et al. (eds.), *Kommunismi must raamat: Kuriteod. Terror. Repressionid* (Tallinn, 2000), pp. 823–894; Olev Liivik, *Eesti NSV Ministrite Nõukogu institutsionaalne areng ja kaadrid 1940–1953* (Tartu, 2014); Olev Liivik and Hiljar Tammela (eds.), *Uuemaid aspekte märtsiküüditamise uurimisest* (Tallinn, 2009); Meelis Maripuu (ed.), *Sõja ja rahu vahel: Eesti julgeolekupoliitiline olukord sõja alguseni*, vol. 2 (Tallinn, 2010); Aigi Rahi, *1949. aasta märtsiküüditamine Tartu linnas ja maakonnas* (Tartu, 1998); Vello Salo (ed.), *The White Book: Losses Inflicted on the Estonian Nation by Occupation Regimes 1940–1991* (Tallinn, 2005); Meelis Saueauk, *Propaganda ja terror: Nõukogude julgeolekuorganid ja Eestimaa Kommunistlik Partei Eesti sovetiseerimisel 1944–1953* (Tallinn, 2015); Tõnu Tannberg (ed.), *Sõja ja rahu vahel: Eesti julgeolekupoliitika 1940. aastani*, vol. 1 (Tallinn, 2004); Tõnu Tannberg (ed.), *Eesti NSV aastatel 1940–1953: Sovetiseerimise mehhanismid ja tagajärjed Nõukogude Liidu ja Ida-Euroopa arengute kontekstis* (Tartu, 2007); Tõnu Tannberg (ed.), *Nõukogude Eesti külma sõja ajal* (Tartu, 2015); Enn Tarvel (ed.), *Eestimaa Kommunistliku Partei Keskkomitee organisatsiooniline struktuur 1940–1991* (Tallinn, 2002).

19 Toomas Hiio, Meelis Maripuu, and Indrek Paavle (eds.), *Estonia 1940–1945: Reports of the Estonian International Commission for the Investigation of Crimes Against Humanity* (Tallinn, 2006); Toomas Hiio, Meelis Maripuu, and Indrek Paavle (eds.), *Estonia since 1944: Reports of the Estonian International Commission for the Investigation of Crimes Against Humanity* (Tallinn, 2009); Toomas Hiio and Meelis Saueauk (eds.), *Sovietisation and Violence: The Case of Estonia* (Tartu, 2018); Anu Mai Kõll (ed.), *The Baltic Countries under Occupation: Soviet and Nazi Rule 1939–1991* (Stockholm, 2003); Olaf Mertelsmann (ed.), *The Sovietization of the Baltic States, 1940–1956* (Tartu, 2003); Olaf Mertelsmann (ed.), *Vom Hitler-Stalin-Pakt bis zu Stalins Tod: Estland 1939–1953* (Hamburg, 2005); Olaf Mertelsmann (ed.), *The Baltic States under Stalinist Rule* (Cologne, 2016); Tõnu Tannberg (ed.), *Behind the Iron Curtain: Soviet Estonia in the Era of the Cold War* (Frankfurt, 2015).

research was conducted by historians from abroad: for instance, Elena Zubkova produced the standard account of the Stalinist period in the Baltic republics.[20] The economic history of this period was, for a certain time, not thoroughly covered. One published overview of 20th-century economic history is of low quality and perpetuates Soviet myths.[21] An economic history of the Baltic states covers the Stalinist period, understandably only briefly.[22] A history of Estonian agriculture touches on the topic very briefly.[23] Later, a couple of papers based on archival research appeared,[24] as did a monograph by this

20 Elena Zubkova, *Pribaltika i Kreml' 1940–1953* (Moscow, 2008).

21 Ene Tomson, *Eesti majandusajalugu 20. sajandil* (Tartu, 1998).

22 Juhan Kahk and Enn Tarvel, *An Economic History of the Baltic Countries* (Stockholm, 1997).

23 Rein Lillak, *Eesti põllumajanduse ajalugu* (Tartu, 2003).

24 Martin Klesment, "The Estonian Economy under Soviet Rule: A Historiographic Overview," *Journal of Baltic Studies* 40 (2009), pp. 245–264; Olev Liivik, "EKP Kekskomitee rahvamajanduse valitsemisel," in Tarvel (ed.), *Eestimaa Kommunistliku Partei Keskkomitee*, pp. 209–241; Olaf Mertelsmann, "Was There a Stalinist Industrialization in the Baltic Republics? Estonia—An Example," in Mertelsmann (ed.), *The Sovietization*, pp. 151–170; Olaf Mertelsmann, "Did Estonian Industry Really Grow So Fast after the War? Soviet Statistics and a More Realistic Approach," *The Soviet Occupation Regime in the Baltic States 1944–1959* (Riga, 2003), pp. 232–242; Olaf Mertelsmann, "Estonian Moonshine in the 1940s," *Humanitāro Zinātņu Vēstnesis* 2004, no. 6, pp. 86–95; Olaf Mertelsmann, "Mehrdimensionale Arbeitswelten als Überlebensstrategie während der stalinistischen Industrialisierung am Beispiel Estlands," in Burghart Schmidt and Jürgen Hogeforster (eds.), *Mehrdimensionale Arbeitswelten im baltischen Raum* (Hamburg, 2007), pp. 94–106; Olaf Mertelsmann, "Die Arbeiter des estnischen Ölschieferbeckens—eine Industrieregion des Stalinismus," *Mitteilungsblatt des Instituts für soziale Bewegungen* 2007, no. 37, pp. 113–131; Olaf Mertelsmann, "Transition to Command Economy and Economic Exploitation: The Experience of Estonia 1940–1941," in Dzintars Ērglis (ed.), *History of the Baltic Region of the 1940s–1980s* (Riga, 2009), pp. 349–375; Olaf Mertelsmann, "The Cost of Transition from Market to Command Economy: The Case of Estonia," *Revista Română pentru Studii Baltice şi Nordice* 1 (2009), pp. 8–31; Olaf Mertelsmann, "Searching for Reasons of the Forced Collectivization in the Baltic Republics," in Dzintars Ērglis (ed.), *Occupation Regime in the Baltic States 1940–1991* (Riga, 2009), pp. 634–640; Olaf Mertelsmann, "Living on a Stalinist Kolkhoz: Peasant Survival Strategies in Estonia," *Humanitāro Zinātņu Vēstnesis* 2009, no. 15, pp. 83–94; Olaf Mertelsmann, "Keskmine oodatav eluiga stalinismiaegses Eestis," *Ajalooline Ajakiri* (2010), no. 1, pp. 105–110; Olaf Mertelsmann, "Poslevoennoe vosstanovlenie v pribalttiiskikh respublikakh na primere Estonii," in Beate Fieseler and Nathalie Moine (eds.), *Pobeditely i pobezhdennye: Ot voiny k miru: SSSR, Frantsiia, Velikobritanniia, SShA* (1941–1950) (Moscow, 2010), pp. 213–226; Olaf Mertelsmann,

author.[25] However, the collectivization of agriculture was even covered by two monographs.[26] It has to be said that our knowledge of Estonia's economic history during the Stalinist era has improved greatly. In addition, Martin Klesment attempted to construct a GDP series for the Estonian SSR from 1950 onwards.[27] A document collection offers new insights into the economic relations between the Baltic Soviet republics and the center in Moscow from 1953 to 1964.[28]

Estonia's path from market economy to command economy can only be understood in the context of the Soviet Union as a whole. Thanks to the opening of the archives, there are an increasing number of historical studies on the Soviet Union covering the early era, from 1917 to 1941; still, less research has been done on the postwar period.[29] Certainly, we know less about the late 1940s and early

---

"Creating Malnutrition in an Agricultural Surplus Area: Stalinist Food Policy in Newly Acquired Territory," in Matthias Middell and Feliks Wemheuer (eds.), *Hunger and Scarcity under State-Socialism* (Leipzig, 2012), pp. 225–251; Olaf Mertelsmann, "The Economic Impact of the Early Cold War on the Estonian SSR," in Tannberg (ed.), *Behind the Iron Curtain*, pp. 119–137; Indrek Paavle, "Grain and Eggs in the Service of the Regime: Coercive Procurement in Estonian Villages in the 1940s," in Hiio and Saueauk (eds)., *Sovietisation and Violence*, pp. 235–253; Maie Pihlamägi, "Eesti tööstus murrangulisel 1940–1941. aastal: turumajanduselt plaanimajandusele," *Acta Historica Tallinnensia* 1 (1997), pp. 152–172; Maie Pihlamägi, "Esimene nõukogude aasta Eesti majanduses: 1940–1941," *Acta Historica Tallinnensia* 9 (2005), pp. 187–209; Maie Pihlamägi, "Industry of the Estonian SSR in the Light of the First Post-War Five-Year Plan (1946–1950)," *Acta Historica Tallinnensia* 15 (2010), pp. 1–18; Maie Pihlamägi, "Die Sowjetisierung der Industrie Estlands unter dem ersten Fünfjahresplan (1946–1950)," in Walter M. Iber and Peter Ruggenthaler (eds.), *Stalins Wirtschaftspolitik an der sowjetischen Peripherie: Ein Überblick auf der Basis sowjetischer und osteuropäischer Quellen* (Innsbruck-Vienna-Bozen, 2011), pp. 211--241.

25 Mertelsmann, *Der stalinistische Umbau.*

26 David Feest, *Zwangskollektivierung im Baltikum: Die Sowjetisierung des estnischen Dorfes 1944–1953* (Cologne, 2007); Anu Mai Kõll, *The Village and the Class War: Anti-Kulak Campaign in Estonia* (Budapest, 2013).

27 Martin Klesment, Allan Puur, and Jaak Valge, *Childbearing and Macro-Economic Trends in Estonia in the XX Century* (Tallinn, 2010), p. 44.

28 Elena Zubkova (ed.), *Sovetskaia model' ekonomiki: Soiuznyi tsentr i respubliki Pribaltiki 1953 g.—mart 1965 g.* (Moscow, 2015).

29 For example: Sheila Fitzpatrick, *On Stalin's Team: The Years of Living Dangerously in Soviet Politics* (Princeton, 2015); J. Eric Duskin, *Stalinist Reconstruction and the Confirmation of a New Elite, 1945–1953* (New York, 2001); J. Arch Getty, *Practicing Stalinism: Bolsheviks, Boyars, and the Persistence of Tradition* (New Haven, 2013); Yoram Gorlizki and Oleg Khlevniuk, *Cold Peace: Stalin and the Soviet Ruling Circle, 1945–1953* (Oxford, 2004); Rudol'f G. Pikhoia, *Sovetskii Soius: Istoriia vlasti 1945–1991*

1950s than we do about the 1920s and 1930s. In the field of Soviet economic history, there are many works, both old and new. The developments described in that literature occurred, of course, in Estonia, too. This field is dominated by English-speaking authors.

With the onset of the Cold War, extensive research on the economy of the USSR started, especially in the US. Some of those studies have been groundbreaking.[30] Before the opening of the archives after 1991, the picture of Soviet economic history became more and more elaborated in the West.[31] However, thanks to the access to the original documents, our knowledge of the Stalinist economy has improved greatly. Since the 1990s, important studies by Russian authors have been published.[32] Still, English-speaking authors have led the

---

(Novosibirsk, 2000); Małgorzata Ruchniewicz, *Das Ende der Bauernwelt: Die Sowjetisierung des westweißrussischen Dorfes 1944–1953* (Göttingen, 2015); Amir Weiner, *Making Sense of War: The Second World War and the Fate of the Bolshevik Revolution* (Princeton, 2001); Elena Zubkova, *Russia after the War: Hopes, Illusions and Disappointments, 1945–1957* (Armonk, NY, and London, 1998).

30 For example: Joseph S. Berliner, *Factory and Manager in the USSR* (Cambridge, MA, 1957); Abram Bergson, *The Real National Income of Soviet Russia since 1928* (Cambridge, MA, 1961); Warren G. Nutter, *Growth of Industrial Production in the Soviet Union* (Princeton, 1962); Janet G. Chapman, *Real Wages in Soviet Russia since 1928* (Cambridge, MA, 1963).

31 Vladimir Andrle, *Managerial Power in the Soviet Union* (Westmead, 1976); Vladimir Andrle, *Workers in Stalin's Russia: Industrialization and Social Change in a Planned Economy* (New York, 1988); Timothy Dunmore, *The Stalinist Command Economy: The Soviet State Apparatus and Economic Policy 1945–53* (London, 1980); Donald Filtzer, *Soviet Workers and Stalinist Industrialization: The Formation of Modern Soviet Production Relations, 1928–1941* (London, 1986); Mark Harrison, *Soviet Planning in Peace and War 1938–1945* (Cambridge, 1985); Jerzy F. Karcz, *The Economics of Communist Agriculture* (Bloomington, 1979); Stephan Merl, *Bauern unter Stalin: Die Formierung des sowjetischen Kolchossystems* (Berlin, 1990); Alec Nove, *An Economic History of the USSR 1917–1991* (London, 1992); Alec Nove, *Das sowjetische Wirtschaftssystem* (Baden-Baden, 1980); Eugène Zaleski, *Stalinist Planning for Economic Growth, 1933–1952* (Chapel Hill, 1980).

32 Rifat Guseinov, *Istoriia Ekonomiki Rossii* (Moscow, 1999); N.A. Ivnitskii, *Kollektivizatsiia i raskulachivanie (nachalo 30-kh godov)* (Moscow, 1996); Valentin Katasonov, *Ekonomika Stalina* (Moscow, 2016); G.I. Khanin, *Ekonomicheskaia istoriia Rossii v noveishee vremia: Ekonomika SSR v kontse 1930-kh gg.–1987* (Novosibirsk, 2008); Andrei Markevich, "Byla li sovetskaia ėkonomika planovoi? Praktika planirovaniia v narkomatakh v 1930-gg," *Ekonomicheskaia istoriia. Ezhegodnik* 2003, pp. 20–54; Andrei Markevich, "Soviet Planning Archives: The Files That Bergson Could Not See," *Comparative Economic Studies* 47 (2005), pp. 364–386; Andrei Markevich, "How Much

way. An important contribution is the work of Mark Harrison, whose research concentrates on the war economy and the defense industry but also analyzes mechanisms of planning and pricing, as well as covering everyday life.[33] Julie Hessler's social history of trade in the USSR is a pioneering work on a rarely studied topic.[34] Donald Filtzer has investigated the situation of workers under postwar Stalinism and the living conditions in Russian towns in this period.[35] There is, of course, more research on Soviet workers during this period.[36] Paul R. Gregory has offered deep insights into the mechanisms of the Stalinist command economy.[37] Robert C. Allen has attempted a new interpretation of Stalinist

---

Control Is Enough? Monitoring and Enforcement under Stalin," *Europe-Asia Studies* 63 (2011), pp. 1449–1468; Elena Osokina, *Za fassadom "stalinskogo izobiliia": Raspredelenie i rynok v snabzhenii naseleniia v gody industrializatsii 1927–1941* (Moscow, 1998); Vassilii P. Popov, *Ekonomicheskaia politika sovetskogo gosudarstvo 1946–1953 gg.* (Moscow-Tambov, 2000); Nikolai S. Simonov, *Voenno-promyshlennyi kompleks SSSR v 20–50-e gody* (Moscow, 1996); O.M. Verbitskaia, *Rossiiskoe krest'ianstvo: ot Stalina k Khrushkhevu* (Moscow, 1992).

33 Mark Harrison, *Accounting for War: Soviet Production, Employment, and the Defence Burden, 1940–1945* (Cambridge, 1996); Mark Harrison, "Prices, Planners, and Producers: An Agency Problem in Soviet Industry, 1928–1950," *Journal of Economic History* 58 (1998), pp. 1032–1062; Mark Harrison, "Soviet Industrial Production, 1928 to 1955: Real Growth and Hidden Inflation," *Journal of Contemporary Economics* 28 (2000), pp. 134–155; Mark Harrison (ed.), *The Economics of World War II: Six Great Powers in International Comparison* (Cambridge, 1998); John Barber and Mark Harrison (eds.), *The Soviet Defence-Industry Complex from Stalin to Khrushchev* (London and New York, 2000); Mark Harrison (ed.), *Guns and Rubles: The Defense Industry in the Stalinist State* (New Haven, 2008); Mark Harrison, "Forging Success: Soviet Managers and Accounting Fraud, 1943 to 1962," *Journal of Comparative Economics* 39 (2011), pp. 43–64; Mark Harrison, *One Day We Will Live Without Fear: Everyday Lives Under the Soviet Police State* (Stanford, 2016).

34 Julie Hessler, *A Social History of Soviet Trade: Trade Policy, Retail Practices, and Consumption, 1917–1953* (Princeton and Oxford, 2004).

35 Donald Filtzer, *Soviet Workers and Late Stalinism: Labour and the Restoration of the Stalinist System after World War II* (Cambridge, 2002); Donald Filtzer, "The Standard of Living of Soviet Industrial Workers in the Immediate Postwar Period, 1945–1948," *Europe-Asia Studies* 51 (1999), pp. 1013–1038; Donald Filtzer, *The Hazards of Urban Life in Late Stalinist Russia: Health, Hygiene, and Living Standards, 1943–1953* (Cambridge, 2010).

36 Tanja Penter, *Kohle für Stalin und Hitler: Arbeiten und Leben im Donbass 1929 bis 1953* (Essen, 2010).

37 Paul R. Gregory, *Before Command: An Economic History of Russia from Emancipation to the First Five-Year Plan* (Princeton, 1994); Paul R. Gregory, *The Political Economy of*

industrialization, but despite interesting ideas, it is not entirely convincing.[38] Thanks to those newer works, we are able to understand the economic development under Stalin much better. The population obviously had to pay a high price for Stalin's brutal industrialization drive, the forced collectivization of agriculture, and excessive defense spending. The result was far from impressive. The economy did not grow as expected; nor did the desired well-being materialize. Instead, the command economy was erected on "faulty foundations,"[39] which could not contribute to the necessary increase in economic efficiency.

The Sources

Archives in Estonia and Moscow were used for this work. The documents are in Russian or Estonian; all translations are my own. In Estonia there are no restrictions on access to sources from this period, unlike in some other former Soviet republics, and research is eased by the extremely user-friendly approach of the Estonian National Archives (*Rahvusarhiiv*). Unfortunately, there are gaps in the documentation. Research in Moscow was less convenient. There are undoubtedly many important documents and statistics in Moscow that will become available sometime in the future. However, the archival holdings in Estonia are rich enough to base this book mainly on them.

The former party archives of the Estonian Communist Party (ECP) are now part of the National Archives and are known as the Branch of Estonian State Archives.[40] Because the party headed by the first secretary of the Central Committee's Bureau (CC Bureau) was the most important center of power inside the Estonian SSR, the archival holdings of the party archives are more important than the documents of the government of this Soviet republic. The protocols, stenographs, and additional documents of the CC Bureau's meetings represent the most important group of sources.[41] The CC served as the local center of power and information. The CC possessed its own apparatus of different departments, which were regularly restructured. Correspondence and reports of the

---

Stalinism: Evidence from the Soviet Secret Archives (Cambridge, 2004); Paul R. Gregory (ed.), *Behind the Façade of Stalin's Command Economy* (Stanford, 2001).

38 Robert C. Allen, *Farm to Factory: A Reinterpretation of the Soviet Industrial Revolution* (Princeton, 2003).

39 Holland Hunter and Janusz M. Szyrmer, *Faulty Foundations: Soviet Economic Politics, 1928–1940* (Princeton, 1992).

40 Rahvusarhiiv, Eesti Riigiarhiivi Filiaal (ERAF).

41 ERAF 1-4.

ministries and other institutions can be found in these archives. Apart from the documents of the administrative apparatus, the party archives also hold the documents of local party organizations, which give us a glimpse of the situation and problems on the ground.

The former Estonian State Archives,[42] now under the aegis of the National Archives, is home to the documents of the Council of Ministers, the Supreme Soviet, and the ministries of the Estonian SSR. These holdings are as important for this research as those of the Statistical Office. Nevertheless, the "government" was subordinated to the party leadership, even when many leading politicians held party and government offices at the same time. In addition, during waste-paper campaigns in the Soviet period, vast quantities of documents from these institutions were destroyed, thus demonstrating that the "formal" government was less important than the party. The surviving records pertaining to many years are uninteresting accounting material. However, in most ministries, even the protocols of the regular meetings of the department heads have disappeared.

In Moscow, valuable information was found in the Russian State Archive of Socio-Political History,[43] containing, among other things, the documentation on the Communist Party and the Politburo until 1952. Those sources reveal the perspective of the central authorities. The Russian State Archive of Economics[44] and the State Archives of the Russian Federation[45] house additional sources for this research.

Soviet archival documents come with certain problems.[46] On occasion, the process of decision-making was not documented, because in a system of personalized rule, orders were given often verbally. Sources might paint an overoptimistic picture of reality or are not easy to interpret due to the highly ideological use of language. The effects of administrative chaos and inefficiency on the archival holdings should not be underestimated. One key question is how reliable the statistical information in the documents is. Roughly, we might place Soviet statistics in three categories. There is quite reliable data, such as in financial accounting or in budget surveys of workers' and collectivized peasants'

---

42 Rahvusarhiiv, Eesti Riigiarhiiv (ERA).

43 Rossiiskii gosudarstvennyi arkhiv sotsial'no-politicheskoi istorii (RGASPI).

44 Rossiiskii gosudarstvennyi arkhiv ekonomiki (RGAE).

45 Gosudarstvennyi arkhiv Rossiiskoi Federatsii (GARF).

46 See Andrea Graziosi, "The New Soviet Archival Sources: Hypotheses for a Critical Assessment," *Cahiers du monde russe* 40 (1999), pp. 13–64; Klaus Gestwa, "Reflektierte Archivarbeit—der 'Königsweg' osteuropäischer Zeitgeschichte," *Osteuropa* 50 (2000), pp. 549–561.

households. Other statistics might be highly problematic due to the methods used, for example, when applying fixed, unchanged prices to measure the growth of industrial gross production. A third group consists of manipulated data and outright forgeries.

One example of the manipulation of data is the reporting of incorrect information concerning the size of land under cultivation—the basis for the calculation of harvests. The Ministry of Agriculture of the Estonian SSR used inflated numbers collected during spring in the countryside. Gosplan drew on other samples each summer and found much smaller but more realistic figures.[47] Although the Estonian leadership was aware of the difference, the overestimates were always used as a basis for the calculation of agricultural output and reported to higher authorities in Moscow. A discrepancy of more than one-fifth was thus simply ignored. But the superior agency in Moscow could insist that the Estonian institutions manipulate their reports to a certain degree in order to present "better" figures to the Politburo. Comrade Malyshev said in the meeting of the Estonian CC Bureau: "Concerning the question of the area [of cultivated land], it is like this: we have sent final data to Moscow, and Moscow has to confirm them. During private talks in Moscow I was told that we have to add 3 percent. I promised to send the revised data."[48] Because of this, we must approach the statistical sources with extreme caution, and we must concede that sometimes only rough estimates can be derived from them.

In addition, for this study I used ego-documents, surveys, and interviews. At first glance, it may seem strange to use oral history for a work on economic history. Still, there are good reasons to do so. As mentioned, Soviet sources come with enormous problems, and they mostly ignore the perspective of the population. Oral history is able to provide important background information and to close some gaps. Of course, we should not forget that, aside from diaries, such sources are based on memories accessed long after the fact and that have thus been transformed by narrative structures. People remember the past only in fragments. It is mainly important events that are remembered, while long-lasting processes normally are not remembered as strongly or are not even mentioned,

47 Report on the problems with Gosplan, documents for the meeting of the CC Bureau of the ECP, September 28, 1950, ERAF 1-4-1045, l. 17.

48 Meeting, February 2, 1948, ERAF 1-4-652, l. 36. On the sources of Estonian agrarian history in the postwar period and their plausibility, see Ants Ruusmann, "Eesti agraarajaloo allikad aastail 1945–1950: Kasutatavus uurimustes," in Enn Tarvel (ed.), *Ajaloolise tõe otsinguil* (Tallinn, 1999), pp. 73–87.

because the informer has forgotten them or thinks they are well known. Mistakes, myths, and topoi enter the narrative, and qualitative description is usually more important than quantitative information. Images of history from school or the media and the attitudes of society also play a part in shaping our memory.[49] Because of this, I have not quoted those oral or autobiographical sources at length; nevertheless, they offered important context for my understanding of this period.

In the Estonian Literary Museum is the Estonian Archive of Cultural History, which holds the collection "Estonian Life Stories."[50] This collection, started in the late 1980s, contains more than 2,000 autobiographical texts, some of which have already been published in a shortened and edited form. At the center of the life stories from the older generation are World War II and Stalinism. The Estonian National Museum houses the Archive of the Replies of the Correspondents of the Museum.[51] For decades now, surveys have regularly been sent out to the network of correspondents. These surveys originally consisted of ethnological questionnaires, but recently, questions about contemporary history were also asked. The questions are open-ended, motivating the correspondents to write. In addition, in 2003 and 2004 I participated in the collection of life story interviews and conducted numerous interviews with contemporary witnesses.

The Starting Point

As a result of World War I, the momentary weakness of Germany and Russia, and a successful war of independence, Estonia was able to establish independence.[52] The economic development of interwar Estonia has been relatively well

---

49 See Elisabeth Domansky and Harald Welzer, "Die allmähliche Tradierung von Geschichte," in Elisabeth Domansky and Harald Welzer (eds.), *Eine offene Geschichte* (Tübingen, 1999), pp. 7–25.

50 Eesti Kirjandusmuuseum—Eesti Kultuurilooline Arhiiv (KM-EKLA).

51 Eesti Rahva Muuseum—Korrespondentide vastuste arhiiv (ERM-KV).

52 For an historic overview, see Toivo U. Raun, *Estonia and the Estonians* (Stanford, 2001); Georg von Rauch, *Geschichte der baltischen Staaten* (Stuttgart, 1970); Seraina Gilly, *Der Nationalstaat im Wandel: Estland im 20. Jahrhundert* (Bern, 2002); Konrad Maier, "Estland in der Zwischenkriegszeit: Die 'Ära des Schweigens,'" in Mertelsmann (ed.), *Vom Hitler-Stalin-Pakt*, pp. 10–30; Ago Pajur and Tõnu Tannberg (eds.), *Eesti ajalugu VI: Vabadussõjast taasiseseisvumiseni* (Tartu, 2005); Seppo Zetterberg, *Eesti ajalugu* (Tallinn, 2009); Karsten Brüggemann, Ralph Tuchtenhagen, and Anja Wilhelmi (eds.), *Das Baltikum. Geschichte einer europäischen Region, vol. 3: Die Staaten Estland, Lettland und Litauen* (Stuttgart, 2020).

researched.[53] Though Estonia is larger in area than Denmark or the Netherlands, it had only 1.1 million inhabitants and thus had a very low population density. Agriculture dominated the economy in the first half of the 20th century. In the context of establishing independence, Estonia had to solve two major economic questions. The first was how to conduct an agrarian reform.[54] Agriculture was, to a certain extent, dominated by manors and by large landowners—often of Baltic German origin. Land and other property had to be nationalized and then distributed among peasants with the aim of establishing new farmsteads and strengthening the existing ones. The second question was that of economic orientation. Before World War I, the territory of Estonia was part of the natural hinterland of the capital of the Russian Empire—St. Petersburg. Under the tsar, Estonian industry had been protected by tariffs and was oriented towards the Russian market. Since the Bolsheviks had cut traditional economic ties with the Baltic states, Estonia had to search for new markets in the West.

For Estonia, the process of "breaking away from Russia" proved to be difficult. Due to Bolshevik reparation payments mandated by the Tartu Peace Treaty

53 Uno Kaur, *Wirtschaftsstruktur und Wirtschaftspolitik des Freistaates Estland 1918–1940* (Bonn, 1962). An edited volume deals with the interwar period: Anders Johansson, Kārlis Kangeris, Aleksander Loit, and Sven Nordlund (eds.), *Emancipation and Interdependence: The Baltic States as New Entities in the International Economy, 1918–1940* (Uppsala, 1994).
Very important are the works by Anu Mai Kõll, Maie Pihlamägi, Jaak Valge, and Karl Stern: Anu Mai Kõll, "Economy and Ethnicity in the Hands of the State: Economic Change and the National Question in Twentieth-Century Estonia," in Alice Teichova, Herbert Matis, and Jaroslav Pátek (eds.), *Economic Change and the National Question in Twentieth-Century Europe* (Cambridge, 2000), pp. 357–381; Anu Mai Kõll, *Peasants on the World Market: Agricultural Experience of Independent Estonia 1919–1939* (Stockholm, 1994); Anu Mai Kõll and Jaak Valge, *Economic Nationalism and Industrial Growth: State and Industry in Estonia 1934–39* (Stockholm, 1998); Maie Pihlamägi, *Eesti industrialiseerimine 1870–1940* (Tallinn, 1999); Maie Pihlamägi, *Väikeriik maailmaturul: Eesti väliskaubandus 1918–1940* (Tallinn, 2004); Karl Stern, *Mittetariifsete kaubandusmeetmete rakendamine 1930. aastatel Eesti Vabariigi näitel* (Tartu, 2017); Jaak Valge, *Lahtirakendamine: Eesti Vabariigi majanduse stabiliseerimine 1918–1924* (Tallinn, 2003); Jaak Valge, "Uue majanduse lätteil: Eest sisemajanduse kogutoodang aastatel 1923–1938," *Akadeemia* 15 (2003), pp. 2202–2228, 2443–2486, 2712–2735; Jaak Valge, *Breaking away from Russia: Economic Stabilization in Estonia 1918–1924* (Stockholm, 2006).

54 Marju and Olaf Mertelsmann, *Landreform in Estland 1919: Die Reaktion von Esten und Deutschbalten* (Hamburg, 2012).

starting in 1920, the importance of Estonia as a bridgehead for Soviet international trade in the early 1920s, and the role of Estonia in shady economic deals for the Soviets (gold, jewelry, etc.), economic reorientation was delayed. High inflation made the situation more difficult, and instead of helping the newly established farmsteads after the agrarian reform, the state decided to support industry. Murky deals by some in the political elite played a role in this decision. The economy stabilized only in 1924.[55] Thus we can speak of a "delayed launch" in the early years of independent Estonia's economy.

Later economic policies were more successful; agriculture received more support, and a catching-up modernization was favored. Large firms that had previously produced for the Russian market closed shop or downsized. Essentially, there was no other choice. What could a small country do with a Tsarist-era shipyard specialized in submarines, like the one in Tallinn? The second half of the 1920s witnessed a degree of de-industrialization. Denmark served as a model for the primary sector. Co-operatives expanded. Agriculture successfully turned to new markets in Germany and Britain; the relatively high level of organization among the peasants (rural co-operatives) and the state supported this development. In addition, Europe's largest exporter of agrarian products before the war, Russia, had now mostly left the world market. This helped newly independent countries such as the Baltic states and Poland to fill in the gap. The Great Depression hit the agrarian sector severely and led, as in other countries, to economic nationalism.[56]

In 1934, Konstantin Päts, one of the founding fathers of the republic, turned the government in hitherto democratic Estonia into an authoritarian regime. This regime increasingly opted for economic nationalism and for preferential treatment of ethnic Estonians in the economic sphere. Around the world, including in Estonia, the economy recovered from the crisis second half of the 1930s. Economic growth started again, and the standard of living increased. Estonia featured a relatively high level of state intervention, state monopolies, and dirigisme. At the same time, the GDP grew.[57]

---

55 Jaak Valge, *Lahtirakendamine*; Jaak Valge, "Eesti Panga rahakraanide kallal," *Tuna* 5 (2002), no. 3, pp. 28–39; Jaak Valge, "Es ist nicht alles Gold, was glänzt: Das Gold der Bolschewiki in Estland und die Folgen," in Olaf Mertelsmann (ed.), *Estland und Russland: Aspekte der Beziehungen beider Länder* (Hamburg, 2005), pp. 157–192.

56 Kõll, *Peasants on the World Market.*

57 Kõll and Valge, *Economic Nationalism.*

Jaak Valge, who constructed a reliable time series of Estonian per capita GDP for the period of 1923–1938, correctly points out that Finnish economic growth was faster in the interwar period. Valge also shows some comparable figures for other European countries, and they indicate a clear direction.[58] Estonia was less developed than Western Europe but was better off than Eastern Central Europe. Undoubtedly, during independence the standard of living increased for the vast majority of the population, partly as a result of the massive redistribution of property through the land reform.

The large share of the agrarian sector in the GDP and in employment was an indicator of a certain lack of development, but this should not be exaggerated. There was much more agricultural land per capita than in Western Europe. The dominant role of the state could have impeded future development, since corruption and the pursuit of one's own economic interests were obviously not uncommon among the elites. Nevertheless, nothing indicated that a large share of the population wanted a fundamental economic transformation.

Command Economy

The economic order of socialist states is conventionally described as a "planned economy." Sometimes the term "centralized economy" (*Zentralverwaltungswirtschaft*) is used. A planned economy implies the central position of the plan and of the planning authorities. Soviet propaganda and contemporary authors also suggested this. Nevertheless, very early experts like Ludwig von Mises indicated that planned economies are inherently unworkable.[59] A national economy is far too complex to operate all processes according to one plan, even a very broad and extensive one. For one thing, at the start the necessary statistical data is lacking. In addition, there is the problem of prices that are set by the planning authorities. Those fixed prices are, naturally, unable to reflect the scarcity of resources, the relation between supply and demand, and the production costs. Elements of a planned economy can be found in the war economies of the great powers during World Wars I and II. J. Adam Tooze has described the breathtaking development of German statistics from 1900 to 1945. Under the Nazi regime, this led to a radical experiment of economic planning.[60] Still, the

---

58 Valge, "Uue majanduse lätteil," pp. 2726–2727.

59 For example, Ludwig von Mises, *Die Gemeinwirtschaft: Untersuchungen über den Sozialismus* (Jena, 1922).

60 J. Adam Tooze, *Statistics and the German State, 1900–1945: The Making of Modern Economic Knowledge* (Cambridge, 2001).

Third Reich operated in a capitalist framework. When we compare the economic planning of Nazi Germany with the reality of planning in Stalin's Soviet Union, which is also reflected in the documents of the authorities of the Estonian SSR, it becomes clear that the Third Reich's planning was more intensive and efficient than the USSR's. Soviet plans like the famous Five-Year Plan served only as a rough guideline and as an instrument of propaganda; they were not key determinants of the economy, as new research has proven.

The term "centralized economy" stresses the crucial role of the administration. Thus the economic authorities of the socialist countries and not only the planning authorities were decisive. To reach this aim, an efficient administration is needed that follows its own logic in the sense of maintaining a functional bureaucracy. In practice, the socialist countries built up a large-scale bureaucracy. Yet this bureaucracy could not simply follow fixed rules embedded in laws and provisions; it also faced constant interference from above. The interference came not only from Josef Stalin and his associates but also from lower-ranking authorities on the spot, representing the party, the government, or the security forces. The administration did not stand in the center but instead was a "transmission belt" for a leadership that could change course at random and that was not structured uniformly. In practice, in the administration of socialism, informal networks and interventions from above were far more common than standardized procedures. In reality, informal networks helped the state to function. From the outside, the socialist state seems over-centralized and monolithic: even simple decisions had to be made on the highest level. Yet informal networks led to a certain degree of decentralization, which the leadership countered by measures of centralization.[61] Research in the archives proves that the so-called "centralized economy" was not really one, even if those involved and many outsiders might have thought otherwise.

The field of new institutional economics has identified the principal-agent problem in hierarchical organizations. The principal needs to oversee his agents and measure their economic performance, since he has different interests than his agents. The principal wants to carry out his policies and gain the highest possible return; his agents try to follow their own line and seek the biggest possible rewards for their effort. Basically, the principal possesses the opportunity and the power to discipline his agent; at the same time, the agent might demand his share

61 For a brief overview, see Rafael Mrowczynski, "Gordische Knoten: Verwaltungshierarchien und Netzwerke in der UdSSR," *Osteuropa* 55 (2005), no. 10, pp. 31–46.

of the returns.[62] When researching Stalinist economics, one becomes aware how central this problem was, even at the highest level.

Another phenomenon is rent-seeking—the misuse of one's own status to receive gains that are not related to performance. Corruption might be the classic example.[63] In an economy without the disciplining power of the market, like the one during the Stalinist era, the players tend to use rent-seeking behavior at the expense of the dictator. Strict rules could not be effectively enforced because of the multiple hierarchies of party and state, in which every superior could turn into a mini-dictator of his subordinates and which were dominated by networks based on personal power and reciprocal favors. The best solutions were interventions from above, outright orders, and direct pressure.

Paul R. Gregory argues convincingly, based on his own archival work, that Stalin's Soviet Union was a command economy. Yet the dictator did not always achieve his aims, since he had to deal with principal-agent problems even at the highest level. The dictator's best weapon was repression, but this did not always lead to the intended outcomes. The plan provided only imprecise and sometimes difficult-to-check requirements, even though the propaganda stated that "the plan is law." The output plan, the most important of all plans, was measured in rubles at unchanged prices. Thus the producers had considerable influence over what was produced and how. The investment plan, the second most important plan, was given in current prices. In this case, too, the dictator could not control the concrete implementation. He could use orders, interventions, and sheer violence.[64] Today, many experts regard the economy of Stalinism as a command economy, and rightly so.

Viktor, born in 1910, who became the head of a collective farm in 1954, describes the command economy in a 1989 text as an eyewitness: "The management and supervision of agricultural work was completely wrong—the commanders and those who prohibited something, whose orders were supposed to lead the work on the fields, in the stables, and everywhere on the kolkhoz [collective farm], had absolutely no idea about agriculture. They did not know what

---

62 Douglass C. North, *Institutions, Institutional Change and Economic Performance* (Cambridge, 1990), pp. 32–33.

63 James Heinzen, *The Art of the Bribe: Corruption under Stalin, 1943–1953* (New Haven and London, 2016).

64 Gregory, *The Political Economy of Stalinism*. A summarized version is Gregory, "The Political Economy of Stalinism: A Bergson Retrospective," *Comparative Economic Studies* 47 (2005), pp. 402–417.

to plant to gain high yields, not to mention pig and cattle farming. If the orders were difficult and you did not fulfill them, you were ordered to the office and immediately threatened with dismissal."[65] This quote illustrates the principal-agent problem, weakened by the reference to the incompetence of the superior, which seemed to be a frequent issue.

Structure of the Work

The first two chapters of this work describe chronologically the reconstruction of the economy. Due to the wealth of sources and the importance of the break from capitalism, the first Soviet years receive a great deal of coverage. At the end of the chapter, a brief overview of the German occupation is given. The second chapter deals with postwar reconstruction and the continuation of measures to establish the command economy.

The third chapter covers demographic changes. Not only war and state terror but also economic conditions affected the size of the population. Immigration and return-migration played an important role. The fourth chapter analyzes the standard of living, which was directly influenced by the economic transformation and by the war.

Agriculture and forced collectivization are the focus of the fifth chapter. Here I also attempt to estimate the performance of Soviet Estonian agriculture. The sixth chapter deals with industry. Officially, industry experienced tremendous growth under Stalinism. I question whether it is even possible to speak of industrialization in the Stalinist era. The seventh chapter is dedicated to services. This sector of the Soviet economy is not well covered in previous studies or in the primary sources, even though it employed a large share of the labor force. The eighth chapter investigates counterfactual scenarios and presents conclusions.

65 KM-EKLA 350-14.

1 The First Soviet Year 1940/41 and the German Occupation 1941–1944

The First Soviet Year 1940/41

The development of the Estonian economy from the Soviet takeover in June 1940 until the outbreak of war is a rarely researched chapter in Estonia's history. Publications from the Soviet period offer bits of interesting information, but they were intended to present a success story.[66] Some early works describe a fairy tale, reporting, for example, industrial growth of two-thirds in one year.[67] Official Soviet statistics also contain data that is too impressive to be true. It would take considerable economic naivete to believe those fables.

Estonian emigrants, most of whom fled to the West in 1944, had a completely different perspective, but they could not use the archives.[68] Nevertheless, the exile Estonians knew the first Soviet year from their own experience, and some of their articles might be read today as accounts of contemporary witnesses. A popular joke reflects public opinion on the economic situation. In Estonian, the acronym for the Estonian Socialist Soviet Republic (ESSR) was "ENSV." This was said to stand for "Enne Nälg, Siis Viletsus"—"First hunger, then misery."[69] Overviews of economic history deal rarely with the first Soviet year.[70] A more realistic perspective based on archival research has been presented by Maie Pihlamägi.[71] Jüri Ant has extensively researched the political history of the period 1939–1941.[72]

According to the Hitler-Stalin Pact in August 1939, Estonia fell into the Soviet sphere of interest. In September 1939, Stalin demanded the right to station Soviet troops in the country and pledged not to interfere in its internal affairs. After

66 For example, Ruus, *Sotsialistlikud ümberkorraldused*; Kuuli, *Revolutsioon Eestis*. Ruus's study is definitely the superior one and offers many details on economic questions.
67 Leede, *Bor'ba partiinykh organizatsii*, p. 3; Brandt, *Estonskaia SSR*, p. 20.
68 See the contributions by A. Kaelas, G. J. K. Kõll, H. Nurk, J. Nõu, and V. Riismandel, in *Eesti riik ja rahvas teises maailmasõjas*, vol. 3 (Stockholm, 1956).
69 The oldest archival document referring to this motto is dated November 1940, ERAF 1-1-57, l. 18.
70 Kahk and Tarvel, *An Economic History*; Tomson, *Eesti majandusajalugu*.
71 Pihlamägi, "Eesti tööstus"; Pihlamägi, "Esimene nõukogude aasta."
72 Ant, *Eesti 1939–1941*.

Stalin issued an ultimatum, Estonia gave in. The Baltic states de facto became Soviet protectorates without independent foreign policies. In June 1940, the world was watching Hitler's successful campaign in France. At that time Stalin posed a second ultimatum to the Baltic states, demanding that additional Soviet troops be stationed there and new, Soviet-friendly governments installed. In view of the military threat and the international situation, the Baltic governments had no other choice, military resistance would not have changed the outcome on the ground. The occupying Soviet troops in Estonia far outnumbered the Estonian army. Stalin's special envoy in Tallinn, one of his lieutenants, Andrei Zhdanov, organized mass demonstrations with the help of the Red Army to present the image of a "revolution" from below and dictated to President Päts the list of new government members.[73] This pro-Soviet government acted behind a seemingly legal facade, and the president signed its decrees, but in fact it was a puppet government of Moscow, with Zhdanov as the string-puller on the spot. The invasion by additional units of the Red Army effectively meant that the country was under military occupation.

To keep up a facade of legitimacy, sham elections were held in July. The new "parliament" requested Estonia's incorporation into the USSR. This was carried out on August 6, 1940. The process of Sovietization had already started earlier. After the establishment of the new regime and a phase of power consolidation, economic restructuring started, based on the Soviet model. Mass arrests and a mass deportation in June 1941 purged society of real and invented enemies and "socially alien elements."

The German attack on the Soviet Union in June 1941 changed the situation; state terror intensified and local resistance to the Soviets began to be prepared. In July 1941, German troops reached Estonian territory, and they were often greeted as liberators by the population. The German occupation lasted until the fall of 1944. Some of the Soviets' economic measures were reversed, but not the large-scale nationalization of private property, since Berlin had formally recognized the Soviet annexation of the Baltic states, and Estonia, Latvia, and Lithuania did not receive independence or autonomy. They were seen as Soviet territory belonging to the Reich Commissariat Ostland.

73 Ibid., pp. 101–118.

The Transition to a Soviet Economy

Estonia's economy suffered a small initial setback even before the political takeover in June 1940: starting in 1939, the Baltic Germans were resettled by the Third Reich. According to an economic census, approximately one-quarter of all large industrial companies were in German hands.[74] A similar German share might have been in business management. Though this minority was tiny, when it was resettled, Estonia lost a substantial share of managers, medical doctors, civil servants, engineers, lawyers, and other professionals. This loss of human capital was incalculable, since the Baltic Germans were by far the richest and best-educated ethnic group in Estonia.

After June 1940, the economy came under much stronger pressure. The new government initiated the restructuring according to the Soviet model. Yet the new rulers lacked any understanding of the economy. Strictly speaking, most of the so-called "June communists" in Estonia were economically illiterate. Only a few of them had economic experience, and that had been in minor positions. This is one reason why the new regime needed the expertise of civil servants of the Republic of Estonia. Were the June communists thus merely faithful servants, doing only what Moscow ordered them to?[75] Yes and no. The local documentation contains few instructions, and even fewer detailed ones, for the restructuring of the economy. Eastern Poland definitely served as an example. Yet in practice, hardly any information was made available about how the Soviet model operated. The best example of this is the first Estonian plan for industrial output in the fourth quarter of 1940.[76] This plan differed enormously from the Soviet reality of planning and was entirely homegrown. It used the Estonian prices of 1939 as a basis, was oriented toward real output in physical units (the Soviets used gross output), and projected only a minor increase. In those times, this was how a planned economy was imagined in capitalist countries. Another example of the uncertainty in economic policy in the initial months was the laws and regulations published in the *Government Gazette* (*Riigi Teataja*), which had to be constantly changed and amended to fit reality. In addition, the "helpers" from Moscow did not really understand the market economy in Estonia that they were going to restructure.

---

74 Riigi Statistika Keskbüroo, *I majandusloendus Eestis: Tööstus*, booklet 1 (Tallinn, 1939), p. 25.

75 Pihlamägi, "Eesti tööstus," p. 172.

76 See ERA R-973-1-48.

Even when central decisions were made at the highest level in Moscow, like the introduction of the ruble as the official currency and the rules for this measure,[77] the implementation was carried out by the local rulers. There was no master plan for the remodeling of Estonia's economy, in either Tallinn or Moscow. The annexation of eastern Poland served only as a rough model. Instead, only the end goal was known, the Soviet model. Yet to reach this goal, improvisation and trial and error were used. Most of the rulers in Estonia did not even know what they were supposed to be striving for, since they lacked direct experience in the Soviet Union. Thus the plan for the national economy for 1941 was developed according to the Soviet line only by the end of 1940 and with the help of Comrade Kokurkin, head of department in Moscow's Gosplan, who was sent specifically to fulfill this task for Estonia.[78] The approach can hardly be considered systematic when the proposal for establishing a central administration for the construction materials industry contains the following: "Initially the organizational structure remains open; two or three people should be hired to build up the mentioned institution and to form it according to the actual needs. Following the proposals of these people, the central administration of the construction materials industry shall evolve, which should lead the entire branch of industry."[79] The entire state apparatus was reconstructed step-by-step in an improvised manner; it was often restructured several times and, due to written instructions from Moscow and seconded experts, adjusted to the Soviet model. The process was not finished by 1941.

Linguistic problems in the implementation of Moscow's orders should not be underestimated, as they came in Russian. For example, on a copy of Resolution No. 700 of the Council of People's Commissars of the USSR, even very simple words like *promyshlennost'* (industry) are underlined in pencil and translated into Estonian.[80] Whether this Estonian reader even understood the text might be doubted. The role of seconded experts should not be overestimated; some of them had to handle too many tasks at the same time. The newly established Economic Council, a kind of central coordination agency for the entire economy,

---

77 Decision of the Council of People's Commissars of the USSR and of the CC of the VKP(b) on the transition to the Soviet currency, September 1940, ERAF 1-1-169, l. 1ff.

78 Report on the activities of the State Planning Commission of the ESSR 1941–1948, ERA 1-47-29, l. 167.

79 ERA R-1206-1-2, l. 22.

80 Copy, September 2, 1940, ibid., l. 10–11.

had only one Soviet adviser, who, at the same time, served as translator. He was given the following tasks:

1. He must inform us, as well as the heads of departments, about Soviet regulations, laws, and decrees in the field of economics.
2. He checks whether the decrees and regulations concerning the economy of the Estonian SSR correspond with the Soviet economic order and searches for ways to strengthen the economic relations of the ESSR with other union republics. He reports to the head of the economic council concerning necessary changes and about other things attracting his attention.
3. He supports the various departments in the preparation of the solution of economic questions.
4. He completes the translation requests of the economic council and of the individual departments and carries out additional tasks given to him.[81]

One individual could not realistically be expected to master all those tasks at the same time.

There was a striking continuity in the personnel of institutions in the Estonian state apparatus dealing with economic issues. While in the Ministry of Justice and the Ministry of the Interior, the personnel were replaced quickly by new employees, the staff of the Bank of Estonia remained nearly intact. By the end of 1940, only 14 out of 354 co-workers employed before the political takeover were fired, and 81 were newly hired.[82] Like Lenin after the revolution, the Estonian communists hired "bourgeois specialists" for all those issues that they could not master themselves.[83] The 81 newly hired bank employees were obviously there to engage in surveillance of the others.

The report of the People's Commissariat of Finances on the year 1940 describes a similar situation: "There were really good experts—bourgeois experts of finances—yet they had had intensive contacts with the former rulers, and because of that, we had to monitor them at every step. Even those who demonstrated their loyalty to the government of the working people could not adapt so easily to the new conditions."[84]

81 Organizational structure of the Economic Council, ibid., l. 16.

82 Report of the branch of Gosbank of the USSR in Estonia, January 1941, ERAF 1-1-175, l. 116.

83 After the revolution, many of those specialists worked in the economic system of Soviet Russia. See Richard Pipes, *Die Russische Revolution*, vol. 2 (Berlin, 1992), pp. 595–597.

84 Report of the People's Commissariat of Finance of the ESSR, January 1941, ERAF 1-1-175, l. 43.

The delicate work of dismantling the market economy step by step was conducted by the economic experts of the annexed Republic of Estonia. When reading the *Government Gazette* or the reports of the people's commissariats, one can sense, in the use of language and the expertise, whether the author was a representative of the old order or the new one. Another example is meetings of the plenipotentiaries of the various people's commissariats and Gosplan concerning economic issues. Nearly all of the attendees were second-tier leading personnel who demonstrated expertise and competence. At this level, the economic machinery was kept running and restructured according to orders from above.[85]

The first major interference in the economic cycle occurred by the end of June 1940, when retail prices were set at the level of June 15.[86] Officially, this measure served in the fight against profiteering, but in reality, it was meant to reduce inflation. This ended open pricing in most trade sectors, with the exception of peasant markets; thereafter, the state regulated prices.

In July all stocks and bonds had to be registered[87] so they could later be withdrawn from circulation.[88] This makes one characteristic element of the Sovietization of the economy clear: the state was out for booty. Estonian government bonds, for example, were invalidated and could not be redeemed. The regime confiscated all foreign stocks and bonds owned by the citizens. Stocks and bonds of Estonian companies became worthless, to the advantage of businesses that had yet to be nationalized. Shareholders and creditors were expropriated. The same happened to Estonian foreign debt. Another typical element of the approach was the segment of society it targeted. Gradually, the middle and upper classes lost their property. A modern economy is unimaginable without a wide range of financial instruments, economic life became more primitive.

On July 19, a bank moratorium took effect. The maximum withdrawal allowed was 100 kroons (the Estonian currency) per month,[89] approximately equivalent to a little more than a monthly salary. Private companies were also affected. They now needed permits to access their own financial resources, which could be used only to keep the business running. The measure was to prevent the owners from holding on to any of their property upon the announcement of the nationalization of large enterprises and banks, which was officially decided in the state

85 See the protocols in ERA R-1206-1-12.
86 *Riigi Teataja* 1940, 57, 513.
87 *Riigi Teataja* 1940, 69, 678.
88 *Riigi Teataja* 1940, 98, 959, 965.
89 *Riigi Teataja* 1940, 70, 688, 699.

council a few days later. It can easily be imagined what this bank moratorium meant for the functioning of all private companies, including the smaller businesses that were not nationalized. At the end of the year, the state confiscated amounts of more than 1,000 kroons held in bank accounts; the remaining sums were converted into rubles at an exchange rate of one kroon for 1.25 rubles. Of course, the money had far less purchasing power than before the moratorium. At the beginning of December, private savings on Estonian bank accounts totaled 65.6 million kroons, of which 45.9 million kroons was frozen. By the end of June 1941, private individuals' savings added up to only 8.3 million rubles.[90] This sum had the purchasing power of approximately one percent of the savings before the political takeover in June 1940. The Soviet state had simply robbed the new citizens.

To illustrate how the Sovietization of the economy actually worked, let us look at what happened to the banks. On July 21, 1940, the Soviet plenipotentiary received an extremely long telegram describing the economic measures taken by the Red Army in eastern Poland in 1939 and those that happened in Bessarabia in 1940.[91] Previous experience, mainly in eastern Poland, served as a model, and local information was added. Two days later, Zhdanov replied from Tallinn with a telegram to Molotov providing detailed information on Estonian banking and some data on industry.[92] On July 24, 1940, the Politburo in Moscow made a decision on the nationalization of banks and large enterprises in Estonia.[93] In fact, this happened two weeks before Estonia's formal incorporation into the Soviet Union. Many important decisions were thus made in Moscow—of course, with the help of local knowledge. Even minor issues needed the formal approval of the central authorities; however, often the Politburo followed proposals made by the locals. This was, for example, the case with procurement norms for grain in spring 1941; they had been proposed by Johannes Lauristin and Karl Säre.[94] Thus it is not always easy to know whether certain measures were a result of republican initiative or of the center's decision. However, important issues were in the

90 Statistical overview on personal savings, ERAF 1-1-168, l. 6–7.

91 Telegram to Andrei Zhdanov, July 21, 1940, RGASPI f. 77, o. 4, d. 40, l. 62–71.

92 Telegram by Andrei Zhdanov to Viacheslav Molotov, chairman of the Council of People's Commissars, July 23, 1940, RGASPI f. 17, o. 163, d. 1272, l. 187.

93 Meeting of Politburo, protocol no. 19, decision 61, July 24, 1940, RGASPI f. 17, o. 3, d. 1026, l. 14.

94 Meeting of Politburo, protocol no. 29, decision 317, March 31, 1941, RGASPI f. 17, o. 3., d. 1036, l. 379–383.

hands of Moscow. Especially in the second half of 1940, the Baltic republics were regularly mentioned in the Politburo minutes.

In July 1940, rents in towns were frozen. They could be raised only with the approval of the tenants, and the landlord also needed their agreement to terminate the lease.[95] Due to the onset of inflation, the results were clear. Rent control in times of inflation is economically unsound; the landlord will stop investing in keeping up the property, and private individuals will stop building additional flats to let. The measure targeted the middle and upper classes, but it also affected some poor people who rented out a room or a part of their small wooden house to earn additional income. Many people rented out apartments as a way to generate income for retirement. In September all profitable apartment houses were put under state surveillance,[96] and in October the government announced the nationalization of large houses.[97] The term "nationalization" is misleading, even when used by the regime. Nationalization normally implies that compensation is paid to the owner and that the measure serves the public good. Taking away private houses without compensation is better characterized as confiscation. The policy applied to houses with a living space of more than 220 m^2 in Tallinn, Tartu, Narva, and Pärnu and of more than 170 m^2 in other towns or settlements. Initially, tenants were happy about the low rents, but as time went on, the condition of the properties severely deterioriated. By March 1941, the state controlled half of the urban living space.[98] When the state becomes the sole landlord and lacks sufficient financial resources, living space gradually deteriorates, and fewer new flats are built than would be in a market economy.[99] Not until the late 1970s did the average urban Estonian have at his disposal the same amount of living space as he did before the war.[100] For the remaining rooms and flats rented out privately, a black market was established, in which state price regulations were quickly ignored.

Urban residents soon experienced the negative effects caused by state control of living space. With the "Instructions to Increase Population Density and the Use of Free Living Space" issued in October, each person in the towns was

---

95 *Riigi Teataja* 1940, 86, 817.

96 *ENSV Teataja* 1940, 12, 121.

97 *ENSV Teataja* 1940, 37, 10, 40.

98 Ruus, *Sotsialistlikud ümberkorraldused*, p. 66.

99 Arnold Purre has estimated that between 1946 and 1965, 1.4 million m^2 of living space completely deteriorated, while 2.9 million m^2 were built. Arnold Purre, "Ehitustegevus ja korteriolud," *Eesti saatusaastad, 1945–1960*, vol. 5 (Stockholm, 1968), p. 48.

100 Misiunas and Taagepera, *The Baltic States*, p. 364.

allowed a maximum of 9 m^2 of living space.[101] This was the Soviet norm, making it possible to bring Soviet military and seconded comrades in large numbers to the Estonian towns. Along with the nationalization of houses, these instructions allowed the new elite to live in comfortable flats and houses that had been stolen from their former owners. In addition, the maximum of 9 m^2 of living space did not apply to them. The average citizen had to sacrifice about 40 percent of his living space. The reality was harsher. According to the statistical data of the economic authorities, by the end of December 1940, each inhabitant of Tallinn had an average of only 5 m^2 at his disposal, because the town's population had increased by 30 percent. In addition, the Red Army and all kinds of authorities and institutions possessed an insatiable appetite for houses and flats.[102]

By August 1940, the first effects of the restructuring of the economy became visible. The Political Police, still existing from independent Estonia, reported from the small town of Viljandi: "Concerning economic life, people believe that it is declining."[103] One further step in establishing state control over the economy was the nationalization of large industrial enterprises, banks, and, later, large trading companies. In this context, "large" often meant those with 20 or more employees or workers. The August 1, 1940, Law on the Execution of Nationalization describes the procedure. The Ministry of Economics took over the nationalized enterprise and the property and had previously established a committee responsible for this task. Within the enterprise, a nationalization committee was formed, headed by a commissar. This committee prepared an act of takeover, a balance sheet, and a list of property and goods. Until the takeover of the business was final, the former owner remained responsible for the smooth operation of production; after this, the commissar took over. Debts and other financial demands were taken over, but the minister of economics could declare a debt moratorium of up to two years.[104] In some cases, the former owners became responsible for the debts of their nationalized enterprises.[105]

101 *ENSV Teataja* 1940, 24, 272.

102 Protocol, December 28, 1940, ERA R-1206-1-12, l. 77–78.

103 Announcement, August 15, 1940, ERAF 1-1-61, l. 9.

104 *Riigi Teataja* 1940, 89, 870. See also Ruus, *Sotsialistlikud ümberkorraldused*, pp. 51–52; Pihlamägi, "Eesti tööstus," pp. 154–155. A good source for an example of the process of takeover are the protocols of the meeting of management and nationalization committee of the Franz Krull enterprise, ERA R-828-1-32.

105 See the balance sheets of nationalized enterprises, ERA R-10-1-99.

The first wave of nationalization affected 487 industrial businesses and all 103 Estonian banks. By the end of the year, 181 industrial enterprises followed.[106] The takeover usually happened in an orderly manner; no "acts of sabotage" by the former owners were noted. Significantly, the past debts of the newly nationalized enterprises were later renounced, meaning that the state expropriated the assets not only of owners but also of creditors. The same happened with large trading companies; until June 1941, 703 were nationalized and approximately 300 put under state control.[107] In September 1940, the Politburo had decided that some of the nationalized Baltic firms should be subordinated to union people's commissariats.[108] The state took control of a large share of the economy without paying compensation. But what were the effects?

Many, but not all, owners and managers lost their positions; some of them were later arrested, deported, or killed. In this way, Estonia lost much of its economic expertise. The incompetence of the commissars and later of the new directors was, in many cases, legendary. One narrator of a life story, a former accountant, recalls that a commissar named Jõesaar, who headed four companies in the wood-processing industry, "barely understood financial accounting and calculations."[109] The quality of management declined everywhere. This opened the door for corruption and embezzlement—a deeply ingrained part of a command economy—and complicated a regular working procedure. The loss of owners and managers meant the loss not only of expertise but also of contacts and networks facilitating the ordering of raw materials, components, and materials. This was one reason for the many supply problems and the resulting interruptions of production. In Estonia at that time, a business with 20 or more employees or workers was termed a "large enterprise."[110] However, this was at odds with international standards, which categorize enterprises with a staff of up to one thousand as "medium-sized." If the staff totaled a couple of hundred, workers and employees knew managers and owners personally. If the new management was obviously incompetent, work morale declined.

The large-scale nationalizations created a huge problem for the state: overnight, hundreds of companies had to be managed and the state was completely

---

106 Ruus, *Sotsialistlikud ümberkorraldused Eestis*, pp. 52–53.

107 Ibid., p. 61.

108 Meeting of the Politburo, protocol no. 20, decision 263, September 24, 1940, RGASPI f. 17, o. 3, d. 1027, l. 75.

109 Villu (born 1916), then an accountant, KM-EKLA 350-678, l. 17.

110 Riigi Statistika Keskbüroo, *I majandusloendus Eestis: Tööstus*, p. 10.

unprepared for this task. The resulting organizational chaos can be easily imagined, especially because state institutions like the newly established People's Commissariat for Light Industry and the People's Commissariat for Local Industry were competing with each other[111] and thus increased the disorder. The response seemed to be to fight every new problem with a new bureaucratic organization on the enterprise and the state level. For instance, an Economic Council of the Estonian SSR, headed by Johannes Lauristin, was established in October 1940[112]—even though an Economic Council already existed in independent Estonia. Economic life became more bureaucratic. At that time, under capitalist conditions, less than 10 percent of the staff of industry were white-collar workers, yet the figure for the Soviet Union was a staggering 21 percent.[113] In Estonia, too, the number of white-collar workers was to increase substantially.[114] A contemporary witness talks about the situation in a tobacco factory: "They established a department for planning, one for statistics, one for accounting, and so on. Before, those tasks had been carried out by five employees; now the paperwork was done by 50. Until my mobilization into the army, those five still calculated workloads and wages so that the workers would receive their pay in time. The new departments made those calculations retroactively."[115] Understandably, bureaucratization led to increased transaction costs and declining efficiency.

Even when the Stalinist principle of one-person leadership demanded that the directors assert themselves, often the opposite happened. A private company needs to generate fresh ideas and take risks; otherwise it is driven out of the market. In a command economy, there is no real competition between enterprises, economic efficiency is of marginal importance, and though the management of a business might order the staff around, in the end it is an organ of administration without much initiative. The heads of the People's Commissariat for Local Industry complained: "The first managers are really spoiled, because for every little matter they come to the people's commissariat to receive our support."[116]

---

111 Pihlamägi, "Eesti tööstus," p. 157.

112 Copy of the decision of the Council of People's Commissars of the ESSR, October 2, 1940, ERA R-1206-1-2, l. 3.

113 CSU SSSR, *Narodnoe khoziastvo SSSR v 1956 godu*, p. 50.

114 H. Nurk, "Eesti majandus punasel aastal," *Eesti riik ja rahvas teises maailmasõjas*, vol. 3, p. 119.

115 Enn (born 1914), then an accountant, KM-EKLA 350-899, l. 32.

116 Protocol of the meeting of department heads, March 22, 1941, ERA R-12-1-33, l. 97.

The nationalization drive worsened the Estonian economy; step by step, Soviet patterns of behavior were taken over, neglecting economic efficiency. According to Joseph S. Berliner, the main aim of a Soviet manager was to receive a bonus for successfully fulfilling the plan. Viability or even profits were less important. For this reason, workers and inventories were hoarded, quality was neglected, and informal ways were used.[117] These developments unfolded no differently in Estonia.

In December 1940, a joint decision was made in Moscow by the Politburo and the Council of People's Commissars that has influenced Estonia ever since, even though the country was not even mentioned. During the arms race of the late 1930s, the Soviet leadership felt the need to increase the production of fossil fuels and to utilize the Soviet reserves of oil shale for this. With an increasing number of tanks, trucks, and other equipment, the Soviet oil industry could no longer produce enough fuel.[118] The decision states that, in the "old" republics of the USSR, the expansion of oil shale mining, the exploitation of new mines, and the growth of oil shale processing had not succeeded. The target was an increase in oil shale mining from 700,000 tons in 1940 to 10 million tons in 1945. The processing facilities were not yet operational, but they were supposed to process 272,500 tons of gasoline, oil, diesel, bitumen, and other fuels in the future. Electricity was to be produced from oil shale as well. One hundred thirty million rubles was to be used for new mines and processing facilities.[119] In 1940, the oil shale mining and processing sector in the Estonian SSR was larger than in the rest of the USSR put together. However, the center had not noticed this, probably because the oil shale sector was under republican jurisdiction and fulfilled orders for the German navy.

Another joint decision of the Council of People's Commissars and the Politburo on the economic plan for the Estonian SSR in 1941 foresaw, among other things, the "speeding up" of the development of oil shale mining and processing to reach an output of 2.7 million tons of oil shale and more than 200,000 tons of processed fuels.[120] This decision was made just one month later. Estonian oil

---

117 See Berliner, *Factory and Manager in the USSR*.

118 A.A. Igolkin and A.K. Sokolov, "Neftianoi shturm i ego posledstviia," *Ekonomicheskaia istoriia: Ezhegodnik* 2006, pp. 385–438.

119 Joint decision of the Politburo and the Council of People's Commissars, signed by Stalin and Molotov, December 29, 1940, RGASPI f. 17, o. 3., d. 1031, l. 208–215.

120 Materials on the decisions of Politburo, protocol 26, decision 91, January 28, 1941, RGASPI f. 17, o. 163, d. 1294, l. 53–54.

shale became part of the Union-wide oil shale scheme, and output needed to increase by one-half. In May the Politburo committed 18 million rubles to the expansion of oil shale mining and processing.[121] Plans for the Estonian oil shale industry projected the mining of eight million tons of oil shale and the processing of 755,000 tons of fuels by 1945.[122] This would have meant a nearly fourfold increase of output and large-scale investment in only five years. Due to the outbreak of war, those plans were not realized then, but they became a starting point for postwar planning. In other words, I argue that the postwar expansion of the oil shale sector in Estonia was related to prewar thoughts and planning.

Not only domestic problems but also the drastic decline of international trade with Western countries hamstrung the economy and the population. Many goods were not produced in Estonia and had to be imported. These were not only consumer goods but also machinery, spare parts, and special tools for agriculture and industry, raw materials, other materials, and artificial fertilizer. The gradual closing of the borders, the end of the exchange of foreign currency, and the system of import permissions complicated international trade. Since August 1, 1940, the monopoly of international trade was in the hands of the state, and every import needed the written permission of the Ministry of Economics. Just 23 days later, Estonia became part of the all-Union monopoly, and the previous permissions became invalid. In December the Soviet customs system came into force.[123] As a result, production stagnated. The reason was that Estonian enterprises preferred foreign supplies to Soviet ones, because the latter came too late, in too small amounts, and in substandard quality.[124] The Soviet aim was clear: Estonia needed to reorientate its economy to accept Soviet goods, as Anastas Mikoian wrote to Johannes Lauristin.[125]

Yet this reorientation did not go smoothly. At the beginning, the official line was that imports from the Soviet Union were easy to organize and to be ordered from only one center. Later, it became clear that the Estonian economy had to order from 60 different supply centers and that the order forms had to be filled out again. In addition, it was unclear which goods could be ordered through a

121 Meeting of Politburo, protocol 33, decision 14, May 16, 1941, RGASPI f. 17, o. 3, d. 1040, l. 5.

122 Document on occupation damage in the sphere of the People's Commissariat for Oil Shale and Chemical Industry, March 15, 1945, GARF f. R-7021, o. 97, d. 865, l31.

123 Ruus, *Sotsialistlikud ümberkorraldused*, pp. 61–64.

124 Pihlamägi, "Eesti tööstus," p. 160.

125 Letter, June 17, 1941, ERA R-1-5-14.

special supply chain and which could not. Order forms arrived in Estonia weeks after the deadline. The responsible managers did not know how to fill them in. Apart from food and spices, deliveries arrived irregularly. Only if the representatives of the people's commissariats lobbied in Moscow would the deliveries improve.[126]

Trade with the Soviet Union was an important means to utilize Estonia for the Soviet economy. Until June 21, 1940, trade between Estonia and the USSR was conducted on the basis of the U.S. dollar; thereafter, it followed the transition to the calculation in kroons according to the official Soviet exchange rate of 1.25 rubles for one kroon.[127] In 1939 Estonia imported goods from the Soviet Union for 1.4 million dollars (5.1 million kroons) and exported products for 1.6 million dollars (5.8 million kroons).[128] Trade remained at a low level until the political takeover in June 1940; then the conditions changed, and trade skyrocketed. In 1940, Estonia imported Soviet goods for 47.5 million kroons and exported products to the USSR for 66.8 million kroons. It might be said that the increase in trade with the Soviet Union was quite natural because Estonia became a Soviet republic. The explanation lies in the exchange rate. In June the kroon was worth 10–15 rubles, and in December it was still worth more than two rubles. Not only were exports to the USSR nominally one-quarter larger than imports, but the real value of exports was several times higher than those of imports. Soviet goods were bought at too high a price and Estonian goods sold for too low a price. If we calculate based on an average purchasing power parity of three rubles per kroon, Estonian exports in 1940 would be worth 200.4 million rubles and imports from the USSR only 59.4 million rubles. As detailed trade statistics are unavailable, those figures remain rough estimates.[129] Starting in 1941, trade was conducted exclusively in rubles. Meanwhile, Estonia delivered mostly processed agricultural products like butter, meat, or bacon, which were highly undervalued in the Soviet price system. Until the outbreak of war, trade with the Soviet Union obviously took place on terms unfavorable to Estonia.

---

126 Meeting of the department heads in the Ministry for Local Industry, March 20, 1941, ERA. R-12-1-31, l. 12ff.

127 H. Nurk, "Eesti majandus punasel aastal," p. 120.

128 Trade statistics for 1939 and 1940: Ruus, *Sotsialistlikud ümberkorraldused*, p. 170.

129 The relevant holding in the Estonian National Archives (ERA. R-1105) of the Soviet plenipotentiary for international trade in Estonia offers no concrete data. It is possible that no one dared to calculate how much was earned because of the terms of trade.

The academic literature remarks that the Soviet planned economy was introduced by fall 1940. First of all, it might be asked whether the Stalinist "planned economy" actually was one, an economy in which all the economic processes were headed by a center, namely Gosplan. New research based on work in the respective archives suggests it was not. The dictator and his associates gave the orders in the socialist command economy, but via Gosplan they checked only a few planning targets. Meanwhile, enterprises had ample opportunities to misuse the organization of production.[130] The planners used few real output figures but used mainly the plan prices; therefore, it was much harder to check the results.[131] In addition, the plan prices were not related to production costs,[132] which limited the ability to manage the economy. The Soviet economy can be considered more a "managed" than a "planned" economy.[133]

In Estonia the State Planning Commission of the ESSR (Gosplan) developed from the State Central Office for Statistics. At first, Gosplan was located in the Ministry of Economics, and its first task was the development of a plan for the national economy for the fourth quarter of 1940. The first draft of the plan for 1941 was worked out under the instruction of Comrade Kokurin, head of department of Gosplan, seconded from Moscow. At that time the Estonian planning authorities had 52 co-workers, yet the structure had to be reorganized several times. The tasks of lower-ranking organizations had not yet been developed, and there was a lack of experienced employees. Knowledge of the condition, the equipment, and the potential of the enterprises was fragmentary, because everywhere, the management was mostly replaced by newcomers. Shortcomings in planning needed to be corrected over and over, yet it was impossible to harmonize the plan with the possibilities of the economy. The official fulfillment of the plan progressed steadily, yet problems persisted with the organizational restructuring of the enterprises, the continuous change of prices and tariffs, and the reorientation towards Estonia's own raw materials. Gosplan was unable to effectively carry out its main functions, and under the circumstances, it often had to carry out duties outside its competence, like the allocation of raw materials. Because of this, the

---

130 Paul R. Gregory, "The Dictator's Orders," in Gregory (ed.), *Behind the Façade*, p. 32.

131 Harrison, "Prices, Planners and Producers," pp. 1032, 1036.

132 Ibid., p. 1058.

133 Joseph S. Berliner, "The Contribution of the Soviet Archives," in Gregory (ed.), *Behind the Façade*, p. 8.

main tasks were not completely fulfilled, and the managers had to choose their priorities.[134]

In other words, real planning according to the Soviet model did not start in the first Soviet year. In addition to the organizational chaos resulting from the restructuring, the ignorance of those involved of exactly how the Soviet model functioned, and the lack of personnel, one major problem was that Soviet prices and tariffs, including plan prices, had not been adopted yet. Realistically speaking, the Soviet managed planned economy, the command economy, did not truly take over until the postwar period. Before that, there was an improvised, transitional model.

State price-setting was particularly problematic in times of high inflation. Soviet plan prices were not fully introduced until the German invasion; the Estonian SSR regulated retail and wholesale prices. Retail and wholesale prices were to be related to production costs, and they were fixed by the people's commissariats on the basis of calculations of enterprises. In January 1941 in the People's Commissariat of Trade, only two civil servants processed the price lists.[135] These two were unable to examine the calculations in depth; thus the enterprises were able to make the calculations in their own favor and to operate uneconomically, because it was much easier to generate an increase of productivity on paper than to actually raise efficiency. Moreover, the two civil servants could not set prices in time, which meant that at a time of high inflation, enterprises were forced to sell their output at prices below cost, and they had to deal with the losses. Estonian industry alone produced 17,000 types of goods, so with the existing workforce, it was virtually impossible to check the price calculations.[136] Nearly everywhere, price-setting was delayed for several weeks due to lack of personnel.[137]

One problem mentioned by Maie Pihlamägi was that some prices were higher in Estonia than in the old republics of the USSR.[138] This might be explained by the peculiarities of price calculation. While the retail and wholesale prices in Estonia were at least theoretically related to production costs, the situation in the old Soviet republics was different. Prices of raw materials and energy were fixed

134 Report on the State Planning Commission of the ESSR 1941–1948, ERAF 1-47-29, l. 167–168.

135 See the protocol of the meeting concerning price questions, January 18, 1941, ERA R-1206-1-12, l. 11f.

136 Meeting of the price commission, February 27, 1941, ERA R-1206-1-26, l. 1.

137 Letter of Gosplan ESSR to the Council of People's Commissars of the ESSR, February 13, 1941, ERA R-1206-1-20, l. 90.

138 Pihlamägi, "Eesti tööstus," pp. 162–163.

at a very low level without any connection to production costs; in this way some goods could be produced cheaper even when the overall price level was higher.

The transition to a Soviet economy did not happen smoothly as mentioned above. The scale of the problems becomes clear when looking at the unemployment statistics. Kulno Kala and Raul Juursoo state that as of December 1, 1940, there were 6,595 unemployed, including many skilled workers.[139] Yet the real unemployment rate must have been much higher. At that time the small town of Viljandi reported 900 unemployed, 650 of whom were women;[140] this was an unemployment rate of approximately 15 percent. In Harju County there was high unemployment in the countryside.[141] Valga County, too, reported high unemployment.[142] In May 1941 there was officially a labor shortage; still, at the job center, 11,533 unemployed were registered (2.3 percent). Thus the People's Commissariat for Labor proposed to simply dissolve the job center.[143] If the unemployed were not registered, then officially, there would be no unemployment. Certainly, most unemployed people did not register. Real unemployment was thus much higher than suggested by Kala and Juursoo and must have exceeded 10 percent in many places.

Where did the jobless come from? The restructuring of the economy hit small private enterprises, like retail trade and craftsmen's businesses, especially hard. They had to lay off personnel or close shop completely. Because of this, many skilled workers lost their jobs. Some "former people" who lost their jobs, like owners of businesses or higher civil servants, faced enormous difficulties in finding comparable positions but nevertheless would not register themselves as unemployed. Because of the nationalizations, the upper and middle classes grew poorer and could no longer afford servants or cleaners; this is why unemployment hit more women than men. Due to the drastic decline of the private economy, possibilities for occasional labor decreased. Generally, unemployment served as an indicator of the difficulties of economic restructuring, especially because the Soviet economy usually had a structural labor shortage.

139 Kala and Juursoo, "Nõukogude Eesti töölisklass," p. 136.

140 Report on the situation in Viljandi County, December 8, 1940, ERAF 1-1-57, l. 30.

141 Report on the situation in Harju County, December 2, 1940, ERAF 1-1-45, l. 20.

142 Discussion of the party secretaries of the town and county committees, October 3, 1940, ERAF 1-4-29, l. 16.

143 Letter to the CC of the ECP, May 26, 1941, ERAF 1-1-276, l. 9.

The State, Inflation, and Shortages

Starting in the fall of 1939, prices in Estonia increased due to the outbreak of war in Europe and the difficulties with international trade. The cost of living index increased until June 1940 by nearly one-fifth.[144] But even Soviet statistics indicated that real incomes declined by only a few percent, due to the rise of incomes.[145] After the political takeover, the situation changed, and inflation gathered speed. By December 1940, average prices in trade were 4.4 times higher than they had been one year earlier.[146] In this context, it must be noted that there were extreme shortages of many products, and these could be bought only at higher prices on the market or under the counter. The real rate of inflation was obviously higher. In the future, prices would increase further. Closely related to inflation was the phenomenon of ubiquitous shortages. One of the first measures introduced to fight the shortages and to follow the Soviet model was the introduction of purchase quantity restrictions (see Table 1). The purchase of high-quality goods was even registered in one's passport. On the one hand, Estonia followed the guidelines set in the "old" Soviet Union; on the other hand, the government took action against hoarding.

Table 1: Restrictions on Purchases, October 1940

Butter	500 g	Tea	50 g
Pearl barley, etc.	1 kg	Canned food	1 piece
Noodles	500 g	Cookies	500 g
Cereal coffee substitutes	400 g	Cocoa	100 g
Real coffee	200 g	Soap	1 piece

Source: *ENSV Teataja* 1940, 19, 217.

There were multiple reasons for inflation, but the main cause was plainly the state. It is quite normal for prices to rise in turbulent times or during a dramatic

144 Index compiled in fall 1940, ERA R-973-1-27, l. 9.

145 Statistics of real wages, ibid., l. 10.

146 Information on the increase of prices, ERA R-973-1-112, l. 162. Those figures are supported by a conversion table of turnover by the People's Commissariat of Trade (ERA R-13-1-19, l. 23). However, the food prices fixed by the state come out lower.

political transformation. Later, the price level normalizes. This did not happen in Estonia, because economic conditions remained unstable.

The nationalization of large trading companies caused enormous difficulties in wholesale trade. Ultimately, competent personnel were fired, the state began to dictate the prices, and inexperienced commissars and emissaries hindered a smooth workflow. In January 1941 the People's Commissariat of Trade stated: "Industrial enterprises have attempted to market their products on their own initiative, because these goods are distributed unevenly within the borders of the ESSR."[147] In other words, wholesale trade no longer functioned smoothly. In addition, transport problems occurred and storage space was lacking, even after the volume of trade sharply declined. The question arises why these problems did not occur earlier, under the market economy. The answer is easy: in a command economy they are inherent to the system.

The state's attempt to regulate prices tried to compensate for this. On June 29, 1940, the prices were frozen at the level of June 15, a clear indicator of inflation. In the summer of 1940, retail trade was still in private hands; when the state tried to fix or to dictate prices, the normal reaction of shop owners would be to hold goods back and wait for higher prices. Starting in October 1940, the Soviet Union introduced quantity restrictions on purchasing goods; this regulation was also valid in Estonia.[148] Such strict regulations automatically led to the establishment of a black market, where goods in short supply were available at higher prices. This kind of economic policy created speculators, whom the regime then demonized. The government took action against "excessive" prices in trade with its own price inspection. Within 10 days (October 11–20), it had levied a total of 37 fines by court order.[149]

The nationalization of banks also disrupted trade and thus accelerated inflation. A smoothly functioning banking system is the backbone of every modern economy. The Estonian financial sector had caught up to Western European standards of the time.[150] At the same time the banks were nationalized, a bank moratorium was declared. Thus not only individuals' accounts but also those of

---

147 Overview on the work of the People's Commissariat of Trade from August to December 1940, ERAF 1-1-175, l. 24.

148 Osokina, *Za fassadom*, p. 258; *ENSV Teataja* 1940, 23, 264; Pihlamägi, "Eesti tööstus," p. 158; Tomson, *Eesti majandusajalugu*, p. 78.

149 Report on activities, ERA R-13-1-159, l. 2.

150 See G.J.K. Kõll, "Eesti pangaduse ja rahanduse likvideerimine," *Eesti riik ja rahvas teises maailmasõjas*, vol. 3, p. 129–138.

private businesses were effectively frozen. Within a matter of weeks, the communists destroyed a functioning financial system, made financial transactions much more difficult, and forced trade to return completely to cash, and later even sometimes to bartering.

Other factors that accelerated inflation were the stationed Soviet troops and seconded specialists and advisors. They received a certain amount of kroons at the official exchange rate of 1.25 rubles to the kroon and thus could shop very cheaply.[151] Many life stories mention the "shopping sprees" of the Soviets. Given the nearly 10 percent increase of population and the increased amount of money in circulation, coupled with a decrease in the amount of goods to be sold due to trade disruption, lack of imports, and so on, the result was inevitable: prices increased.

Another reason for inflation was the introduction of Soviet retail prices. As mentioned above, they were 10–15 times higher than the Estonian prices in kroons. For right from the start, the official exchange rate of 1.25 rubles per kroon was used, and later, the ruble was also introduced as the sole currency at the same rate. Thus the prices had to increase dramatically. The adoption of the Soviet price level was a clear aim of the rulers' economic policy. How the inflation had to proceed was ordered from Moscow in September by a decision of the CC and the Council of People's Commissars.[152] At first, the prices of consumer goods increased and, by November 25, 1940, officially reached the Soviet level. For food, there was a special Baltic solution.[153] Until the outbreak of war, food prices were cheaper than in the "old" republics. Moreover, many consumer goods remained cheaper.

The value of the Estonian kroon was also undermined by the government in Tallinn continuously printing new money. In that case, the order for the massive issue of new money came from Moscow.[154] The draft of the state budget of the Estonian SSR for the fourth quarter of 1940 stipulated for the period from October 1 to November 15 the issue of 35.8 million kroons. Karl Säre and Johannes Lauristin even asked Moscow for permission to print 50.8 million kroons.[155] To

---

151 Misiunas and Taagepera, *The Baltic States*, p. 31.

152 Decision of the Council of People's Commissars of the USSR and of the CC of the VKP(b) on the transition to the Soviet currency, September 1940, ERAF 1-1-169, l. 1ff.

153 Overview on the work of the People's Commissariat of Trade from August to December 1940, ERAF 1-1-175, l. 21f.

154 Decision of the Council of People's Commissars of the USSR and of the CC of the VKP(b) on the transition to the Soviet currency, September 1940, ERAF 1-1-169, l. 1.

155 See copy of the letter by Säre and Lauristin to Vishynskii, Council of People's Commissars, end of September 1940, ERAF 1-1-272, l. 1–4.

better understand the dimensions of this inflationary policy: within six weeks, 50 million kroons needed to be put into circulation—the equivalent of 700,000 average monthly salaries or half of the annual state budget in the late 1930s. The reason for the inflationary policy was simple: two-thirds of the planned budget for the fourth quarter of 1940—111.2 million kroons—was not covered by any revenues. As long as the real value of the kroon was higher than the official exchange rate of the Soviet ruble and the ruble was not yet introduced as the only legal tender, the government in Tallinn could finance its activities by printing additional money. This inflationary policy eased some reforms that were meant only for show, like the introduction of free health care. However, it also increased the money supply enormously and thus increased inflation. After the ruble became the sole currency, the Tallinn government lost this financing option.

The aforementioned draft of the state budget for the fourth quarter of 1940 offers us an important indicator of the actual economic crisis. The regular revenues were estimated to be roughly as high as they had been before Sovietization began.[156] The existing Estonian tax laws remained in force until the end of the year.[157] Even if most of the profit from private enterprises vanished because of the wide-ranging nationalization, this budget draft, made in a period of high inflation, indicates that economic activities had declined considerably.

The problem of shortages in retail trade was closely connected to the aforementioned problems, especially inflation. In literature and in the Estonian collective memory, those shortages were often associated with the stationed Red Army soldiers and the specialists sent from the rest of the USSR,[158] who emptied the shops. But could they have been the main reason? With the invasion of the Red Army and the arrival of Soviet experts, the population increased by about one-tenth. The typical army private usually did not have enough money for a shopping spree. Of course, this factor played a role but clearly was not the main reason. Shortages were caused by a couple of factors. First, the exports to the rest of the USSR increased, while imports from there remained at a low level. Second, the nationalizations and the restructuring of trade disrupted the organization of wholesale trade. For instance, a daily report on trade from November 1, 1940, stated: “The turnover of ordered goods in the provinces has become slower than

---

156 Ibid., l. 3.

157 Report of the People’s Commissariat of Finance, January 1941, ERAF 1-1-175, l. 42.

158 For example, Pihlamägi, “Eesti tööstus,” p. 158.

in the past. The reason is the transition from the existing trade system to the building-up of a trade network."[159]

Due to nationalization and the closing of shops, the number of retail stores declined by approximately one-fourth from 1937 to January 1, 1941.[160] This decline continued thereafter as well. As a result, more and more villages found themselves without a shop. The lack of transportation and storage space was also a source of complaints.[161] The high inflation, combined with price controls, caused private dealers and producers (in agriculture and in industry) to hold back their products and to reduce output. This can be proven for agriculture (see below). Without a hard and potentially convertible currency, selling was less profitable. The virtual end of international trade increased the shortages of imported goods, which could not always be replaced by local products. The widespread nationalization of the economy changed the relationship between producer and consumer. In a market economy, one basis for production is demand (a buyer's market), while in a state-run economy, the state decides what is to be produced (which leads to a seller's market). In this case, the state often acted chaotically and thus intensified the shortages.[162] Another possible reason for the shortages was the overall decrease of economic activity and production.[163] An additional problem was panic buying. This phenomenon appeared in Estonia in uncertain times—for example, in reaction to the announcement of a currency conversion and the introduction of the ruble in November 1940,[164] other significant incidents, or war rumors. People bought available goods to stock up for an uncertain future, or they purchased products that were expected to be in short supply whenever they appeared in the shops. An economy of shortages was to persist in Estonia until the currency reform in 1992. The quality and quantity of the offered goods were oriented towards what the state provided to the citizens.

---

159 Daily report of the People's Commissariat of Trade of the ESSR, November 1, 1940, ERAF 1-1-73, l. 2.

160 See overview on the work of the People's Commissariat of Trade from August to December 1940, ERAF 1-1-175, l. 9, 18.

161 Ibid., l. 24.

162 See Carl Mothander, *Parunid, eestlased ja enamlased* (Tartu, 2nd edition, 1998), p. 208, 234.

163 Because there are no reliable statistics on the main products, this hypothesis cannot be proven. Due to the overall problems during the restructuring of the economy, a decline in output seems very likely.

164 Daily report of the People's Commissariat of Trade of the ESSR, November 29, 1940, ERAF 1-1-73, l. 24.

The first news of food scarcity arrived in August 1940 from the island of Saaremaa.[165] In the fall, reports stated that everywhere in the country, consistently long lines were forming in front of shops. In December, a shortage of replacement shoe soles prevented some children in the Lääne and Harju counties from attending school.[166] Because of the cold, they could not walk barefoot. Soon afterward, the secretary of the ECP in Lääne County, Oskar Cher, commented: "The mood of the majority [of the population] is bad because of the new prices and the shortages of goods. People complain that prices are very high and that there is nothing to buy."[167] A December 1940 overview of the products on offer stated that there were shortages of nearly all convenience goods, for various reasons (such as too-low purchase prices for the producers, the weather, bad organization, the liquidation of small enterprises, lack of materials, import problems, and panic buying).[168] In spring 1941, a lack of meat soured the public mood in Valga County.[169] In Tallinn the meat shortage caused long lines in front of shops.[170] In Aruküla the workers at the peat factory threatened to strike because of the lack of meat.[171] According to the reports from the counties, the situation improved in some places, but all in all, in 1941 the supply of goods was considerably worse than in the fall of 1940.

Standard of Living and Work Discipline

As a result of shortages and inflation, the standard of living declined. The increase of nominal wages (for example, the average wage in industry in May 1941 was 358 rubles[172]) could not stop this development. As Carl Mothander recalled, Estonian workers were used to a diet rich in fats and proteins;[173] now

165 Report of the Political Police, August 17, 1940, ERAF 1-1-61, l. 14.

166 Report on the situation in Lääne County, December 2, 1940, ERAF 1-1-48, l. 19; Report on the situation in Harju County, December 9, 1940, ERAF 1-1-45, l. 24.

167 Report, December 17, 1940, ERAF 1-1-48, l. 25.

168 Meeting of the extraordinary commission, December 4, 1940, ERA R-1206-1-13, l. 131–157.

169 Report on the situation in Valga County, April 15, 1941, ERAF 1-1-56, l. 45.

170 Reports on the situation in Tallinn, April 3 and 9, 1941, ERAF 1-1-54, l. 21–22.

171 Report on the situation in Harju County, May 27, 1941, ERAF 1-1-45, l. 108.

172 Pullat (ed.), *Istorija rabochego klassa*, p. 66.

173 Mothander, *Parunid, eestlased ja enamlased*, p. 230. Indeed, statistical research on 290 households of workers and employees at the end of the 1930s indicates that the food consumption pattern in Estonia was comparable with Western European standards. Riigi Statistika Keskbüroo, *I majandusloendus Eestis: Büdžetiuurimus*, booklet 4 (Tallinn, 1940), p. 83.

the population did not outright starve, but their diet grew worse and worse because of Sovietization. The decline of the standard of living hit hardest among the vulnerable: retired people, small children, casual laborers, the unemployed, or those living on social benefits. Annexation by the Soviet Union happened at an inopportune time, because the Soviet economy was in crisis. Starting in 1939, defense spending increased continuously, and as a result, real incomes declined, and the supply of goods worsened. In the "old" republics, cases of malnutrition were not rare, and in individual cases, people died of starvation.[174]

An indicator of the dramatic decline in Estonia's standard of living was the change in the crude death rate. There are usually small fluctuations during the year due to waves of diseases or the weather. Until the summer of 1940, the crude death rate in Estonia had been, for a couple of years, between 14 and 15 cases per 1,000 inhabitants. In the fall, the numbers stayed around the same range, but in December 1940 the crude death rate increased to 27.7, nearly twice the usual level. The weather and infectious diseases were cited as an explanation. The death rate especially increased among the elderly and small children.[175] From January to April, the crude death rate averaged 20.0,[176] which was still one-third higher than normal; for the period from May until the outbreak of the German-Soviet war, no information is available. According to the Soviet definition, the armed forces, prisoners, and victims of state terror were not included in the crude death rate of the civilian population. Natural mortality was even higher than the average for the years 1901–1914, under the tsar.[177] Such an increase cannot be explained by a wave of diseases; a large epidemic is not documented in the archives and not mentioned in the life stories. A dramatic deterioration of medical care cannot be the explanation: first, medical treatment had recently become free of charge, and second, in contrast with the situation during war or a natural disaster, the number of physicians or hospital beds did not decline. The decrease of foreign trade reduced the availability of some medicines, of course. The weather might have played a minor role, since the winter was extremely cold and the supply of firewood had worsened considerably compared to the previous year. Yet such an increase of mortality over the short span of five months could have only one cause: a dramatic decline in the standard of living and a resulting

174 Elena Osokina, "Tsena 'bol'shogo skachka,'" in Iurii Afanas'ev (ed.), *Sovetskoe Obshchestvo: Vozniknovenie, razvite, istoricheskii final*, vol. 1 (Moscow, 1997), p. 236.

175 See statistical information on mortality in December 1940, ERA R-10-1-486, l. 1–4.

176 Analysis of the cases of death in the first four months of 1941, ERAF 1-1-187, l. 3.

177 Information on these years in Veimer, *Kompleksnoe razvitie*, p. 77.

deterioriation of the quantity and quality of the food supply. The fact that small children and the elderly were hit first confirms this line of argumentation. Both groups could not handle a drastic decline in nutrition in the way that healthy adults in their prime could, and because of that, they more easily fell prey to infectious diseases, which were a major cause of death in December. This is also a possible explanation for the decline of mortality until April. After the weakest parts of society had already died, the situation stabilized again, although the standard of living did not really improve. Within half a year, Estonia's level of mortality reached that of Russia.[178]

The decline in the standard of living and the increased mortality indicate that during the first Soviet year, Estonia was in a deep economic crisis. This crisis hit the population harder than the Great Depression did. Mortality was lower back then.[179] This decline of the standard of living had consequences. In peacetime in an open society, such a decrease would usually lead to mass strikes and perhaps riots or even uprisings. Only under a dictatorship like Stalin's could the population be increasingly impoverished without much unrest. But when people cannot resist openly, the logical result is an increase in job turnover, as well as passivity on the job, as reflected in the popular Soviet saying: "You pretend to pay us and we pretend to work."

In January 1941, 13 percent of all workers changed their job; in February it was 14 percent.[180] In May 1941, 28 percent of all enterprises reported disruptions of work discipline; the daily rate of absenteeism in many factories was 10–12 percent.[181] This is only the official and reported information; for the managers it made more sense to report as few of the problems as possible. The Kommunaar Textile Factory in Tartu reported an increase of waste during production in spring 1941. In April, for example, the waste rate was 18 percent for underwear, 24.7 percent for socks and stockings, and 61.8 percent for artificial silk.[182] We would expect to find that work discipline and thus work quality and productivity were much lower during the first Soviet year than before Sovietization, because the most important incentive for hard work was lacking—an adequate income.

---

178 Vladimir A. Isupov, *Demograficheskie katastrofy i krizisy v Rossii v pervoi polovine XX veka* (Novosibirsk, 2000), p. 126.

179 Odile Frank and Marta Gacic Dobo, "Historical Records, Mortality Decline and Changing Causes of Death: Estonia and Uruguay in the Twentieth Century," *World Health Statistics Quarterly* 51 (1998), p. 152.

180 Plenum of the CC of the ECP, March 24, 1941, ERAF 1-4-54, l. 9.

181 Meeting of the CC Bureau of the ECP, May 29 and June 5, 1941, ERAF 1-4-71, l. 64.

182 Report on the situation in Tallinn, May 15, 1941, ERAF 1-1-54, l. 34.

Shock work and the Stakhanovist movement fulfilled mainly propaganda purposes; they were even interpreted as reasons for the declining quality of industrial products.[183] In addition, those measures were not popular at all. A message from March 1941 reports: "Among the workers in Kohtla-Järve, the hatred of the Stakhanovist movement is really big; they have no interest in workplace competitions, and shock workers were threatened with being beaten up."[184]

Although the enterprises' problems were mostly caused by the restructuring of the economy and factors inherent to the system, shortcomings were blamed on supposed "saboteurs." In the Stalinist environment this was a natural reaction; the command economy could not be held responsible for any problems. Nikolai Karotamm found after an inspection of a business in Klooga that "anti-Soviet" elements were responsible for the occurrence of all kinds of abnormal difficulties: heavy drinking, absenteeism, inaccurate accounting of wages, low quality and irregular delivery of output, and a bad supply of the workers with necessary goods. He called for Klooga to be purged of "anti-Soviet elements and illegal vodka dealers."[185] In reality, what Karotamm encountered in Klooga was not saboteurs but rent-seekers.

The regime reacted to the decline in work discipline by introducing employment record books (this was not fully implemented until June 1941[186]), increasing the use of piecework, and introducing draconian Soviet labor legislation. According to the first prosecutor of the Estonian SSR, Kaarel Paas, those laws were valid only formally in Estonia and rarely executed.[187] In May 1941 Karl Säre, Oskar Sepre, and Vladimir Bochkarev asked Georgii Malenkov in Moscow whether they really had to implement those laws in Estonia to the full extent.[188] This would have made work conditions much worse. The transition to individual piece rates did not happen everywhere. In oil shale-mining the *artel'*-system persisted beyond the spring of 1941.[189] This was a piece rate that took into account the output of each worker in a group and divided the rate proportionally among the members of the *artel'*.

---

183 Report on the situation in Viljandi County, October 5, 1940, ERAF 1-1-57, l. 4.
184 Report on the situation in Viru County, March 21, 1941, ERAF 1-1-58, l. 21.
185 Meeting of the CC Bureau of the ECP, October 14, 1940, ERAF 1-4-1, l. 43–44.
186 Meeting of the CC Bureau of the ECP, May 29 and June 5, 1941, ERAF 1-4-71, l. 65.
187 Letter, January 25, 1941, ERAF 1-4-276, l. 2.
188 Ibid., l. 13.
189 Meeting of the CC Bureau of the ECP, May 21 and 22, 1941, ERAF 1-4-74, l. 33.

Agriculture

When banks and factories were nationalized, there was little resistance; especially in the countryside, no one felt they had a personal stake in the matter.[190] In the first meeting of the State Assembly (*Riigivolikogu*), all land and mineral resources were nationalized, but this remained widely unnoticed. The rural population ignored the first expropriations of neglected farms by the presidential decree of July 12, 1940.[191] It covered 3,779 farms and homesteads.[192] The peasants received their first taste of state interference in September. They were obligated to sell sheep wool, 160–200 g per hectare of land owned,[193] regardless of whether they were keeping sheep. If a peasant did not own sheep, he had to buy wool on the market and fulfill the selling commitment in another way, either in kind or in money. This was the first additional tax for farmers; many others were to follow.

In fact, the peasants quickly realized the consequences of the new economic policy. First of all, they were trapped since summer 1940 in asystem of inflation and price regulation. Estonian farmers sold their products mainly to state commissions buying up goods, to co-operatives, and to wholesale traders. In these contexts, price controls could be more easily enforced. Because the peasants produced most of the needed food on their own, they bought mostly consumer goods, but the price increases among those goods were definitely higher. "All farmers said that this was a day of judgment, because the prices of their own product did not increase," states a report on public sentiment in Harju County.[194] The difference between the price at which they could sell their agricultural goods and the costs of their own purchases was to increase further in the future. In addition, there were shortages of many consumer goods in the countryside. Farmers could have only two logical reactions to a severe decline in their incomes. One was to reduce production slightly in the future, consume more of their own output, and sell less. The other was to hoard products in anticipation that prices would be higher in the future[195] and to channel their sales not to the large trade organization but to the peasant market and to the black market. The hoarding of food because of excessively low prices quickly led to food shortages

---

190 Misiunas and Taagepera, *The Baltic States*, p. 34.

191 *Riigi Teataja* 1940, 67, 646.

192 J. Nõu, "Hoop Eesti põllumajandusele," *Eesti riik ja rahvas teises maailmasõjas*, vol. 3, p. 88.

193 *ENSV Teataja* 1940, 6, 52.

194 Report on the situation in Harju County, October 6, 1940, ERAF 1-1-45, l. 1.

195 Report on the situation in Järva County, October 13, 1940, ERAF 1-1-46, l. 10.

in the towns.[196] The inflation had one positive effect: the agricultural mortgages and credits extended by the Agricultural Bank (*Maapank*), which held debts of 95 million kroons against 75,000 farms,[197] rapidly lost their real value. Later, the government completely canceled two-thirds of agricultural debts.[198]

For seasonal laborers in agriculture, inflation had an even larger impact. As part of the poorest strata in rural society, they should have benefited the most from the new government. In spring and summer they worked on a farm and received free board and accommodation. After the harvest, they were assigned all kinds of casual labor and paid an agreed-upon sum of money that would allow them to survive the winter. "The mood among farmhands is bad. The reason is the price increase. Those who worked for the winter have been hit very hard by inflation. The autumn work will soon end, and the peasants will not hire any farmhands for winter."[199]

In October 1940, the land reform started right after the harvest. When it became known that there was land to be distributed, the majority of peasants tried to claim some of the holdings of their neighbors. Approximately 98,000 applications were filed, 40,000 by landless agricultural laborers and 58,000 by farmers; this was the majority of rural households. Forty-one percent of the existing farms applied for additional land.[200] In fact, one-quarter of the agricultural area was expropriated, mostly from farms with more than 30 hectares of land.[201] The number of farms increased from 139,000 to 164,000, while the average farm size decreased, because those receiving additional land got only a few hectares.

Was the land reform positive or negative for the development of agriculture? Of course, those who received land were happy; at first glance, their conditions improved. Economically, though, this land reform was not sound. Those who received land through it were mostly agricultural laborers. Due to inflation, they found it difficult even to survive the winter and could not even hope to establish a functioning farm. The Ministry of Agriculture calculated that to acquire a very modest house and the living and dead inventory of a small farm would take 5,500 not-inflated kroons.[202] This meant an agricultural credit by the state

196 Report on the situation in Viljandi County, December 1, 1940, ERAF 1-1-57, l. 26.
197 Situation in agriculture before June 21, 1940, ERAF 1-1-265, l. 28.
198 Overview on the damage to agriculture in the years 1941–1944, ERA R-6-16-1, l. 1.
199 Report on the situation in Harju County, October 6, 1940, ERAF 1-1-45, l. 2.
200 Situation on October 26, 1940, ERA R-6-1-467, l. 36.
201 Tomson, *Eesti majandusajalugu*, p. 76.
202 Information on the land reform, ERA R-6-1-467, l. 14–19.

of 137.5 million old kroons just to cover all newly established homesteads. But others who received land were in need of cash, too. The government designated only a sum of 7.2 million inflated kroons in the state budget for this purpose;[203] this was less than 2 percent of the sum needed in practice. All those receiving land would have no proper inventory and too few farm animals, seeds, fertilizer, and tools, not to mention buildings or machinery, to work properly on the land. With this decision, the decline of agricultural output and productivity was inevitable. The more successful farmers could not be sure that they would be able to harvest what they sowed; after all, the next year could bring a new land reform. Peasants facing an uncertain future tend to let their output shrink instead of increasing it. The formation of the first kolkhozes, sovkhozes, and Machine-Tractor Stations (MTS) remained economically insignificant, but the resulting rumors of a possible collectivization upset the farmers even more.

In addition, in wintertime the firewood campaigns produced unrest in the countryside. Because the state-run forestry no longer functioned properly and there was a shortage of fuel, many rural inhabitants were sent into the forests more or less by force to cut timber, for daily wages that were far too low. Essentially, this was a kind of corvée for the state. According to a report from Harju County: "This led to a situation in which people got very agitated and said, 'If you force us to go to the forest, then we will simply knock down the officials.'"[204]

For another problem the regime could not be held responsible: due to the weather, there were two bad hay harvests in 1939 and 1940. According to Soviet estimates, the gross production of agriculture declined from 1939 to 1940 by about one-tenth. Because of this, there was a lack of fodder, especially for cows. Concentrated feed had to be imported.[205] At this point the new government took power. Imports started slowly, and local organizations were badly prepared and showed virtually no interest in the ordering and distribution of concentrated feed. In addition, there were norms limiting the selling.[206] The administrative chaos under socialism exacerbated the fodder crisis. Even in January 1941, there was only 20 kg of concentrated feed for each cattle. The pragmatic, calculating farmers reacted by reducing the number of milk cows. In October and November

203 Copy of a letter by Karl Säre and Johannes Lauristin to Andrei Vyshinskii, November 1940, ERAF 1-1-272, l. 2.

204 Report on the situation in Harju County, not dated, probably November or December 1940, ERAF 1-1-45, l. 19.

205 Plan for the development of agriculture 1941, ERA R-6-1-187, l. 5, 12, 30.

206 Report for the People's Commissar of the ESSR of Agriculture, ERA R-6-1-189, l. 1.

1940, twice as many cows were slaughtered as in the same period of the previous year, according to statistical data by the slaughterhouses.[207] In spring 1941, the shortage of concentrated feed continued.[208] In April it was reported from Võru County: "To avoid the decimation of livestock, we urgently need 1,200 tons of concentrated feed, before the animals are let again onto the pastures. Everywhere in the county, livestock are dying of malnutrition. On many farms, the animals get sick due to the poor food and lie on the ground. Diseases and deaths among the livestock will increase if we do not receive enough concentrated feed."[209] The decrease in the number of livestock continued, but because of the outbreak of war shortly thereafter, proper statistics are not available. Estonian livestock would face an even larger hunger crisis after the forced collectivization of agriculture in the 1950s.

Table 2: Import of Concentrated Feed from Other Soviet Republics

Month	Fodder (tons)	Month	Fodder (tons)
August 1940	50	November 1940	1,888
September	145	December	6,693
October	744	January 1941	10,802

Source: Report for the People's Commissar of the ESSR of Agriculture, ERA R-6-1-189, l. 1.

The bleak prospects were reflected in the decrease in the number of livestock. From July 1939 to January 1941, the number of horses declined by 7 percent, the one of cows by 16 percent, and that of pigs by 32 percent. Of course, in the fall and before Christmas, many pigs were slaughtered anyway (see Table 3). At first the farmers slaughtered the animals they needed the least. Because Estonia's agriculture was based on animal husbandry, this mass slaughter meant a decline of potential productivity and of natural fertilizer, manure.

207 ERAF 1-1-265, l. 52.

208 Report on the situation in Pärnu County, May 15, 1941, ERAF 1-1-52, l. 51.

209 Report on the situation in Võru County, April 12, 1941, ERAF 1-1-59, l. 59.

Table 3: Livestock in Estonia in Thousands

Date	Horses	Cattle	Of them, cows	Pigs	Sheep and goats
July 1, 1939	210.8	675.4	458.9	425.9	657.9
January 1, 1941	196.1	504.8	382.4	290.4	316.1

Source: ERA F 1-47-49, l. 61.

The aforementioned statistics originate from Gosplan. J. Nõu provides a higher figure for 1939 (Nõu, "Hoop Eesti põllumajandusele," p. 91).

In the spring of 1941, the peasants faced new challenges. A plowing plan caused disorder. This raises the question of what right the state had to instruct free peasants when and how to till the soil and which crops to grow. As a result, plowing was done badly[210] and the plan was fulfilled only on paper. Full of pride, the Soviet agrarian experts proclaimed that plowing now took only 25 days, as compared to the 50 it took in "bourgeois times."[211]

The second measure was the forced procurement norms for the peasants, which were introduced on April 18, 1941, but made retroactively valid back to January. The purchasing prices were well below the market prices.[212] Despite all the state's forceful measures and interventions, the sale of agricultural products to the state declined by one-half in 1940/41 from the same period one year before.[213] The mood of the rural population darkened considerably upon the announcement of procurement norms in April; in June many peasants realized that they would have enormous troubles meeting those norms.[214] Especially hard hit were the small peasants who had a little land to start with and then received more through the land reform. Because they lacked animals, tools, and buildings, their harvest was smaller; but unlike those establishing a new homestead, they were not exempted from the norms. "The fulfillment of the norms would ruin many of them economically," stated a report from Pärnu County.[215]

---

210 Nõu, "Hoop Eesti põllumajandusele," p. 95.

211 Overview on the damage of agriculture in the years 1941–1944, ERA R-6-16-1, l, 2.

212 See the price list, ERA R-1-9-8, l. 8–9.

213 Ant, *Eesti 1939–1941*, p. 150.

214 Reports on the situation on the island of Saaremaa, April 28 and June 9, 1941, ERAF 1-1-53, l. 52, 78.

215 Report on the situation in Pärnu County, June 5, 1941, ERAF 1-1-52, l. 57.

The first Soviet year saw a severe decline in agriculture—the extent is hard to estimate. Even without the destruction of war and the human losses sustained since June 1941, the productivity of agriculture was shrinking. Because of the economic circumstances, the farmers scaled back their efforts. The amount of livestock declined because of the lack of fodder. Thousands of farms were badly equipped and unable to survive. New machinery and work tools could not be obtained due to the import restrictions. The peasants had no money, because purchasing prices were low and regulated. In spring, the delivery of needed artificial fertilizer was delayed because of the recurring organization problems.[216] As result, the sown area was reduced by approximately 7 percent.[217] In September 1941, during the German occupation, the harvest was half that of 1939.[218] It seems possible that the data was revised downward in order to claim a larger damage. In my view, we can realistically estimate a one-quarter to one-third decline of agricultural potential before the outbreak of war.

Industry

Among the great successes claimed by the Soviet system was extraordinary industrial growth. E. Leede even claimed that during the first Soviet year, Estonian industry grew by 66.8 percent.[219] To check this claim on the basis of existing statistics, we first need some context. The performance of Soviet industry was measured not as a net figure, the sum of all delivered goods minus costs, but as a gross figure, the sum of all industrial products without regard to costs (Russian: *valovaia produktsiia*). The measurement occurred at prices set by the state, regardless of whether the goods were sold.[220] So the concept of value added did not really figure in published Soviet statistics of industrial production. Statistics in the press on how many thousands of tractors or millions of tons of steel there were in the USSR was often outright propaganda. Initially, what was counted was the sum of rubles at plan prices. Using this method led to many inaccuracies, and hidden inflation distorted the result. Because the output of all producers and suppliers was simply totaled up, a certain amount of double-counting

216 Agricultural Supply Office to the People's Commissar of the ESSR of Agriculture, May 16, 1941, ERA R-6-1-107, l. 35.

217 Nõu, "Hoop Eesti põllumajandusele," p. 94.

218 Ibid., p. 91.

219 Leede, *Bor'ba partiinykh organizatsii*, p. 3.

220 Nove, *Das sowjetische Wirtschaftssystem*, p. 116.

occurred.[221] The state gave every new product a fixed price based on production costs, including a calculated profit and depreciation. On this basis, lists of fixed prices emerged containing thousands of goods (and later, hundreds of thousands of goods). Because the production of a new good is always more expensive at the beginning than in later mass production, the fixed prices were often too high.[222] This allowed managers to fulfill the plan more easily, and the total output was inflated. Whether those products were sold, kept in storehouses, or redefined as a delivery of materials was immaterial. In 1940 in the USSR, the lists of unchanged fixed prices of 1926–1927 were valid. Because of the more expensive pilot production mentioned above, the price lists did not remain unchanged. Another measure to increase the output at "unchanged prices" was to simulate technical improvement in order to introduce a "new" product at higher prices.[223] As a result, the price lists were distorted by inflation, which could be higher than 100 percent during a long period. In addition, to demonstrate how absurd this measure was, imagine if a company producing mobile phones were to sell 15-year-old models at the same price as when they were first introduced.

Until the end of 1940, Estonian industrial production was measured in kroons. All later information is expressed in rubles in unchanged fixed prices of 1926/27, a unit that existed until 1950. How big was Estonian industrial output in kroons, and how was this recalculated? For 1936, Estonian statisticians calculated a gross production of 193 million kroons at then-current prices,[224] for 1939 they calculated 269 million kroons, and for 1940 they expected 275 million kroons at 1939 prices.[225] The growth of gross production in 1940 was estimated at only 2 percent, although industrial employment increased in the fourth quarter. The two figures are hard to compare. Until 1940 there was a buyer's market in Estonia: there were few shortages—they mainly involved imported goods that became hard to get as the war in Europe unfolded—and production was oriented towards demand. The main aim of a business was to generate profit and thus to produce goods that could be sold. As the command economy began, so did shortages. The buyer's market turned into a seller's market. The logic of the planned economy prioritized plan fulfillment without taking notice of profits or losses.[226] Output

221 Ibid., p. 440.

222 Harrison, "Soviet Industrial Production," p. 139.

223 Ibid., p. 146.

224 Riigi Statistika Keskbüroo, *I majandusloendus Eestis: Tööstus*, p. 10.

225 The two last figures both originate from the draft of a speech by Karl Säre. They are definitely not as exact as the data for 1936 but are still realistic. ERAF 1-4-49, l. 65.

226 Nove, *Das sowjetische Wirtschaftssystem*, p. 26.

was to be improved regardless of cost-effectiveness.[227] Because of this, many unnecessary goods were produced in an inefficient way, and without any thought to whether they could be sold. In certain cases, the statistics were simply doctored to make the plan appear fulfilled. Under those changed circumstances, we need to evaluate the production of 1940 not as slightly increasing but as slightly shrinking.

During the transition to the ruble and to the command economy at the end of 1940, the statisticians had to recalculate these output figures. The methodologically sound way would have been to find or define a price for all Estonian products according to the list of fixed, unchanged prices. However, this would have required a great deal of time, information, and human resources. Another, much easier way was to convert kroons to plan price rubles at a fixed rate. If we compare data for different years, such as gross production in 1945 and 1950 and official growth since 1940,[228] in both cases we find the value of 355 million rubles in unchanged prices of 1926/27 for 1940. When we divide the sum by the official exchange rate of 1.25 rubles per kroon, we get the sum of 268 million kroons for 1940 industrial production. This value is suspiciously close to the official Estonian data for 1939 and 1940. Obviously the Soviet statisticians did not the effort to convert kroon prices to plan prices, they multiplied just by 1.25. That this method of conversion was used is also proven by a protocol of a meeting of heads of department in the People's Commissariat of Local Industry.[229] This method not only saved time but also delivered the desired results: a low industrial production during independence and rapid industrial growth after Sovietization. A similar method was obviously also used in Latvia and Lithuania to produce the same fairy-tale scenario. A correct conversion of kroons into fixed ruble prices is no longer possible, but a rough estimate can be attempted.

In 1940 the ratio between the fixed ruble prices of 1926/27 and the current ruble prices was, on average, 2.86. This means that 1940 prices were 2.86 times as high.[230] Naturally, this conversion can only provide an approximate result, because depending on the category of goods (for instance, food or ship

227 ENSV Majandusnõukogu bülletänn no. 1 (October 8, 1940), ERA R-1206-1-8.

228 Gross production in 1945 was 245 million rubles and in 1950 was 1,145 million rubles in unchanged prices of 1926/27. In 1945, the output should have been 73 percent of that in 1940, and in 1950, it should have been 342 percent of that in 1940: overview on the development of industry, ERAF 1-72-37, l. 142.

229 Meeting, January 15, 1941, ERA R-12-1-31, l. 58.

230 Simonov presents the national income of the USSR in current and unchanged prices: Simonov, *Voenno-promyshlennyi kompleks*, p. 181.

construction), this ratio could vary by several times.[231] If we calculate using this not-very-reliable conversion factor, the real value of the kroon would be 10 rubles, and the result would be:

> 1 kroon = 10 rubles of 1940, divided by 2.86 = 3.50 rubles in unchanged prices of 1926/27.

Then we have to account for the fact that industrial products possessed a higher plan price on average. In this case, a conversion factor of 6 seems reasonable.

At such an exchange rate for the kroon, 270 million kroons would be 1.62 billion rubles in unchanged, fixed rubles of 1926/27. If the exchange rate of the kroon was more favorable, the amount would increase. This value would mean that Estonian per capita industrial production was twice as high as the Soviet average.[232]

If the output of Estonian industry in the first five months of 1941 was 202 million rubles in 1926/27 prices,[233] this indicates not growth but shrinking. The reality was even more complicated. The products of Estonian industry did not conform to Soviet standards, and the prices did not conform to the plan prices. To assign a realistic value to each and every product was a long process. This means the transition from the old price system to the new one occurred very gradually. In addition, in Estonia there was a lack of information about Soviet prices and standards. For example, in March 1941 it was still impossible to calculate the cost of industrial buildings according to Soviet standards because the necessary data was lacking.[234] Under these circumstances, there was no way to calculate reliable figures for the first months of 1941. Industrial output might have increased by one-third or declined by one-tenth; there is no way to detect this with the available data. The transition to a new price system provided an opportunity to fabricate economic growth. How inaccurate the gathering of data was and which illusions were fostered is revealed by a statement by Oskar Sepre, the official responsible for planning and statistics, at the Plenum of the Estonian CC in March 1941: "We know that in comparison to 1940, the plan of 1941 prescribes an increase of 30 percent. Now the plan is already overfulfilled, so we can reach an increase of 40–50 percent. These are not precise figures,

---

231 Harrison, "Prices, Planners and Producers," p. 1057.

232 The total industrial output of the USSR was 138.5 billion rubles in prices of 1926/27. Donald Filtzer, "Wirtschaft und Gesellschaft der Nachkriegszeit," in Stefan Plaggenborg (ed.), *Handbuch der Geschichte, Russlands*, vol. 5, part 1 (Stuttgart, 2002), p. 83.

233 Ruus, *Sotsialistlikud ümberkorraldused*, pp. 89–90.

234 Meeting about large building projects, March 10, 1941, ERA R-1206-1-13, l. 46.

only approximate ones."[235] Is it possible that Sepre believed those fantasy figures himself?

One has to assume that in reality, industrial production declined heavily, as a result of chaotic conditions, low work discipline, and irregular deliveries. For example, the metal- and construction-material factory Tehnika reported: "[...] the state of affairs is really bad, especially concerning materials. [...] In summary, we state that the situation is this: we cannot fulfill any orders to be produced quickly and in time, and we are definitely unable to fulfill the plan, too. [...] The most insane is the situation in the commissariat. They demand all kinds of plans; when going there asking, the answer is always: 'Try to cope on your own; we have no specific prescriptions either.' [...] How is it possible to demand one thing exactly when their own affairs are in disorder? This is hard to understand, and at the same time, the plan has to be fulfilled exactly."[236] The lack of spare parts and tools was one major problem[237] caused by the termination of Western imports.

Another indicator suggesting the shrinking of production was investment. To compensate for the natural wear and tear of machinery and equipment, a sum of approximately 5 percent of the capital stock of industry should have been invested annually. The available statistics and investment plans indicate a lower degree of investment.[238] In addition, for administrative reasons, those sums were rarely used. The deputy head of the Council of People's Commissars, Kress, stated that as of March 5, 1941, only 7.5 million rubles, out of a planned 170 million rubles, had been used for investment.[239] Thus in summer 1941, the capital stock of Estonian industry was in much worse shape than one year previously. This too means that there could not have been any increase in output.

The capacity of power stations did not increase but stayed the same.[240] Which sources of energy were responsible for the increase in production? Oil shale mining increased until the summer of 1941, but oil shale processing stagnated

---

235 Plenum of the CC of the ECP, March 24, 1941, ERAF 1-4-54, l. 3.

236 Report by A. Kask, February 11, 1941, ERAF 1-1-55, l. 39.

237 For instance, at the Proletaar ("Proletarian") Machinery Factory, ERAF 1-1-52, l. 37.

238 The data is hard to work with because of inflation and needs to be recalculated. However, neither the real investment in the third and fourth quarter of 1940 (ERA R-9-1-32, Bl. 64) nor the investment plan for 1941 (ERAF 1-4-26, l. 8) foresaw sufficient financial means. In addition, many investment plans were not fulfilled, and many projects did not start on time because of the lack of information (see ERA R-1206-1-13, l. 41–48).

239 Meeting about large construction projects, March 10, 1941, ERA R-1206-1-13, l. 41.

240 Report of the Estonian energy producers, October 12, 1948, ERAF 1-47-29, l. 92.

starting in 1940.[241] Wood as a source of energy for industry can be eliminated because of the lack of firewood in winter.

It is also quite unlikely that productivity per worker increased. In the Soviet Union, productivity per worker stayed at nearly the same level from 1929 to 1950; a slight increase was achieved only by increasing working hours.[242] If the Soviet dictator was unable to increase per capita productivity in their own country for 21 years, he could hardly have done so amid declining living conditions within a few months in Estonia. Starting in July 1940, the Soviet Union had a 56-hour working week,[243] while before the political takeover, Estonia had a 48-hour working week.

The huge increase in industrial employment, as announced in some Soviet sources, cannot be seen as a motor of industrial growth.[244] One reason for this increase was a large number of unproductive white-collar workers. Another reason was that many small enterprises that were not categorized as industry were now merged into trusts and counted as large industrial enterprises. Kala and Juursoo state, plausibly, that the number of workers increased from 46,000 in October 1940 to 58,200 in April 1952.[245] If the workers of small enterprises are taken into consideration, the real increase of productive workers in industry was smaller, as the two authors maintain, and amounted to a few percent. Given the decline in productivity per laborer, this small increase could not lead to a rise in overall output.

Because certain branches faced a labor shortage in the spring of 1941, the Soviet system of labor reserves was to be adopted. Factory schools providing six months of training and vocational schools providing two years of training were to be established by the end of summer for about 5,000 students in Estonia. Half of the youths aged 14 to 15 were to be mobilized by force into those schools; this amounted to one-third of the respective age group.[246] The outbreak of war ended those plans; they were postponed for later.

---

241 For 1941, there is no information on processing: report of the Ministry for Oil Shale and Chemical Industry of the ESSR on the period 1940–1948, ERAF 1-47-30, l. 117ff.

242 See Mark Harrison, "Wartime Mobilization: A German Comparison," in Barber and Harrison (eds.), *The Soviet Defense-Industry Complex*, p. 110.

243 Guseinov, *Istoriia Ekonomiki Rossii*, p. 297.

244 Leede claims an increase from 49,800 employed on October 1, 1940, to 80,200 on January 1, 1941 (Leede, *Bor'ba partiinykh organizatsii*, p. 4).

245 Kala and Juursoo, "Nõukogude Eesti töölisklass," p. 136.

246 Meeting of the CC Bureau of the ECP, April 15–17, 1941, ERAF 1-4-62, l. 164–167, 183.

One relatively little-known fact is that private industry continued to operate. Officially, private industry accounted for only 1.7 percent of total output.[247] Internally, its contribution was estimated to be 6 percent and should be improved by more regular deliveries.[248] In reality, its significance was larger, since private enterprises operated partly on the black market to evade higher taxation.

In summary, even with slightly increased employment, Estonian industry produced much less than it had before June 1940, and definitely not those goods that were most in demand among the population. This correlates with the experience of shortages throughout the country.

The Service Sector

The development of the service sector during the first Soviet year is statistically not well documented. One reason was that, reflecting Marxist ideology, an emphasis was placed on material production, and services were considered less important. Paradoxically, one part of the service sector expanded in the USSR as in hardly any other contemporary country—administration.

Another reason for the imprecise documentation lay in the fact that, for a long time, many services stayed in private hands, and state records did not take this into account. In October 1940 the Central Tax Administration estimated that the private economy, excluding agriculture, employed approximately 40,000 people, but data on self-employed people and craftsmen was virtually unavailable.[249] By comparison, the total number of workers and employees in Estonia for 1940 was given as 176,000.[250] Due to the imprecise reporting, any information on the private share of the economy should be handled with caution. Outside agriculture, the share might have been one-sixth or one-fifth.

In addition to state regulation and tax increases,[251] the decline in the standard of living hurt the service sector. Demand fell because of the diminished purchasing power not only of the middle and upper classes but also of the rest of the population. In other words, if you are struggling to afford meat or shoe soles, you are not going to hire a craftsman and will rarely, if ever, visit a café. The decline of services might be illustrated using the example of craftsmen. According to the

247 See Pihlamägi, "Eesti tööstus," p. 170.

248 Meeting of the economic council, January 14, 1941, ERA R-1206-1-10, l. 12.

249 Report on the possible revenue from the income tax for 1941, November 20, 1940, ERA R-4-1-280, l. 205–206.

250 TsSU ESSR, *Estonskaia SSR*, p. 127.

251 *ENSV Teataja* 1940, 58, 701.

1936 census of the economy, there were 27,000 employed in crafts.[252] By contrast, in 1941 there were 409 *artel's* of craftsmen, employing 5,273, of whom one-third provided services.[253] We might add to this figure several thousand independent craftsmen. Obviously, under the new regime, the service sector declined faster than other sectors.

Conclusions on the First Soviet Year

Economically, the first Soviet year was a catastrophe; this was reflected even in the mortality of the population. Economic performance may have declined by at least one-fourth. The standard of living declined even more. Not only for political reasons did Estonians resist the Soviet regime and greet the Germans in the summer of 1941 as "liberators"; economic reasons were also definitely important. Apart from a small political elite, who were taken care of by *spetstorg* (a special retail trade network with more than 500 employees[254]), the economic situation worsened for nearly everyone. Mass arrests and the mass deportation in June 1941 contributed to the decline of available labor. Taking a model from a less developed country and applying it to a more developed country naturally led to a setback. The governing communists blamed "sabotage" for the problems that they themselves were causing.

The fact that the Soviet Union generated only a small per capita growth of the economy has long been known. Abram Bergson estimated in 1961 that the per capita GNP of the USSR increased from 1937 to 1940 at factor costs of 1937 by only 3 percent and decreased at factor costs of 1950 by as much as 0.5 percent.[255] The Estonian economy faced a large restructuring to fit into the Soviet model. In this context, a decline of economic performance in the first Soviet year was a logical consequence. The transition in the opposite direction—from command to market economy in the 1990s—also lasted a long time and was accompanied by several years of declines in the GDP.

Nevertheless, the first Soviet year was, in another way, an exception during the Stalinist phase of economics. After the war, the majority of industrial enterprises would be subordinated to union ministries. However, the investment plan

252 V. Raud, "Majanduselust Eestis," *Eesti riik ja rahvas teises maailmasõjas*, vol. 1 (Stockholm, 1954), p. 119.

253 Report on the *artel's* of craftsmen 1940–1948, ERA 1-47-29, l. 61, 66.

254 Overview on special trade, ERAF 1-1-288, l. 17.

255 Bergson, *The Real National Income*, p. 225.

for 1941 called for 173 million out of 241 million rubles to be invested in republican enterprises.[256] This meant that approximately 70 percent of industry was under the control of the republic. Only during the *sovnarkhozy* experiment under Khrushchev would the Estonian leadership regain such influence on its industry.

The German Occupation 1941–1944

Because the main topic of this monograph is the Stalinist restructuring of the economy, we can deal only briefly with the German occupation and the impact of this period. On the German occupation, we have monographs by Seppo Myllyniemi,[257] Alvin Isberg,[258] Ruth Bettina Birn,[259] Meelis Maripuu,[260] and Anton Weiss-Wendt,[261] various articles,[262] and a multiauthor volume.[263] Isberg, in his well-sourced work, covers economic questions in more depth; Misiunas and Taagepera[264] deal with them in their overview only briefly. Two lengthy sections of Volume 5 of "Germany and the Second World War," the series edited

256 "On the Economic Plan for the Estonian SSR in 1941," annex to decision 91, protocol 26, meeting of Politburo, January 28, 1941, RGASPI f. 17, o. 3, d. 1033, l. 152–155.

257 Seppo Myllyniemi, *Die Neuordnung der baltischen Länder 1941–1944: Zum nationalsozialtischen Inhalt der deutschen Besatzungspolitik* (Helsinki, 1973).

258 Alvin Isberg, *Zu den Bedingungen des Befreiers: Kollaboration und Freiheitsstreben in dem von Deutschland besetzten Estland 1941 bis 1944* (Stockholm, 1992).

259 Ruth Bettina Birn, *Die Sicherheitspolizei in Estland, 1941–1944: Eine Studie zur Kollaboration im Osten* (Paderborn, 2006).

260 Meelis Maripuu, *Omavalitsuseta omavalitsused: halduskorraldus Eestis Saksa okupatsiooni ajal 1941–1944* (Tartu, 2012).

261 Anton Weiss-Wendt, *Murder without Hatred: Estonians and the Holocaust* (Syracuse, 2009).

262 For example, Oskar Angelus, "Wirtschaftsfragen im deutschbesetzten Estland 1941–1944," *Acta Baltica* 16 (1976), pp. 147–171; Martin Seckendorf, "Deutsche Baltikumskonzeption 1941–1944 im Spiegel von Dokumenten der zivilen Okkupationsverwaltung. Eine Dokumentation," *1999* 16 (2001), pp. 140–172; Meelis Maripuu and Indrek Paavle, "Die deutsche Zivilverwaltung in Estland und die estnische Selbstverwaltung," in Mertelsmann (ed.), *Vom Hitler-Stalin-Pakt*, pp. 96–129; Olaf Mertelsmann, "Das 'kleinere Übel'? Das Generalkommissariat Estland im estnischen Vergangenheitsdiskurs," in Sebastian Lehmann, Rainer Bohn, and Uwe Danker (eds.), *Reichskommissariat Ostland: Tatort und Erinnerungsort* (Paderborn, 2012), pp. 349–366.

263 Hiio, Maripuu, and Paavle (eds.), *Estonia 1940–1945*.

264 Misiunas and Taagepera, *The Baltic States*.

by the German Military History Research Office, deal with the war economy and German-occupied countries;[265] naturally, they did not separately cover the situation in *Generalbezirk Estland*. Klaus Jochen Arnold covers economic questions, among other topics, in his monograph.[266] Roswitha Czollek's overview[267] is only of limited use because of her ideological approach. Political actors, such as politicians of the Estonian Self-Administration or of the Reich Ministry for the Occupied Eastern Territories, also left memoirs;[268] these should be treated with great caution.

In July 1941, the Wehrmacht reached at the Estonian borders, and by the end of August, they were in Tallinn. In October the Germans took over the remaining Estonian islands. After initial successes, the German advance in Estonia came to a halt for several weeks. This gave the Bolsheviks enough time to forcibly mobilize men in northern Estonia into the Red Army and to conduct evacuation measures.[269] The war disrupted the harvest and led to livestock losses. Industry suffered from fighting, targeted destruction, and the evacuation of workers. Seventeen enterprises essential for the war effort were counted as completely or partly destroyed. Nevertheless, the oil shale industry was taken over nearly intact.[270] On the whole, the fighting increased the economic losses of the first year of Soviet rule. The most important was the loss of population—about 100,000 people (see Chapter 3). This would later lead to an enormous labor shortage, because most of those lost were working-age males. The war damage was not

265 Bernhard R. Kroener, Rolf Dieter Müller, and Hans Umbreit, *Organisation und Mobilisierung des deutschen Machtbereichs: Kriegsverwaltung, Wirtschaft und personelle Ressourcen*, first part, 1939–1941 (Stuttgart, 1988); second part, 1942–1944/45 (Stuttgart, 1999).

266 Klaus Jochen Arnold, *Die Wehrmacht und die Besatzungspolitik in den besetzten Gebieten der Sowjetunion: Kriegführung und Radikalisierung im "Unternehmen Barbarossa"* (Berlin, 2005).

267 Roswitha Czollek, *Faschismus und Okkupation: Wirtschaftspolitische Zielsetzung und Praxis des faschistischen deutschen Besatzungsregimes in den baltischen Sowjetrepubliken während des zweiten Weltkrieges* (Berlin, 1974).

268 Oskar Angelus, *Tuhande valitseja maa: Mälestusi Saksa okupatsiooni ajast 1941–1944* (Stockholm, 1956); Hjalmar Mäe, *Kuidas kõik teostus: Minu mälestusi* (Stockholm, 1993); Peter Kleist, *Zwischen Hitler und Stalin 1939–1945* (Bonn, 1950).

269 On the German advance, see Toomas Hiio, "Ein kurzer Überblick über Truppenverbände und Kampfhandlungen 1939–1941," in Mertelsmann (ed.), *Vom Hitler-Stalin-Pakt*, pp. 67–95.

270 Isberg, *Zu den Bedingungen*, pp. 52, 61.

comparable to that on Russian, Belorussian, or Ukrainian territory, because in Estonia, scorched-earth tactics were not used on a large scale.

Officially, until December 1941, Estonia stood under the military administration of the Army Group Rear Area Command of Army Group North, Lieutenant General Franz von Roques. During this period the Estonian Self-Administration under the leadership of Hjalmar Mäe was officially installed; it would remain in office until the end of the German occupation. In fact, the German term for this institution—*landeseigene Verwaltung* or national administration—describes the task better than the Estonian term—*Eesti omavalitsus* or Estonian Self-Administration. Estonian bureaucrats were to support German administrators and reduce the need for German manpower. No one in Berlin considered allowing Estonia genuine self-administration. On December 5, 1941, the military authorities handed their tasks over to the German Civil Administration under General Commissar and SA-Obergruppenführer Karl-Siegfried Litzmann, who was subordinated to the Reichskommissariat Ostland with a center in Riga under Reichskommissar Hinrich Lohse, the gauleiter of Schleswig-Holstein. The Reichskommissariat was subordinated to the Reich Ministry for the Occupied Eastern Territories under Alfred Rosenberg.

As in all other German-occupied territories, there were other competing institutions side by side with the German Civilian Administration and the Estonian Self-Administration, the army, and representatives of the SS and of the commissioner of the Four-Year Plan, Hermann Göring, who was responsible for economic questions. As a result there was a clutter of competences; serious power conflicts occurred between the different institutions, and there were many cases in which one order contradicted another.[271] The administration was not unified. The question of what would happen with the occupied territories was delayed until the "final victory." Estonia, like the other Baltic states, was considered a region for future German settlement. Only the lack of personnel caused by the war and considerations of expediency prevented the complete takeover of the country's administration.[272]

The German planning for wartime in the East foresaw securing the food supply of the German army from the occupied Eastern territories, starting in fall 1941.[273] In this way the Reich was to be relieved and profit in the long run

271 Hans Umbreit, "Auf dem Weg zur Kontinentalherrschaft," in Kroener, Müller, and Umbreit (eds.), *Organisation und Mobilierung des deutschen Machtbereichs*, first part, p. 79.

272 Ibid., pp. 100ff.

273 Ibid., p. 84.

from food imports from the East. Academic studies also describe the war in the East as a war for food supplies conceived as a blitzkrieg.[274] In addition to food, another main economic interest was in products of the oil shale industry and of other goods important to the war effort. In all the territories they occupied, the Germans planned to reduce local consumption. However, in the Baltic states, a disruption of the economy was to be avoided.[275] By contrast, in the "old" Soviet republics, the German occupiers barely considered the situation of the population.

In the preparation phase of Operation Barbarossa, the German leadership tried to treat the nationalities in the East differently. Hitler declared in March 1941: "The Baltic Sea states have been taken over by us with their administration."[276] In particular, the state secretary of the Reich Ministry for Food and Agriculture, Herbert Backe, was a driving force in planning the exploitation policy to improve the balance of Germany's food supply. Because many regions in the East were agricultural surplus areas, economic exploitation and a pragmatic treatment of the local population were not mutually exclusive.[277]

The "Green Folder" that was issued to the Wehrmacht in June 1941 on the orders of Hermann Göring for "Operation Barbarossa" stated:

> According to the orders of the Führer, all measures should be undertaken that are necessary for the *immediate and greatest possible exploitation of the occupied territories* in favor of Germany. By contrast, one must refrain from or postpone all measures that could jeopardize this goal. [...] It also entails that those tasks that are not fundamentally compatible with the given strategic goal or that complicate their fulfillment should thus be disregarded, even when it might seem desirable to carry them out. It would be completely improper to think that what matters in the occupied territories is to follow the single position that they should be put quickly in order and quickly reconstructed. On the contrary, the treatment of individual regions must be, by all means, different. The only areas that will be economically supported and urgently kept in order are those in which we can tap into important food and mineral oil resources. In other regions, which cannot feed themselves—such as large parts of northern and central Russia—economic management has to be restricted to exploiting the found supplies. [...] The first task to be

274 Christoph Dieckmann, "Deutsche und litauische Interessen: Grundlinien der Besatzungspolitik in Litauen 1941 bis 1944," in Vincas Bartusevičius, Joachim Tauber and Wolfram Wette (eds.), *Holocaust in Litauen: Krieg, Judenmorde und Kollaboration im Jahre 1941* (Cologne, 2003), p. 67.

275 Umbreit, "Auf dem Weg," p. 241.

276 Arnold, *Die Wehrmacht und die besetzten Gebiete*, pp. 85–86.

277 Ibid., p. 87.

achieved as quickly as possible is to *feed the German troops* entirely from the occupied territories to ease the food situation in Europe and to relieve the transport routes.[278]

The Germans' exploitation policy used similar techniques as the Soviets had used previously. Prices were frozen at a level of 40 percent below the prices of Germany. This allowed for low-priced exports to Germany and for *Schleusengewinne* (lock profits or sluice gate profits).[279] Procurement and sales quotas existed for agriculture, the most important sector of the economy. The majority of the forced procurement went to the army. The Soviet land reform was partly reversed—the former owners were allowed to use the land but not regain ownership of it. Occupation costs were covered by the occupied country. Almost all of the economy that had been nationalized remained so, and the "red" commissars were simply replaced by "brown" ones. According to an August 1941 provision by the Reich Ministry for the Occupied Eastern Territories, state property, which had mostly been seized through nationalization one year earlier, was put under a trust management and provisionally handed over to trustees. Monopoly companies like the Energieversorgung Ostland GmbH (Energy Supply Ostland Ltd.) or the Deutsche Torf GmbH (German Peat Ltd.) were established until owners could be identified. A widespread play on words accurately referred to those companies as "GmbH—Greif mit beiden Händen" (grab with both hands). Another provision from November 1941 prohibited the establishment and the private ownership of larger enterprises; the Estonians were allowed to possess only small enterprises or act as craftsmen. Especially on economic questions, the Estonian Self-Administration had extremely little to say.[280] Concerning reprivatization, the occupiers took a wait-and-see attitude.[281] The control of trade and finances, the issue of *Reichskreditkassenscheine* (Reich credit treasury notes) as a means of payment as an inflationary financing of the war, and the fixing of the exchange rate of the ruble at 10 reichspfennig secured further revenues. The aim of both regimes was to drain purchasing power and goods from the occupied Baltic states.

German economic policy and the effect of combat on economic activities led to a high unemployment rate in the towns. Starting in September 1941, the unemployed were required to register themselves. In 1942 the Germans introduced the obligation to work, and those so obliged could also be forced to work

278 Quoted in ibid., p. 99. Italics original.
279 Myllyniemi, *Die Neuordnung der baltischen Länder*, p. 102.
280 Isberg, *Zu den Bedingungen*, pp. 59–60.
281 See Myllyniemi, *Die Neuordnung der baltischen Länder*, pp. 220–225.

outside Estonia. In 1943 the Germans established draft commissions, consisting of representatives of the employment agency, the police, the Estonian Self-Administration and the German army. People who were obliged to work and who were born in 1919–1924 were to be mobilized into the war industry in Estonia or recruited for German military units. The work assignment of Estonians in Germany did not play an important role.[282] Inside Estonia there was a labor shortage, especially in agriculture and the armament industry. In 1943 the oil shale industry was declared to be of military significance (*kriegswichtig*); its labor shortage was compensated for by approximately 10,000 Jewish slave laborers from the Vaivara concentration camp system, who came mostly from Latvia and Lithuania. They were partly evacuated in 1944; the remaining inmates were murdered.[283] Many branches of industry were not sufficiently reopened, and in comparison to the prewar period, the number of "free" industrial workers declined and was only 26,000–28,000.[284] As the processing of oil shale intensified during the last year of German occupation, industrial employment increased again. The large enterprises thus registered in April 1944 a total of 30,400 workers, of whom 4.5 percent were prisoners of war, 1.5 percent were prisoners, and 4.5 percent were workers from other occupied territories.[285] Obviously the inmates of concentration camps were not accounted for in those statistics; they represented nearly one-fourth of the workforce of industry and mining.

Not surprisingly, German and Soviet economic policies caused the same problems. Keeping purchasing prices for agrarian products artificially low, in combination with the extremely limited range of products, basically led to a situation in which the peasants did not expand production and turned to the black market and moonshining.[286] About this, endless descriptions can be found in the collection of Estonian life stories. Other reasons for the low productivity of agriculture were the labor shortage, which was only partially compensated by Soviet prisoners of war, and the lack of fertilizer and machinery.

The economic framework for agriculture under German occupation was definitely worse than during the 1930s, but the data from the Soviet war damage report comparing the agricultural statistics of 1942 and 1943 with those of

282 Isberg, *Zu den Bedingungen*, pp. 89–90.

283 Argo Kuusik, "Die deutsche Vernichtungspolitik in Estland 1941–1944," in Mertelsmann (ed.), *Vom Hitler-Stalin-Pakt*, pp. 147ff.

284 Kala and Juursoo, "Nõukogude Eesti töölisklass," p. 137.

285 Tomson, *Eesti majandusajalugu*, p. 79.

286 On bootlegging during the 1940s, see Mertelsmann, "Estonian Moonshine."

1935–1940 do not yet sound catastrophic. Since 1939, the area of cultivated land had declined by one-sixth; the production of fodder, and accordingly the animal stock, had decreased by one-fourth; and the harvest was down by one-third.[287] In the years before and immediately after the forced collectivization of agriculture, agricultural output was on a similar level (see Chapter 5). This meant that the German robber economy and the postwar command economy led to a similar level of agrarian production. The explanation lies in the prevalence of private farms and a comparative framework. For the peasants, the main difference between the two systems was that the Germans restricted trade on small markets more but imposed smaller fines for non-fulfillment of the delivery quota and used far less violence against them. For example, in the spring of 1944, peasants not fulfilling their quota could be punished with a fine of 50 reichsmarks or arrested by the village elder for up to three days. In reality, those punishments were rarely imposed.[288] Given that after the war, the same behavior would lead to several months of imprisonment and the possible expropriation of the farm, German authority was relatively restrained.

Due to the state's suppression of private consumption and the resulting low real incomes, labor productivity in industry naturally remained low as well. The official food rations for the urban population, amounting to about 1,200 calories per day, would not have been enough for survival without contacts in the countryside, private gardens, and the black market (see Chapter 4). Nevertheless, war and occupation led to a dramatic decline in the population's health and hygienic conditions.[289]

One major problem during the German occupation was the lack of real value of money. As a result, the situation that had started under the Soviet occupation continued: barter trade expanded and alcohol and tobacco served as a substitute

---

287 Overview on the damage of agriculture in the years 1941–1944, ERA R-6-16-1, l. 1–14.

288 Report of the SD on the economic situation in May 1944, report from Tartu, May 11, 1944, ERAF 1-1-829, l. 131.

289 Allegedly, in 1943–1944, one-fifth of students in Tallinn had skin diseases and fleas, 8 percent suffered from diseases of the lungs, and 27 percent had anemia (First Women's Congress of the ESSR, April 3–4, 1945, ERAF 1-4-242, l. 66). According to People's Commissar of Health Hion, 7 percent of the population suffered from tuberculosis, and in a small town like Võru, 28 percent had fleas and lice (Fifth Plenum of the CC of the ECP, December 1–2, 1944, ERAF 1-4-107, l. 132–133). This information cannot be dismissed as sheer communist propaganda, because other reports and the life stories of contemporaries describe a similar situation.

currency. Services were often paid for in kind. The black market made some people rich, yet the prices were often unaffordable for ordinary people.[290]

Both Soviets and Germans faced a dilemma that was caused by their policies of exploitation and inefficient organization of the economy. A low standard of living, combined with administrative chaos and lack of incentives, led to low productivity. The milk cow was not yet slaughtered, but it produced less milk than expected. The common circumstance in both cases was foreign rule. In times of war or crisis, societies may be willing to cut consumption, but only in their own interest. The Estonians were not willing to sacrifice in the name of the German "master race" or of communist "functionaries" who treated the locals as inferiors and were much better provided for than the locals. In addition, the German personnel in the field of economics did not know the local conditions and often were not highly qualified.

Unlike in the other Soviet territories they occupied, in the Baltic states the Germans took a pragmatic approach, economically speaking, toward the local population, with the exception of Jews and Romani. There were no large-scale policies deliberately imposing hunger or destruction, because plans called for these territories to be later incorporated into the Reich and Germanized. It was not only direct war damage, deliberate destruction during the German retreat, and the loss of population that hampered the further development of Estonia's economy; so did the German version of the command economy and the low rate of investment starting in 1940. The lack of investment led to incalculable losses in the capital stock of agriculture, industry, and trade. With less exploitation, more incentives for production in the form of higher prices, and a more intensive use of market elements, the German occupiers could have better mobilized the Estonian economy for the war effort.

290 Arvo Mägi, "Mis meelde jäänud," *Akadeemia* 9 (1997), pp. 438–439.

2 Postwar Reconstruction

In fall 1944, the German occupation ended after heavy fighting, especially in northeastern Estonia and around the town of Narva, which went on for months and inflicted heavy destruction there. The resulting invasion by the Red Army meant not liberation but the replacement of one occupier by another. Even as fighting continued, a wave of political arrests started, with 13,700 victims in 1944/45.[291] The arrestees were mainly accused, rightly or wrongly, of collaboration with the Germans. Meanwhile, many Soviet soldiers behaved not as if they were in a liberated Soviet republic but as if they were on enemy territory: they stole, robbed, murdered, and raped. According to statistics by the People's Commissariat of the Interior of the ESSR, they conducted the majority of registered crimes in the fourth quarter of 1944.[292] In the Baltic Soviet republics, martial law was officially suspended on June 27, 1946,[293] yet armed conflicts with anti-Soviet partisans, known as the Forest Brothers, lasted well into the 1950s.[294] In 1947, approximately 95,000 Soviet troops were based in Estonia.[295] This was roughly equivalent to one-tenth of the civilian population. Those troops were obviously supplied mostly with Estonian resources, and because of their sheer number, the bases demanded by Moscow, and the need to house them, they posed a substantial obstacle to reconstruction. However, in the immediate postwar period, "construction battalions" participated in the reconstruction of destroyed infrastructure and buildings. Estonian archives do not contain enough information on these battalions to allow us to estimate their share in the reconstruction effort.

Unlike in 1940, this time the communists in the Soviet hinterland thoroughly prepared for their takeover of Estonia. Starting in the spring of 1943, party and Komsomol activists, lawyers, financial experts, and even tractor drivers trained

---

291 Leo Õispuu (ed.), *Nõukogude Okupatsioonivõimu poliitilised arreteerimised Eestis*, vol. 2 (Tallinn, 1998), p. D5; see also Olaf Mertelsmann and Aigi Rahi-Tamm, "Cleansing and Compromise: The Estonian SSR in 1944–1945," *Cahiers du Monde Russe* 49 (2008), pp. 319–340.

292 Report on the work of the militiia, January 6, 1945, ERA 1-3-435, l. 1.

293 Bernd Bonwetsch, "Sowjetunion—Triumph im Elend," in Ulrich Herbert and Axel Schildt (eds.), *Kriegsende in Europa* (Essen, 1998), p. 62.

294 See Laar, *War in the Woods*.

295 David Vseviov, *Kirde-Eesti urbaanse anomaalia kujunemine ning struktuur pärast Teist maailmasõda* (Tallinn, 2002), p. 45.

in three-month courses for their future tasks in Estonia.[296] Most of these people had previously been evacuated voluntarily or not from Estonia. In December 1943, cadres for security services were made available to be replenished by additional participants of courses and increasing recruitment. The republican NKVD (People's Commissariat for Internal Affairs) already had about 400 employees.[297] In contrast to 1940, the existing state apparatus was not to be remodeled and restructured. Instead, the party was to march into Estonia having already formed the nucleus of an administration. This administration was to be supplemented by existing institutions and further recruitment. For example, the state planning committee thoroughly prepared itself for the future task even before the invasion of Tallinn. As soon as the town was taken, the committee would be able to start activities, register the condition of enterprises and take inventory, plan reconstruction work, and develop plans for the fourth quarter of 1944 and for 1945. Execution of the plans was impeded by the lack of recruitment for people's commissariats.[298]

The communists established power first in the towns, while in the countryside, life continued for a long time as usual. Although a second land reform started immediately, as did the system of forced procurement and work norms, the party and state were initially too weak to concretely assert their authority in the countryside. This aim was achieved with a second mass deportation in March 1949[299] and the beginning of forced collectivization of agriculture, for which, as a preliminary step, agricultural taxes had been increased enormously starting in 1947.[300] In 1950 the leadership of the Estonian Communist Party was replaced in the framework of the Estonian affair; Nikolai Karotamm was replaced as first party secretary by Johannes Käbin. A wave of purges started in the party, state,

---

296 Meeting of the CC Bureau of the ECP, April 16, 1943, ERAF 1-4-88, l. 30.

297 Meeting of the CC Bureau of the ECP, December 24 and 28, 1943, ERAF 1-4-97, l. 85–86.

298 Overview of the activities of Gosplan until 1948, ERAF 1-47-30, October 28, 1948, l. 168–169.

299 On repressions, see Aigi Rahi, *1949. aasta märtsiküüditamine Tartu linnas ja maakonnas* (Tartu, 1998); Aigi Rahi-Tamm, *Teise maailmasõja järgsed massirepressioonid Eestis: allikad ja uurimisseis* (Tartu, 2004); Aigi Rahi-Tamm, "Deportation und Verfolgung in Estland 1940–1953," in Mertelsmann (ed.), *Vom Hitler-Stalin-Pakt*, pp. 211–237; Olaf Mertelsmann and Aigi Rahi-Tamm, "Soviet Mass Violence in Estonia Revisited", *Journal of Genocide Research* 11 (2009), pp. 307–322.

300 Taagepera, "Soviet Collectivization of Estonian Agriculture: The Taxation Phase," pp. 263–282.

culture, and education, continuing until 1952.[301] Many lines of continuity with the period of independence were broken by the purge.

The collectivization of agriculture was mostly finished by the early 1950s. Partisan activity declined. After the death of Stalin in 1953, amnesties began immediately, but it took a couple of years before actual de-Stalinization and clear policy changes occurred. The regime stopped employing mass terror and started cautious reforms. By the middle of the decade, the majority of the Estonian population had evidently adapted themselves to the Soviet conditions. The Estonian SSR was on the way to becoming a model Soviet republic with an above-average standard of living and economic development. The Stalinist restructuring of the economy was completed, too.

This chapter offers an overview of postwar reconstruction; the thematic chapters that folllow it go more into detail. The available sources are of poorer quality than for the first Soviet year and the documentation is more incomplete. Before the war, the existing state apparatus was remodeled and restructured into that of a union republic. Many statistical overviews also dealt with the period of independence. There was some continuity in bureaucratic procedures, and they were changed only gradually. Many more files survived, obviously to document the historical development. After the Red Army's second occupation of Estonia, Soviet bureaucratic procedures were implemented immediately, and the credentials of the civil servants in question were lower. Since more and more enterprises fell under the jurisdiction of ministries in Moscow, the relevant documents in Estonia are scattered. In addition, the Estonian leadership's influence on economic policies declined, and thus many developments are scarcely reflected in Estonian archival holdings. Furthermore, the archival holdings of republican ministries were culled to generate waste paper. These are the main reasons why the processes were not as well documented as in the first Soviet year. Additional research in Moscow might round out the picture in the future. But it is questionable whether this will change the main findings.

---

301 Elena Zubkova, "Fenomen 'mestnogo natsionalizma': 'estonskoe delo' 1949–1952 godov v kontekste sovetizatsii Baltii," *Otechestvennaia istoriia* 10 (2001), no. 3, pp. 89–102; Elena Zubkova, "Kaderpolitik und Säuberungen in der KPdSU (1945–1953)," in Hermann Weber and Ulrich Mählert (eds.), *Terror: Stalinistische Parteisäuberungen 1936–1953* (Paderborn, 1998), pp. 187–236.

The Amount of War Damage

As a total war, World War II led to severe damage and population losses in the Soviet Union. According to estimates by Mark Harrison, the Soviet GDP in 1945 might have been approximately one-sixth smaller than in 1940.[302] Due to the high defense expenses, ordinary people, as consumers, were disproportionately affected.[303] In 1946–1947, a famine in parts of Russia, Ukraine, and Moldavia killed more than one million people.[304] Millions had fled because of hunger and the outcomes of war.

War damages in Estonia were according to official information extraordinary. Only 55 percent of industrial capacity, 7 percent of the means of transportation, 60 percent of cultivated land, and 45 percent of urban living space remained.[305] According to the documentation of the Extraordinary Commission for War Damage, 130,000 citizens of the Estonian SSR were deported to carry out forced labor in Germany, 61,000 citizens were killed by the Germans, and an additional 64,000 Soviet citizens (meaning those from other republics) and Soviet prisoners of war died in Estonia.[306] In most cases, those figures do not stand up to a critical examination. They were obviously substantially inflated. This happened for several reasons. Explanations were needed for the massive loss of population due to the mass flight of refugees to the West in 1944 and the Stalinist terror, to hide the relatively low degree of destruction, and to apply for the reconstruction funds from the central authorities.

New research finds that German state terror killed approximately 8,000 Estonian citizens (see Chapter 3). The number of deaths among Soviet prisoners of war and "Soviet citizens," mostly Jews from Latvia and Lithuania, is not known exactly but was probably less than 30,000. Forced labor in Germany did not play an important role in Estonia; the statistical headings "killed by the Germans" and "deported to conduct forced labor" were used to hide the losses of refugees, veterans of the Wehrmacht and the Waffen-SS, war deaths, victims of the Soviets, and people who were evacuated to the Soviet hinterland. Undoubtedly, Estonia

---

302 Mark Harrison, "The Soviet Union: The Defeated Victor," in Harrison (ed.), *The Economics of World War II*, p. 283.

303 Ibid., p. 297.

304 V.F. Zima, *Golod v SSSR 1946–1947 godov: proiskhodeshchdenie i posledstviia* (Moscow, 1996).

305 Misiunas and Taagepera, *The Baltic States*, p. 74.

306 Quoted in Pavel Polian, *Zhertvy dvuch diktatur: Ostarbeitery i voennoplennye v Tret'em Reikhe i ikh repatriatsiia* (Moscow, 1996), p. 369.

suffered enormous population losses, but they were caused more by Stalin's policies than by the war.

The officially declared percentage loss of industrial capacity seems realistic. Starting in 1940, wear and tear outpaced investment, and both sides destroyed and evacuated machinery and equipment. The Ministry for Local Industries stated in 1948: "At the time of liberation, industry was in a neglected condition. Some large factories were completely destroyed during the German occupation. Others sustained varying degrees of damage, and the machinery was transported to Germany. The production capacities of those enterprises that remained fully intact were reduced to a minimum through improper handling of the machinery during occupation." There was a lack of raw materials, skilled labor, engineers, cars, and fuel. One-sixth of the enterprises could not be reconstructed.[307] Electric power stations lost 38 percent of their capacity, five out of seven oil shale mines were damaged, and two out of seven oil shale processing facilities were in operation in early 1945.[308] The real decline of means of transport cannot be established. In this category the Soviets probably included cars, trucks, and railway stock. Given the low level of motorization and the importance of horse power in agriculture and even in towns for transport, the statistic claiming the destruction of 93 percent of all means of transport is not realistic.

Concerning agriculture, Soviet sources are clear. During and after the German occupation, the amount of cultivated land stayed, with slight fluctuations, at around 700,000 hectares, and this size was closely related to the economic conditions of a command economy. The building stock of agriculture was barely damaged by the war (see Table 4). Information is not complete—reports are missing from 15 percent of the parishes—but the picture is quite clear. Approximately 4,600 farms were affected in some way, and in most cases, only parts of the buildings were destroyed. Since there were roughly 140,000 farms in all, the damage to the building stock might have been 3 percent.

---

307 Report on activities 1940–1948, Ministry for Local Industry, October 7, 1948, ERAF 1-47-30, l. 26ff.

308 Report of the Bureau of the CC of the VKP(b) for Estonia about the work from January 1 to May 1, 1945, RGASPI f. 598, op. 1, d. 2, l. 13.

Table 4: War Damage in the Countryside (Information on 85 percent of all parishes)

Category	Completely destroyed	Damaged
Dwellings	3,120	2,405
Stables and barns	3,550	1,765
Sheds	2,280	1,070
Other buildings	4,390	2,100

Affected farms 4,045 of more than 140,000 farms.

Source: ERA R-6-16-1, l. 11a.

The number of farm animals declined between January 1941 and 1944. Although we do not have figures for June 1941, by that time Soviet agricultural policies had already caused a decline of the animal stock. In the fall of 1944, there were reportedly only two-thirds of the horses and cows and 55 percent of the pigs that there had been in January 1941.[309] It might be expected that, after four years of experience with a command economy, peasants underreported their stocks of animals, because the amount of forced procurement and taxes also depended on the number of animals. A contemporary witness remembered: "To conceal the actual number of animals was a necessary duty."[310] Interestingly, the number of tractors declined by only one-quarter, to 1,310.[311] The loss of cattle or of work horses definitely caused hardship for the affected families, but it was nothing compared to the scorched-earth tactics used by Germans and Soviets alike in Russia and Ukraine. Exceptionally, in Estonia there was no large-scale destruction of villages in 1941 or 1944. Given that the population had shrunk from 1.1 million to 854,000,[312] the decline of agricultural potential would not threaten food supplies, since Estonia had been a natural food-surplus region before the war. The decline appears to be less dramatic, as suggested by the halving of agricultural output from 1940 to 1945,[313] since buildings and machinery were less

309 Data for January 1941, ERA R1-47-49, l. 61; for October 1944, 1944, ERA R-1-5-93, unnumbered.

310 KV 904, l. 104.

311 ERA R-1-5-93.

312 Statistical overview, ERA R-10-43-155, l. 1.

313 Data on agricultural output 1940 and 1945, ERA R-6-16-17, l. 78.

affected. The problems of Estonian agriculture and food supply were caused less by the war than by the economic and political framework.

The scale of destruction of urban living space is also exaggerated. From a letter by Nikolai Karotamm to the CC of the VKP(b) (All-Russian Communist Party [Bolsheviks]) we know that in Tallinn, what was destroyed was not half of living space but only 500,000 m^2 out of 1.8 million m^2, or 27 percent.[314] The Extraordinary Commission was even more precise. It found that 451,492 m^2 out of 1,755,000 m^2 of living space was demolished in Tallinn[315]—exactly 25.7 percent. There is no question that Narva and Paldiski were nearly completely destroyed, but the loss of urban living space due to the war was definitely less than 30 percent. In a statistical overview, the Extraordinary Commission reports 9,200 destroyed houses in 31 Estonian towns, out of a total of 39,500.[316] This means that just 23 percent of all urban houses were destroyed. In addition, in fighting and during bombing raids, the Soviet demolished more housing than the Germans. The difference between the official and the actual figures emerged because flats for functionaries and the military and buildings used by state institutions no longer showed up in the housing stock (Russian: *zhilfond*). The Soviet state and the army took over the allegedly destroyed houses. This new use was secret. Thus the Germans could be blamed for the lack of housing and not the party, state, and army who occupied a quarter of living space.

To sum up, the scale of war destruction was not extraordinarily high. Bottlenecks in transport and destroyed power stations and electricity lines, along with the substantial population loss, were the biggest problems. The largest and most important sector of the economy, agriculture, suffered much less damage than industry.

As a result of the war, the Estonian SSR was able to use prisoners of war for reconstruction work—38,000 in 1945 and nearly 46,000 in the following year.[317] In 1945, there were even plans to house a projected figure of 71,400 prisoners in

---

314 Karotamm to Pozdniak, administration for the control of party organs at the CC of the VKP(b), May 21, 1947, ERAF 1-5-77, l. 159–160.

315 Report, GARF f. R-7021, o. 97, d. 6, l. 24.

316 Statistical overview, GARF f. R-7021, o. 97, d. 6, l. 24.

317 Deputy People's Commissar for Internal Affairs Ivanov to Karotamm, May 30, 1945, ERAF 1-3-438, l. 4; statistics on prisoners of war for 1946, ERAF 1-1/4-47, l. 8. On prisoners of war, see also Peeter Kaasik, *Nõukogude Liidu sõjavangidepoliitika teise maailmasõja ajal ja sõjajärgsetel aastatel: Sõjavangide kinnipidamissüsteem Eesti näitel ja hinnang sõjavangide kohtlemisele rahvusvahelise õiguse järgi* (Tallinn, 2012).

eight camps.[318] These were not only Germans and Austrians but also members of other nationalities fighting in German uniform. Three-quarters of the prisoners' labor was directed toward the oil shale industry and building projects in northeastern Estonia, and only a smaller share went toward the reconstruction of towns.[319] The productivity of prisoners in the USSR was approximately one-half that of free workers, and the gulag needed subsidies,[320] although the central camp administration was paid for prison labor according to the fulfillment of work norms. Because of this, the importance of forced labor for the reconstruction of Estonia should not be overstated, even when the Estonian leadership estimated the productivity of prisoners to be two-thirds that of ordinary workers.[321] When the last prisoners of war were freed and repatriated in 1949, an optimistic report stated that their work in Estonia contributed the equivalent of 100 million rubles for the state budget.[322] This was obviously wishful thinking. Starting in 1949, the prisoners of war were replaced by an unknown number of inmates of camps for corrective labor.[323] In addition, in the postwar years, filtration camps and labor battalions operated in Estonia and represented additional sources of labor.

In addition to prisoners of war, dismantled machinery and equipment from Germany and Central Europe brought some compensation for war losses.[324] The sources do not quantify how much Estonia profited from this dismantling. However, one report on local industry in 1945 states that war damage of this people's commissariat amounted to 2.5 million rubles and that German equipment arriving in 1945 was worth 2.7 million rubles.[325] German machinery and equipment

---

318 *Retours d'URSS: Les prisonniers de guerre et les internés français dans les archives soviétiques 1945–1951* (Paris, 2001), p. 107.

319 Ivanov to Karotamm, ERAF 1-3-438, l. 4.

320 G.M. Ivanova, *GULAG v sisteme totalitarnogo gosudarstva* (Moscow, 1997), pp. 102, 145.
For more on the economics of the Stalinist camp system, see Paul R. Gregory and Valery Lazarev (eds.), *The Economics of Forced Labor: The Soviet Gulag* (Stanford, 2003).

321 Statement of Arnold Veimer, meeting of the CC Bureau of the ECP, July 29, 1948, ERAF 1-4-656, l. 47.

322 Report of the political department of the POW camps in Estonia, October 22, 1949, ERAF 1-14-76, l. 7.

323 Vseviov, *Kirde-Eesti*, p. 40.

324 Misiunas and Taagepera, *The Baltic States*, p. 110.

325 Titov to Chairman Perov, report on local industry in 1945 and in the first quarter of 1946, April 17, 1946, RGASPI f. 598, o. 1, d. 10, l. 48.

are mentioned in life stories, sometimes with the comment that they were difficult to use due to the lack of instructions.

Planning for Reconstruction

Victory in World War II reinforced the conviction of Stalin and his associates that Soviet economic policies, which called for strengthening heavy industry, the arms industry, and the command economy, were the right way forward. They saw no reason to diverge from the industrialization drive of the 1930s. Keeping the standard of living of the population artificially low, along with the procurement prices of agricultural products, was an essential part of this economic system. The era of shortages that lay ahead was indicated by the plan targets published in newspapers in 1946. In 1950 one pair of shoes and one pair of socks was to be produced per inhabitant of Estonia, as well as one bicycle for every 400 inhabitants. Many other output targets for products were well below the prewar level.[326] Due to the start of the Cold War in 1946–1947, the defense industry remained highly important. The Soviet Five-Year Plan for 1946–1950 called for heavy industry to receive a staggering 88 percent of all industrial investment.[327] In the long run, Estonia had to follow the Soviet model, even though the economy had a different structure than in the "old" republics, with private farms, a higher share of light industry, and the production of consumer goods. In 1945, three-quarters of the "products of general demand," though low in volume, including products of the food industry, were manufactured by cooperatives of craftsmen (*artel'*).[328] This would change in the future.

In their interpretation of industrialization, the Bolsheviks followed a concept that was widespread in the first half of the 20th century. Based on the development of Great Britain and later of Germany, where mining, metal works, the energy sector, and heavy industry in general played an important role, they decided to develop these "key industries" at the expense of other sectors of the economy.[329] They ignored the fact that the conditions in Britain and Germany

326 "Seadus. Eesti NSV rahvamajanduse taastamine ja arendamine viie aasta plaani kohta 1946-1950.a.," *Postimees*, July 18, 1946.

327 Filtzer, "Wirtschaft und Gesellschaft," p. 80.

328 Meeting of the CC Bureau of the ECP, October 31, 1945, ERAF 1-4-217, l. 10.

329 See the definition in the *Great Soviet Encyclopedia*: "Socialist industrialization: The process of building up and developing a strong engineering industry and especially heavy industry, securing a deep transformation and the growth of the entire national economy on the basis of developed technology and a socialist way of economic activities." *Bol'shaia Sovetskaia Entsiklopediia*, vol. 40 (Moscow, 1957), p. 168.

in the 19th century were completely different, that their interpretation of the industrialization was selective, and that a once-successful path could not simply be copied. In addition, the Bolsheviks did not note that the industrialization of the 19th century was accompanied by an institutional revolution.[330]

Another typical feature of the socialist model was extensive development. The increase of a factory's output was the result not so much of intensifying production and achieving higher efficiency through investment into technologies and machinery as of simply increasing the labor force. Mark Harrison has calculated that over a span of 20 years, productivity per Soviet laborer did not meaningfully increase (see Table 5). Industrial production increased only if more workers were hired. To increase growth in one sector, scarce labor needed be drawn from another sector. This was one main task of postwar planning: employment in agriculture had to decline for the sake of industry and the state service sector.

Table 5: Productivity per Work Hour in Soviet Industry, 1928–1950

Year	Index of productivity 1950 = 100	Year	Index of productivity 1950 = 100
1928	94	1940	91
1929	102	1941	85
1930	107	1942	100
1931	94	1943	107
1932	71	1944	106
1933	74	1945	89
1934	80	1946	69
1935	89	1947	75
1936	99	1948	85
1937	100	1949	96

330 See Clemens Wischerding and Anne Nieberling, *Die institutionelle Revolution: Eine Einführung in die deutsche Wirtschaftsgeschichte des 19. und 20. Jahrhunderts* (Stuttgart, 2004); North, *Institutions, Instituional Change.*

Table 5: Continued

Year	Index of productivity 1950 = 100	Year	Index of productivity 1950 = 100
1938	101	1950	100
1939	104		

Source: Mark Harrison, "Wartime Mobilization: A German Comparison," Barber and Harrison (eds.), *The Soviet Defence Industry Complex*, p. 110.

The plan for the national economy of the Estonian SSR set down the order of the priorities of the reconstruction of industry. In first place were energy companies, followed by the oil shale industry, construction, and suppliers, then engineering companies and metal works; last on the list were textile and food processing industries.[331] On December 8, 1944, for example, the power station of Kohtla-Järve oil shale plant started to operate.[332] The scale of the defense industry could not be determined from the sources. Secret defense installations like the uranium enrichment factory in Sillamäe do appear in Estonian documents, but they were subordinated to Moscow and were not accountable to the Estonian SSR.

Nevertheless, we know something about this large project. In northeastern Estonia, one layer of earth originating from plankton contains radioactive metals, including uranium. In 1946, construction started on an uranium enrichment facility in Sillamäe, siphoning resources from the nearly completely destroyed town of Narva. On this large construction site, more than 20,000 people worked, most of them prisoners and members of labor and construction battalions. For a time, only 2 percent of the workers were free workers. In 1948–1952, uranium was extracted from local rocks, a process that turned out to be uneconomical. Because of that, the mining was stopped in 1952, and rocks were used that had been mined in other locations in the USSR. This project was connected to the Soviet nuclear-arms program; the factory was in use until 1991.[333]

---

331 Explanatory report on the plan for the national economy for 1945, May 16, 1945, ERAF 1-3-429, l. 1.

332 Toomas Vaimann and Endel Risthein, *Eesti energeetika 100 aastat* (Tallinn, 2018), p. 98.

333 Ello Maremäe, "Sillamäe uraanitehaste asutamine ja töö aastatel 1946–1952 (1973): Eesti diktüoneemakilda kasutamine," *Akadeemia* 12 (2000), pp. 476–512. On the reconstruction of Narva, see Karsten Brüggemann, "Der Wiederaufbau Narvas nach 1944 und die Utopie der 'sozialistischen Stadt,'" in Karsten Brüggemann (ed.), *Narva und die Ostseeregion* (Narva, 2004), pp. 81–103.

To quote Estonian party leader Karotamm from October 1945: "The plan of electrification of the republic foresees the securing of the energy supply of the naval base, of the republican and all-union industrial enterprises, of transport, including the electrification of the Tallinn-Leningrad and Tallinn-Keila railway lines, of urban development, and of municipal supplies." To this end, existing capacities had to be expanded, and an oil-shale-based electricity plant in Ahtme and a peat-based power station in Lavasaare had to be built.[334] The order of the list was not a coincidence: first came the military, then industry, transport, and urban construction, and last came the population.

After combat ended, the reopening of power plants was understandably of the highest priority. But one main aim of postwar reconstruction was the major expansion of the energy sector, mainly through the use of oil shale mined in northeastern Estonia and the expansion of the oil shale industry. Only after this were the other branches of industry to be developed, concentrating on certain fields.[335] This led to an asymmetric development: Tallinn and the northeast received preferential support, while the relatively well-developed sphere of agriculture was neglected. At the same time, "large building sites of socialism" emerged.[336]

As a result, oil shale occupied a central position in the planning for the republic. Oil shale could be used to produce electricity or gas or to provide the basic material for concrete or for the chemical industry. Oil, grease, and kerosene could be produced from oil shale. The Soviet planners continued down the path set in the prewar period. However, the use of oil shale required state subsidies and was largely uneconomical, because its fuel value was low compared to coal. By 1950, 40 percent of all industrial investment in the republic was going to the oil shale industry. Starting in 1948, Leningrad was supplied with gas made from Estonian oil shale; meanwhile, Tallinn was connected only years later. Obviously, under the Soviets, the utilization of oil shale also accrued enormous real economic losses. Due to the problems with accounting everything at fixed prices, these losses could not be detected properly. It was a huge misallocation of scarce investment capital and, in practical terms, a permanent loss of value.[337]

334 Copy, Karotamm to Pavlenko, member of the CC of the VKP(b), October 13, 1945, ERAF 1-3-423, l. 123.

335 Report on the first years of the Five-Year Plan (1951–1955), ERAF 1-1-26-33, l. 119.

336 On the large projects, see Klaus Gestwa, "Herrschaft und Technik in der spät- und poststalinistischen Sowjetunion: Machtverhältnisse auf den 'Großbaustellen des Kommunismus,' 1948–1964," *Osteuropa* 51 (2001), pp. 171–197.

337 Olaf Mertelsmann, "Die Herausbildung des Sonderstatus der Nordostregion innerhalb der Estnischen SSR," in Brüggemann (ed.), *Narva und die Ostseergion*, pp. 108–109.

The priority put on oil shale followed Soviet plans from late 1940 and early 1941, as mentioned above. On June 10, 1945, the State Defense Committee, a kind of a Soviet war cabinet headed by Stalin, issued Decision No. 9049s "On the Reconstruction and Development of the Oil Shale Industry of the Estonian SSR and of Leningrad Oblast and on the Supply of Leningrad with Gas, on Special Tasks and Objects of Reconstruction Work, as Well as on Objects of New Construction in the Years 1945–1948." This led to the construction or reconstruction of the following installations in Estonia:

1. Two new facilities to produce gas from oil shale in Kohtla-Järve and Ahtme for the annual production of 800 million m^3 of gas.
2. The reconstruction and expansion of oil shale processing facilities with a capacity of 585,000 tons.
3. Construction Project 14, new mines with annual capacity of 7.8 million tons of oil shale.
4. Reconstruction of the old mines.
5. Reconstruction and construction of power plants.[338]

Shortly after the end of the war in Europe, when the State Defense Committee ordered an expansion of oil shale mining and processing, it seems clear that not only economic but also military interests were involved. Oil shale was seen as a source of fossil fuels for the military, be it the navy, the air force, or the army. There is clear evidence of the use of prison labor: the NKVD of the USSR was responsible for the administration of the construction of gas works and gasification plants.[339] About 80 percent of the roughly 17,000 workers of the oil shale industry consisted of prisoners of war. In 1946 alone, 146 million rubles was invested in the Estonian oil shale industry. "The further reconstruction and development of the oil shale industry will depend on the growth of the energetic base in the oil shale region," concludes the report.[340] This is what happened in the subsequent years. By 1951, 55 percent of all power plants were located in northeastern Estonia.[341]

Another report from 1946 describes the conditions in oil shale construction. Starting in October 1945, more than 11,000 prisoners of war worked on

338 Overview of oil shale industry in the Estonian SSR, A. Skripnin, April 22, 1946, RGASPI f. 598, o. 1, d. 10 l. 126–127.

339 Ibid., l. 128.

340 Ibid., l. 131–132, 135.

341 Vaimann and Risthein, *Eesti energeetika 100 aastat*, pp. 109–110.

the construction sites of Estonian Oil Shale Construction; the daily output per worker was worth less than 10 rubles. The report said: "This catastrophically low indicator of productivity is primarily related to [the workers'] physical exhaustion." Irregular food supplies and extremely small rations had caused this situation. Epidemic diseases like dysentery flourished, hygienic conditions left much to be desired, and there was not even proper drinking water. Even a diet of 2,200 to 2,800 calories per day was not sufficient for physical recovery. More food was needed, as well as more soap and more frequent disinfection, along with other measures.[342]

The planning and execution of the expansion of the oil shale industry was not centralized. At least 29 different Soviet institutions, such as ministries and chief administrations (Russian: *glavki*), were involved in the process.[343] The resulting turf war can easily be imagined. Some enterprises were subordinated to the republic, others to ministries in Moscow, and a third group (such as the uranium enrichment factory in Sillamäe) belonged to the military-industrial complex. Depending on the position of the responsible institution in the supply hierarchy and the importance of the individual enterprise, the situation on the ground proved very different.

Because the living and working conditions in the oil shale region were the worst in all of Estonia, there were considerable problems recruiting labor. Even mobilization by force from other regions of Estonia did not help. Since there was a famine in parts of Russia along with the opportunity to migrate, many Russian-speaking immigrants found their first employment in this region. The vast majority of this immigration was not managed by the Soviet state but occurred spontaneously and at the immigrants' own initiative. As a result, the towns in Ida-Virumaa became largely Russian-speaking.[344] The assumption by Misiunas and Taagepera that migrants were "mostly" imported by the state[345] was not confirmed in the archives.

Concerning Soviet economic policy in Estonia, some academic literature simply describes it as a sort of "colonial economy" or a "colonization."[346] Here I

---

342 Report of the Estonian Oil Shale Construction Trust to Chairman Perov, undated, before July 9, 1946, RGASPI f. 598, o. 1, d. 10, l. 138–141.

343 Tomson, *Eesti majandusajalugu*, p. 85.

344 Mertelsmann, "Die Herausbildung des Sonderstatus," pp. 112–120.

345 Misiunas and Taagepera, *The Baltic States*, p. 111.

346 Kalev Kukk, "Economic Damage," in Vello Salo (ed.), *The White Book: Losses Inflicted on the Estonian Nation by Occupation Regimes 1940–1991* (Tallinn, 2005), p. 143; Rahi-Tamm, "Deportation und Verfolgung," p. 237; Laar, "Eesti ja kommunism," p. 869.

must strenuously object. Undoubtedly, Estonia's economy suffered heavy losses under the Soviets, and for the first Soviet year in 1940/41, there was a demonstrable policy of exploitation. However, Estonia was not a Soviet colony to be ransacked but a Soviet republic taking part in a utopian project. The intention was that Estonia should benefit from the project. The postwar plans no longer foresaw outright "exploitation." On the contrary, the internal trade balance by Gosplan indicated a substantial excess of imports for the period 1944–1948;[347] for later times, reliable statistics are not available. In the framework of the Soviet price systems, it is impossible to establish a precise balance sheet, but Estonia received above-average investment from Moscow because of its existing infrastructure, geographic location, higher level of development, and better-educated workforce.[348] The relatively low economic growth of the Estonian economy during the Soviet period was caused not by colonial dependence but by the poor performance of the Soviet command economy. The support for an uneconomical branch like the oil shale industry provides evidence for this.

Main Lines of Development

The preference granted to energy and heavy industry and the neglect of living standards and consumer goods were typical of the postwar years in Estonia and the entire USSR. First of all, the following tasks had to be carried out: to return the economy to peacetime conditions, to demobilize the army, to stabilize the currency, to reconstruct the infrastructure of trade, to end rationing, and to normalize the price structure. According to a Soviet source, Soviet state retail prices in 1945 were an average of 267 percent what they had been in 1940, resulting in a halving of real incomes.[349] Actually, the Soviet economy was in a sort of permanent supply crisis. Between 1916 (still under the tsarist regime) and 1949, only three years passed without famines or hunger in entire regions. Julie Hessler divides Soviet economic history into two parts: the phase of recurring

347 Balance of trade 1944–1948, compiled by Gosplan, December 9, 1948, ERAF 1-47-29, l. 186ff.

348 An official presentation of Estonian economic development from 1940 to 1960 states that the per capita level of investment was 52 percent above the Soviet average in 1946–1950 and 22 percent above the Soviet average in the five years after that. L. Brutus, "Eesti NSV sotsialistlikust industrialiseerimisest," *Nõukogude Eesti majandus 1940–1960*, p. 56.

349 Harrison, "The Soviet Union," p. 278.

and sometimes life-threatening crises ended by 1948/49 and was followed by a "normal" phase that was still overshadowed by shortages.[350]

The rationing system secured a minimum level of basic supplies for the urban population and state employees, but it led to a distortion of the pricing structure. The rations—when they were available at all—were sold at a low fixed price; other foodstuffs had to be bought on the market at several times the price. Contemporaries complained about "speculators,"[351] whose emergence was a natural outcome of the rationing; the state also made them an image of the enemy in campaigns against them. On the flourishing black market and on the peasant market, nearly everything was available. The state also operated "commercial" shops, in which goods were sold at much higher prices than the ration price. Until the currency reform, privately distilled moonshine was, in some places, used as ersatz currency and was more important than money. Later, the importance of bootlegging declined, although it never disappeared completely.[352] After the currency reform, deflation started. While the prices were falling, urban real incomes increased.

In a local study on Rostov-on-Don, Jeffrey W. Jones describes the illegal economy and the speculators in the time of rationing. His account is comparable to the situation in Estonia after the end of combat. In Rostov-on-Don and in other places, the extreme shortages led to illegal trade. Large-scale profiteering was deemed immoral; other strategies were accepted, such as the black market, the payment of "tips" for public services, or outright corruption. The party and the press did officially acknowledge the thriving of the illegal economy and the availability of countless goods at inflated prices. However, the roots of the problem were ignored, and individuals who engaged in this trade were attacked. Internally, the party stated that the situation was even worse: illicit trade was highly mobile, theft was widespread, and the *militsiia* (Soviet police) were corrupt. There were economic reasons for all this, and the authorities exercised a high level of tolerance toward illegal economic activities. Interviews with

350 Julie Hessler, "Postwar Normalisation and Its Limits in the USSR: The Case of Trade," *Europe-Asia Studies* 53 (2001), pp. 445–446.

351 Diary entry by Jaan Roos, August 30, 1945: "One group of people nevertheless feels fine—the speculators. Never before has speculation bloomed as it does today, and never has it had so much leeway. Life in Russia seems to be based on two pillars: theft and speculation. Whoever masters this has a chance to live. The others starve and are slaves." Jaan Roos, *Läbi punase öö* I (Tartu, 1997), p. 210.

352 See Mertelsmann, "Estonian Moonshine."

contemporary witnesses confirmed the thriving of the black market and the key role of theft.[353]

Bread was the most important food product to be rationed. In spring 1947, approximately 350,000 inhabitants of Estonia, not including army personnel, received their bread with the help of ration cards.[354] Rationing ended in December 1947 in tandem with the currency reform. Back in 1944, the inhabitants of Estonia had experienced how the German occupation currency was taken out of circulation. The renewed currency reform in the entire USSR functioned as a form of confiscation; state debt and savings declined rapidly. However, state and market prices decreased or remained the same as the ration prices.[355] In Estonia, as in the rest of the Soviet Union, economic normalization slowly started. This was demonstrated by the fact that the general public no longer bought up whatever came to the shops. Products of extremely low quality no longer sold well, and the overstocks filled storage facilities.[356]

A relevant difference between the newly acquired territories and the "old" republics was the dominance of the private sector in the economy. Nearly the entire sphere of agriculture was owned by peasants until collectivization. Officially, in 1945, the private economy accounted for 7 percent of the non-agrarian output and was to be nationalized until 1947.[357] That consisted of small enterprises and craftsmen's businesses, which were later collected into co-operatives and large state enterprises. Between 1948 and 1957, the number of workers and employees in this sector increased from 15,600 to 28,700.[358] Even after nationalization, many of those small enterprises were run by private individuals renting them.[359]

---

353 Jeffrey W. Jones, "'People Without a Define Occupation': The Illegal Economy and 'Speculators' in Rostov-on-the-Don, 1943–48," in Donald J. Raleigh (ed.), *Provincial Landscapes: Local Dimensions of Soviet Power, 1917–1953* (Pittsburgh, 2001), pp. 236–254.

354 Sazonov to Kuznetsov, secretary at the CC of the VKP(b), April 23, 1947, ERAF 1-5-77, l. 94.

355 Oleg Chlevnjuk, "Die sowjetische Wirtschaftspolitik im Spätstalinismus und die 'Affäre Gosplan,'" *Osteuropa* 50 (2000), pp. 1035–1036.

356 See the statement of the head of the main administration of the textiles industry, Prokhorov, at a meeting, February 14, 1948, ERA R-12-3-42, l. 24.

357 Tomson, *Eesti majandusajalugu*, p. 87.

358 Kala and Juursoo, "Nõukogude Eesti töölisklass," p. 140.

359 Out of 670 small enterprises, 250 were rented out to private operators in April 1948. Mills could not be nationalized at that time because of a capacity bottleneck. Meeting of the CC Bureau of the ECP, April 17, 1948, ERAF 1-4-654, l. 3, 5.

How important private economic activities really were will be discussed in the following chapters. An important task of economic restructuring after the war was the reduction and subjugation of the private sector. The main measures were nationalization and forced collectivization.

Another problem was the workforce. Because the vast majority of agriculture was in private hands until 1949 and the food supply situation in the countryside was much better than in the towns, it was a constant struggle to find suitable labor for the new projects. The organized recruitment of labor (abbreviated in Russian as *orgnabor*) primarily recruited demobilized soldiers and the agrarian population for work in industry and on construction sites. According to data cited by Donald Filtzer, who thinks the figures are too high, in 1946 about two million workers were recruited with the help of *orgnabor*, and in subsequent years until 1952, an additional 600,000 laborers annually were recruited this way. Those workers usually had to sign five-year contracts and were subject to other restrictions. Labor legislation made the change of workplaces difficult in any case.[360] In Estonia, *orgnabor* helped recruit 10,384 workers from 1945 to 1948[361] and 13,390 workers from 1949 to 1953. Only in the last year could the recruitment plan be fulfilled or over-fulfilled, since 500 amnestied people capable of work were placed in employment after Stalin's death.[362]

Another channel by which workers were hired was job training in labor reserve schools with a two-year program and factory schools with six months of training. From 1946 to 1952, three-fourths of Soviet students came from the countryside. While most of the students at the factory schools had been mobilized by force, the share of those mobilized in labor reserve schools was lower, and living and learning conditions were better. After finishing school, the young person had to work in the enterprise he or she was assigned to. Those who left school or work could be severely punished, especially those who were mobilized; until 1948, those leaving without permission could end up in the camps for several years. Nevertheless, the turnover rate remained high.[363] The authorities ended up relying overwhelmingly on coercive measures. The reconstruction basically happened using forced and compulsory labor.[364] One distinctive

360 Filtzer, *Soviet Workers and Late Stalinism*, pp. 31–34.

361 Report on the activities of the administration for labor reserves, 1948, ERA 1-47-29, l. 142.

362 Report on the activities of *orgnabor*, August 31, 1954, ERA R-1854-1-8, l. 17.

363 Ibid., l. 34–38.

364 Ibid., l. 40.

feature of Estonian vocational schools was that after the war, one-fourth of the students originated from Russia. Only about half of the students in vocational schools had completed elementary school (meaning they had at least six years of schooling).[365] The others were less educated.

The third method of labor recruitment was when the enterprise hired directly at the factory gates. Most jobs were filled in this way. Employment was regulated by draconian labor laws that criminalized normal behavior, such as changing one's job. Because of this, from 1946 to 1952, about 1.5 million industrial workers in the Soviet Union—more than one-tenth of all industrial laborers—were punished with imprisonment.[366] Nevertheless, the high labor turnover could not be reduced. An additional disciplinary measure was the "worker's book," a document every employed person had to possess. Plans called for a general introduction of worker's books in Estonia in the summer of 1941;[367] in practice, this happened only after the war.

Labor turnover afflicted also the higher ranking state organs. On January 1, 1950 all ministries of the Estonian SSR had 2,418 employees. During this year 2,677 persons were fired and 3,152 hired.[368] Even the nomenclature cadres of the Ministry of Wood and Paper Processing stayed barely longer than one year in their position. From 1947 until 1950, every nomenclature position was hold on the average by 3.4 different officials.[369] No "stability of cadres" could be reached in this way.

Work discipline was especially low on the large building sites. According to Gosplan, in 1947 the Estonian Oil Shale Construction Company lost 27.4 percent of work time to idling and 14.2 percent to unexcused absences. In the first seven months of 1948, the figures were even higher—35.9 percent of time lost due to idling and 24.1 percent to unexcused absences. In the Gas-Oil Shale Construction Enterprise, the situation looked similar. According to the source, neither enterprise was prepared to integrate the large number of youths and former prisoners into the work process. There was a shortage of masters and foremen, and the labor was badly organized.[370] In the second half of the 1940s, especially

---

365 Kala and Juursoo, "Nõukogude Eesti töölisklass," pp. 252–253.

366 Filtzer, *Soviet Workers and Late Stalinism*, p. 163.

367 Meeting of the CC Bureau of the ECP, May 29 and June 5, 1941, ERAF 1-4-71, l. 65.

368 Overview on ministries, 1950, ERAF 1-57-18, l. 30.

369 Calculated on the basis of the lists of nomenklatura, materials about the paper industry 1951, ERAF 1-57-18, l. 4-11.

370 Information about the labor reserves of the ESSR, Gosplan, December 4, 1948, ERAF 1-7-27, l. 36–37.

between 1946 and 1948, the work morale in state enterprises reached its lowest level, yet complaints did not end. For the first five months of 1947, the Ministry of Local Industry recorded rates of absenteeism between 9.4 and a staggering 21.3 percent; 5 percent would be a normal rate. In addition, the factories stopped operating completely between 1.2 and 8.8 percent of the time.[371]

Another example of state coercion was the unpaid work that peasants and, later, kolkhoz members were compelled to do. They had to maintain roads and cut and transport timber. From 1945 to 1948, "mobilized" peasants accounted for between 80 and 93 percent of the timber-cutting work and between 81 and 97 percent of the timber transport work in the framework of state forestry.[372] The scale of those works depended on the size of the farm and the status of the owner. Those who did not carry out their duties or failed to fulfill the norms could be punished with correctional labor.[373] Old age or illness was not accepted as an excuse.

The aforementioned measures of labor recruitment and strict work legislation were employed in Estonia. To this day, we do not know how many people were punished. Yet we would expect those figures to be on the scale of the Soviet average, which would mean more than 10,000 victims. As in all formerly German-occupied territories, the population was thoroughly investigated in a search for real and imagined collaborators. Within the authorities and in state enterprises, there was a screening of everyone who had previously worked under the Germans. At the Estonian railways, more than 10,000 people had to be screened.[374]

The demobilization was not conducted smoothly. In the summer of 1945, the CC Bureau of the ECP stated: "As a result of weak control by Soviet and party organs, the demobilized who are sent to work have no living space and no housing, and not enough has been done to arrange the supply of heating fuel. In some places in the countryside, the demobilized soldiers do not receive farm animals and inventory; in the towns of the counties, there is a shortage of living space and goods." *Orgnabor* did not make enough effort to find work for the demobilized: out of 807 demobilized people in Tallinn, up to 200 found a job on their own, and only 159 were recruited. Local party organizations showed a lack of interest.[375]

---

371 Meeting of the activists of local industry, June 20, 1947, ERA R-12-3-27, l. 11ff.
372 Report on the activities of forestry 1940–1948, ERA 1-47-29, l. 107.
373 Examples can be found among the correspondence concerning the legal system, 1945, ERAF 1-3-458.
374 Meeting of the CC Bureau of the ECP, November 10, 1944, ERAF 1-4-120, l. 36.
375 ERAF 1-4-208, l. 77.

The idea that the party and state could control the movements of workers and migration turned out to be an illusion. At the beginning of 1947, it was determined in a meeting of the Estonian CC Bureau that control over the passport system in Tallinn was weak. Enterprises hired workers based on all kinds of documents or with none at all. Throughout the republic, workers were also hired in places where room and board were absolutely inadequate; the actions of the leading personnel were deemed "criminal."[376] The Estonian leadership faced a dilemma. On the one hand, they stated that conditions on the ground were unbearable[377] and that it was impairing work discipline. On the other hand, they requested increases in employment at those enterprises and had caused the bad conditions with a policy of extreme austerity and forced growth.

Tõnis, born in 1927, describes how people worked under Soviet conditions. The working morale in northeastern Estonia was even lower: "Whether you wanted to or not, you had to use your work time for personal things, because the state offices were open only at that time. [...] This was not forbidden; you just had to say when and where you were going. [...] You had to avoid overfulfilling the plan too much, because then the work norms would be raised and you had to work more for the same wage. [...] If my memory is correct, socialist competition happened more on paper than in reality. [...] Every Soviet citizen found something to steal, even if it was only work time. In this way, everyone found something to 'expropriate.' You used the materials of your company to produce something for yourself or for sale. On the invoices and bills, you added a little extra. You used company transportation for personal purposes, without paying for it. This happened with the tacit acceptance of your superiors. They were no better. They did the same or maybe even more so."[378] Jaan Roos stated in April 1945: "The people lack the will and the interest to work."[379] Two years later, he

---

376 Meeting of the CC Bureau of the ECP, February 5, 1947, ERAF 1-4-411, l. 23–26.

377 In 1945, the construction plan for Sillamäe was only 57 percent fulfilled. The workers lived in overcrowded and filthy dormitories without furniture or in former bunkers; the food supply was irregular. Meeting of the Virumaa party committee, March 20, 1946, ERAF 1-1/4-106, l. 139.
In the fall of 1946, the plan fulfillment for the Vivikond pit was 61.7 percent. The management ignored the security of the standard of living of the workers; it was dirty and drinking water was scarce. "The organization of work, the question of the norms, of work discipline, of the conduction of socialist competition in the fulfillment of work duties concerning quality and speed is on a low level." Meeting of the party committee of Virumaa, October 31, 1946, ERAF 1-1/4-107, l. 244–245.

378 ERM-KV 998, l. 164–165.

379 Diary entry, April 30, 1945, Roos, *Läbi punase öö* I, p. 151.

noted a popular saying that summed up the situation: "What things do we have now? Work is a thing of honor, the wage is a very small thing, eating is a necessary thing, and theft is the main thing."[380]

The enterprises of local industry were audited in the spring of 1946. Productivity per worker in the 16 largest enterprises was low—only 76 percent of the level of 1940. The report states that the wages and the organization of work were the main reasons: "The wages are completely unrelated to the quality of the production." Technical equipment was lacking. Employee turnover in the last four months was 16 percent, and absenteeism amounted to 14 percent in the previous year. No one looked out for the material well-being of the workers. The plan for the construction of living space for the employed in 1945 was only fulfilled by 12 percent.[381]

The labor shortage in the oil shale industry and on the construction sites, where the conditions were the most appalling, were to be compensated by forced mobilization into labor reserve schools. In this context, the towns and counties had to fulfill a mobilization plan. In the summer of 1948, for example, the counties of Lääne, Pärnu, and Valga fulfilled, respectively, 30.7, 36.7, and 41.4 percent of the plan. The mobilization plan prescribed in detail how many youngsters from which area were to be sent to which vocational school.[382] The mobilization into vocational schools turned out much smaller than planned, and many graduates from those schools fled their workplace as soon as they had the chance. In spring 1948, the second secretary of the CC of the ECP, Sergei Sazonov, stated that 59 percent of vocational school graduates, who were sent to the northeast to work in mining, long-distance heating, and gasification of oil shale, had quit because of the bad living and working conditions. If the situation in the dormitories did not improve, said Sazonov, the public prosecutor would get involved.[383] In other words, even after using force, the state was unable to keep workers where the regime wanted them to be.

Even as labor shortages plagued the "large building sites of socialism" and it was impossible to hire enough workers and make them stay, there was considerable unemployment in Tallinn. Numerous enterprises declared a hiring freeze.

380 Diary entry, March 27, 1947, Jaan Roos, *Läbi punase öö* II (Tartu, 2000), p. 55.

381 F. Kaloshin, B. Titov, and V. Erit to Chairman Perov, May 20, 1946, RGASPI f. 598, o. 1, d. 10, l. 67–70.

382 Decision of the the Council of Ministers of the ESSR and the CC Bureau of the ECP, June 11, 1948, ERAF 1-4-579, l. 22–26.

383 Meeting of the CC Bureau of the ECP, May 19, 1948, ERAF 1-4-654, l. 136–137.

"Unemployment is not registered; if 17 women are needed, 320 show up. For two jobs, 20 people are coming,"[384] said Comrade Beliakov on a meeting of the CC Bureau.

Propaganda accounts later described reconstruction as a smooth process. However, the economic turn to a peacetime economy encountered many setbacks. For instance, the number of farm animals declined from January to summer 1945; given the season, the figures should have increased.[385] In spring 1945, construction was lagging 40 percent behind the plan. In April and May, industrial output declined, and in April, so did the average wages of industrial workers.[386] "The quality of products is in many cases far below the prewar level and is declining steadily," stated Sazonov in summer 1945 and added that production costs were too high. "A capitalist knows how much production costs and what kind of profit he makes, but here many people are not interested in total production costs and in reasonable accounting."[387]

In this context Sazonov spoke about a fundamental problem of the command economy. Since the enterprises made calculations based on prices fixed by the state, which did not reflect the relation between supply and demand, the scarcity of resources, or production costs, there was no real interest in increasing efficiency or in cutting real costs. In such an economic system, large-scale waste or real losses could go undetected and could even be registered as a success and an overfulfillment of the plan. In light of the huge losses of the Estonian Oil Shale Company, Vassilii Kossov, second secretary of the CC of the ECP, remarked at the beginning of 1952: "Under other circumstances [meaning capitalist ones] they would go bankrupt and be sold at auction."[388] The command economy had no provisions for this option.

Further problems existed: there were irregular supplies of enterprises, an excess inventory of certain goods, and poorly organized operational procedures. This led to an irregular rhythm of production and low quality. Concerning the Estonian food industry in 1949, it was stated that supply contracts were concluded too slowly; the delivered animals were not fed and watered enough and

384 Beliakov on the meeting of the CC Bureau of the ECP, July 29, 1948, ERAF 1-4-656, l. 59.

385 Meeting of the CC Bureau of the ECP, September 10 and 12, 1945, ERAF 1-4-206, l. 6.

386 Protocol of the plenum of the CC of the ECP, July 5–7, 1945, ERAF 1-4-140, l. 84, 86.

387 Stenograph of the plenum of the CC of the ECP, July 5–7, 1945, ERAF 1-4-141, l. 67–70.

388 Meeting of the CC Bureau of the ECP, January 14, 1952, ERAF 1-4-1434, l. 113.

thus lost too much weight; and there were large overstocks of particular products that could not be sold in time. Furthermore, the industry lacked competent and efficient accounting.[389] According to the Ministry of Local Industry, plan fulfillment from 1945 to 1947 was hampered by lack of materials, fuel, energy, and labor, and in 1948 it was also hampered by bottlenecks in the deliveries of materials. Additionally, there were problems of quality, a lack of cooperation between some enterprises, and a labor shortage.[390] Obviously, in production, workers were lacking, but there were too many employees. The newspaper *Rahva Hääl* (People's Voice) asked in January 1947 why the Tallinn Brick Factory did not fulfill the plan. The plant had a staff of 96, of whom 44 served as administrative-technical personnel. Two out of three bookkeepers were "dead souls" who did not work there at all.[391] The question remains why a brick factory needed so many office workers.

Plan fulfillment remained a problem throughout the Soviet period. No Soviet factory was able to fulfill all the contradictory plans. The main planning target was gross production in unchanged, fixed prices in rubles. Yet one-third of all industrial enterprises could not reach this target in the first three quarters of 1952.[392] Two years later, this was the case for 36 percent of all republican enterprises.[393] In 1948 the Estonian planning committee stated that it did not know enough about the economy it was planning for and that information, such as that on the capacity of factories, was insufficient. There were many turf wars with other institutions, and decisions were made without discussing them with Gosplan. In addition, the planning committee did not deal with financial or budgetary questions.[394]

Because of the lack of personnel, the planning committee was unable to fully plan the production of individual goods. For example, in 1950, only 38 of the approximately 1,000 products of the Estonian industrial cooperatives were precisely planned.[395] Even when products were not subject to direct planning, there was a rough plan of the product range. As a rule, the ministries fulfilled their

---

389 Decree of the Council of Ministers, June 1949, ERA R-4-13-6, l. 107–111.

390 Report on the activities of the Ministry for Local Industry, October 7, 1948, ERAF 1-47-30, l. 31–32, 34.

391 *Rahva Hääl*, January 25, 1947.

392 Overview on the ministries, 1952, ERAF 1-58-2, l. 6.

393 Eighth Plenum of the CC of the ECP, November 29–30, 1955, ERAF 1-4-1836, l. 48.

394 Overview on the activities of Gosplan until 1948, October 28, 1948, ERAF 1-47-29, l. 170–171.

395 Meeting of the CC Bureau of the ECP, September 28, 1950, ERAF 1-4-1093, l. 57.

plans in rubles, but that was not the case for the product range. A report from 1944 states that up to 40 percent of production went unfulfilled for important and scarce goods such as meat, soap, and canned fish.[396]

How much decision-making power the Estonian leadership really had is hard to determine from the archival documents. Indicators of the ESSR leaders' sphere of responsibility can be found in the structure of the budget's expenditure. Economics represented 38.6 percent, social questions and culture 51.1 percent, and the state apparatus 8.9 percent of the Estonian SSR's budget.[397] Concerning agriculture and enterprises subjugated to the republic, the local leadership obviously had a say. But even on a question directly impacting Estonia, like the quality of bread, the Estonian communists could not do much. In February 1950, Boris Kumm noted in a meeting of the Estonian CC Bureau that for five years, bread had been of low quality. What emerged from the subsequent debate was that the low quality of grain and the structural deficits of trade were responsible. An audit of retail trade led to charges against roughly 400 people by the public procurator's office.[398] But nothing could be done about the problems caused by the command economy.

After the forced collectivization and a more flexible enforcement of labor laws, together with an increasing standard of living in the towns, the situation normalized. The death of Stalin and increased agrarian prices for forced procurement contributed to this. By the mid-1950s, the process of Stalinist restructuring of the economy and of recovery after the war was nearly finished. This was the goal set in earlier party documents.[399] Apparently, the development level of infrastructure recovered, the standard of living was lower, and the situation of urban living space was much worse than before the war. For the period 1946–1950, the state plan for residential construction foresaw the building of only 240,000 m^2 of living space[400]—less than 1 m^2 per urban dweller. The party's view on how much living space each worker needed can be gleaned from a 1944 plan to recruit more workers for industry and construction. Individual workers were to live in dormitories with 2.5 m^2, and workers with families (average size 2.5 members) were to

396 Amount of the procurement norms, meeting of the CC Bureau of the ECP, September 11, 1944, ERAF 1-4-1045, l. 12.

397 ERA R-4-4-470, l. 8.

398 Meeting of the CC Bureau of the ECP, February 15, 1950, ERAF 1-4-1088, l. 7–10.

399 Resolution of the decision of the Seventh Party Congress of the ECP, September 16–19, 1952, ERAF 1-4-1282, l. 38.

400 Plan of 1946, ERA R-1-5-121, l. 118.

live in small flats or dormitories with 6 m^2 per capita.[401] For an average family, this meant only 15 m^2 of living space. Needless to say, even those targets were not met.

One important tendency of the postwar years was the merger into "large units," referring to collective farms and industry. It was announced in 1950 that the number of industrial enterprises had declined by seven-eighths at the expense of small businesses. The authorities said there were still too many small units with outdated technology and low productivity.[402] Yet such rhetoric was not necessarily credible; the merged enterprises could have survived on their own for a while. It is questionable whether the increase in size always led to gains in efficiency. Very often, managing the new trusts or large enterprises became impossible, or harder than before. Economies of scale might not have been achieved; on the contrary, there was an increasing trend towards the self-sufficiency of large enterprises.

In spite of the large investment in oil shale and heavy industry, the basic structure of Estonian industry changed slowly. From the mid-1930s, the share of fuel production in industrial employment grew from 6.5 to 11.7 percent; the share of metal works and mechanical engineering grew from 11.5 to 17.2 percent.[403] In other words, the vast majority of industrial labor was still in branches of light industry such as food and timber processing or the textile industry. Because the total amount of industrial employment had not increased much (see Chapter 6), structural change was not as extensive as the propaganda suggested. Officially, two-thirds of industrial output in 1955 fell into the category of heavy industry.[404]

The problems inherent in the Soviet economic system became equally rooted in Estonia, as shown by repeated complaints in the sources: shortages and bottlenecks, irregular deliveries and "arrhythmic" production, low work morale and low productivity, problems with quality, resistance to using new technologies, workplace theft, black markets, and preferential access to goods through cronyism. Campaigns to solve these problems could not really help, because they were part and parcel of a command economy.

---

401 Report on industry, transport, and construction in the Estonian SSR 1946, RGASPI f. 598, o. 1, d. 18, l. 52.

402 Meeting of the CC Bureau of the ECP, January 18, 1950, ERAF 1-4-912, l. 20–21.

403 Kala and Juursoo, "Nõukogude Eesti töölisklass," p. 257.

404 Purre, "Estlands Industrie," p. 48.

3 Demographic Changes

Questions of demographic change are an important topic in today's Estonia, and they are debated intensively. The largest change in the composition of the population happened in the 1940s and 1950s: Estonia suffered an enormous loss of population due to war and state terror, and this loss was then compensated for by Russian-speaking immigrants. The decline in population caused by Stalinism was systematically disguised during the Soviet period or blamed on the German occupiers. In 1945 the Extraordinary Commission for the Investigation of War Damage stated that in Estonia, 61,307 "peaceful citizens" and 64,000 Soviet prisoners of war were killed by the Germans, and 130,000 inhabitants were deported to Germany to conduct forced labor.[405] Some publications repeat these figures even today. The Estonian exile community sometimes overstated the number of victims of Soviet deportations and outright persecution. This is not the place to analyze the individual categories of victims and to recalculate the death tolls. That task is handled by more specialized literature. Instead, a brief overview will be presented, also incorporating lesser-known archival sources. As in the case of all Soviet statistics, a certain degree of skepticism is useful. Wartime sources are, unfortunately, fragmentary.

Before the political takeover in 1940, Estonia had only a very small population growth. The birth rate was only slightly higher than the death rate. The total population was 1.13 million. Life expectancy consistently increased; in 1938/39, it reached 58 years, as compared to 43 years in Russia. Infant mortality in Estonia, at 82.4 per 1,000 live births, was only half as high as in Russia.[406] Eighty-eight percent of the population were ethnic Estonians; the Russians were the largest ethnic minority, yet among the elites, the much smaller minorities of Baltic Germans and Jews were strongly overrepresented. World War I and the Estonian War of Independence had left their mark: women far outnumbered men. By 1940, one-third of the population was urban; the remainder lived in the countryside. Since 1913, the urban population had grown by approximately one-half. When the German army entered Estonia in the summer of 1941, only one

---

405 Cited in Polian, *Zhertvy dvukh diktatur*, p. 369.

406 Arvo Kuddo, Aksel Kirch, and Marika Kirch, "Demographic Processes in Estonia," in Kahk (ed.), *World War II*, pp. 42–47; Isupov, *Demograficheskie katastrofy*, p. 127.

million people lived there; the decline was the result of Soviet mobilization, the evacuation of civilians, and Soviet terror.[407]

Losses through War and State Terror

Table 6 offers an overview of the direct and indirect population losses caused by war and state terror. The table has been compiled by Aigi Rahi-Tamm as a summary of the state of research and is based on the preparatory work of several separate projects intending to clarify the fate of Estonia's population. The Soviets deported 33,000 people and arrested 40,000 for political reasons. About 25,000 Estonian citizens died as soldiers in the war. Altogether perhaps 90,000 inhabitants lost their lives, of whom 7,800 were murdered during the German occupation. The victims of Stalin far outnumbered the victims of Hitler. Three historical minorities—Baltic Germans, Jews, and Swedes—virtually disappeared. The Germans were resettled in 1939–1941, the few remaining Baltic Germans were deported in 1945, and the Swedes migrated to Sweden in 1943 and 1944 on the basis of a German-Swedish agreement. The small Jewish minority fell victim to persecution by Hitler and Stalin (the Germans killed roughly 1,000 and the Soviets deported more than 400) or fled the country; probably less than one-fourth returned to Estonia after evacuation. Direct or indirect population losses amounted to roughly 270,000 people, or nearly one-quarter of the prewar population. Not included were all those arrested for non-political reasons during the Stalinist era, be it for criminal offenses, petty theft, tax arrears, non-fulfillment of work or procurement norms or of breaking the labor laws. Official statistics counted them as criminals, even when, in the majority of cases, their deeds were not criminal.[408]

Table 6: Population Losses of Estonia (approximate values)

First Soviet Year 1940/41	
1. Arrests	8,000 (200 survivors)
2. Mass deportation in June 1941	10,000 (4,000 survivors)
3. Resettlers since 1939 (mostly Baltic Germans)	20,000

407 See Ene Tiit, "Eesti rahvastik ja selle probleemid," *Akadeemia* 5 (1993), p. 2118.

408 In the Soviet Union between 1946 and 1952, nearly 10 times as many people were arrested for criminal offenses as for political ones (Filtzer, *Soviet Workers and Late Stalinism*, p. 28). Figures for Estonia are unknown, but it is reasonable to assume that tens of thousands were arrested and punished for minor offenses.

Table 6: Continued

4. Estonian Army	5,600
5. Forcibly mobilized into the Red Army	34,000 (10,000 survivors)
6. Evacuated to the USSR	25,000 (of whom 5,000 died)
7. Unidentified missing	1,100
8. Fled abroad	500
German Occupation 1941–1944	
9. Fallen in the ranks of the German army	14,500
10. Murdered civilians	7,800 (including 1,000 Jews)
11. Labor service in Germany	800
12. Imprisoned in camps	4,000
13. Fled to Finland	4,200
14. Evacuated Estonian Swedes	7,000
15. The big flight to the West	70,000–75,000 (of whom 7,000 died)
Renewed Soviet occupation and postwar period	
16. Political arrests	30,000 (of whom 10,000 died)
17. Deportations 1945–1951	23,000 (of whom 3,000 died)
18. Fallen anti-Soviet partisans	2,000

Source: Compiled according to Rahi-Tamm, "Deportation und Verfolgung in Estland," pp. 212–213.

This enormous population loss was among the highest in Europe. Many of the surviving deportees and arrestees were able to return home after Stalin's death. Numerous soldiers were demobilized after the war or released as former prisoners of war, inmates of filtration camps, or members of labor battalions. Roughly 70,000 people returned by 1950,[409] including 11,000 repatriated people.[410] Yet many were lost forever. What made the loss of this population all the more difficult was its composition. The better educated and the wealthier someone was, the likelier it was that he/she would leave the country or be subjected to state terror. Males were overrepresented among the losses; in a country where most of the labor was conducted physically, this meant a decline of the workforce's potential. Hardest hit were the most economically active age groups, those who were between 20 and 50 years old. As a result, many women did not find a partner, and many children grew up without a father.

409 Kulno Kala, "Eesti rahvuslikust koosseisust pärast Teist maailmasõda," *Akadeemia* 4 (1992), p. 595.

410 Department for repatriation to Karotamm, October 9, 1948, ERAF 1-47-29, l. 45.

The loss of human capital was enormous. Between two-thirds and three-fourths of Estonia's elite war lost. Baltic Germans and Jews, who were highly overrepresented in industry, trade, and among professionals, were especially conspicuous by their absence. So too were engineers, physicians, agricultural experts, and professors. While in 1930s Estonia a common topic of discussion was the glut of university graduates and whether they faced unemployment, after the war there was even a shortage of people with a secondary education. Due to the age and gender demographics of the lost population, the one-fourth decline in the number of inhabitants implied a shrinking of the fully employable population by nearly one-third. In terms of qualifications—which, naturally, is hard to estimate—the economic potential of the remaining inhabitants declined even more.

The Development of the Population after the War

According to Soviet statistics, the development of the population, of inhabitants of rural and urban areas, showed a clear tendency towards urbanization (see Table 7). Following the 1959 census, the figures were slightly corrected. Not included were military personnel, which at times reached nearly 100,000 soldiers,[411] and the inmates of various camps. By the end of the war, Estonia had 270,000 fewer inhabitants than before. However, it must be taken into account that in 1945, Moscow changed the borders. Estonian territories east of the river Narva and a large part of the Setomaa region—with a total of 56,000 inhabitants—were taken over by Russia. By 1945, towns had lost about 100,000 inhabitants, and rural areas lost 120,000. Estonia was very agricultural, and many of those living in towns were in the first generation of their families to do so. Thus in times of a bad supply situation, many of these town dwellers withdrew to the countryside to live with friends or relatives, for example, on the family's farm. In 1945, the Bureau of the CC of the ECP stated that at that time, no one wanted to leave the villages, because life there was better than in the towns.[412] When conditions improved in the towns, many people changed their place of residence again. Due to Stalinist terror, further population losses occurred, but because of immigration, they are

411 As of January 1947. See letter to the Administration for the Verification of Party Organs at the CC of the VKP(b), ERAF 1-5-76, l. 120.

412 Meeting of the CC Bureau of the ECP, November 21 and 26, 1945, ERAF 1-4-237, l. 146.

difficult to identify in the statistics. One explanation for the drop in rural population in 1949 was a mass deportation.

The immigration to Estonia in the second half of the 1940s, especially from 1946 to 1948, is striking. This migration was mostly to towns, but many immigrants and returnees also came to the countryside. However, a rural exodus started some time after the forced collectivization. In less than 10 years, the urban population doubled. By around 1952 or 1953, the urban population outnumbered the rural one.

Table 7: Population, 1945–1956, in Thousands

Year	Urban	Countryside	Total	Urban	Countryside	Total
1945	267	587	854			
1946	305.7	575.3	881			
1947	363.4	593.7	957			
1948	415.9	607	1,022			
1949	439.9	589.2	1,029			
1950	487	593.7	1,080	516.1	580.6	1,096.7
1951	519.1	568.8	1,087.9	548.4	555.6	1.104
1952	550.1	563.5	1,113.6	579.5	542.2	1,129.8
1953	569.6	555.5	1,125.1	599.1	528.2	1,141.3
1954	592.8	541.4	1,134.2	622	528.2	1,150.2
1955	605.2	536.9	1,142.2	634.1	523.2	1,157.3
1956	611.7	535.4	1,147.1	640.3	522.2	1,162.5

Columns 5–7: The figures were adjusted after the population census of 1959.

Source: ERA R-10-43-155, l. 1ff.

The age and gender structure of the rural population on January 1, 1947, indicates a disturbing demographic shift (see Table 8). The age group of up to four years was smaller than that of older children, an indicator of increased infant and child mortality and of the lack of births. The small number of 15-to-19-year-old youngsters might be due to their taking a job or vocational training in town, continuing education there, or doing military service. The age group in their twenties was only half as large as to be expected; that of those in their thirties was, likewise, one-quarter smaller. The rural population tended to be older than the general population, a trend that only increased with time. Even more disastrous was the shortage of males. Among those in their twenties, there was one man for every two women; among those 10 years older, there were two men for every three women. These figures can be explained by the war losses, the fact that males were overrepresented among the victims of terror and refugees, and the fact that men were more likely than women to take a job in a town. The result of the war was clear: in an agricultural system with a low level of mechanization, the absence of so many males and the relatively low number of people of working age led to a labor shortage. In addition, one would expect a decline of the birth rate in the countryside; however, detailed statistical information on this subject is lacking.

Table 8: Age and Gender Structure of the Rural Population, January 1, 1947

Age group	Female	Male	Total
Up to 4 years	22,928	22,873	45,801
5–9 years	27,930	28,124	56,054
10–14	27,821	28,242	56,063
15–19	24,087	22,499	46,586
20–29	36,893	19,367	56,260
30–39	45,135	28,041	73,176
40–49	48,650	35,090	83,740
50–54	22,209	14,909	37,118
55–59	21,858	15,254	37,112
60 years and older	63,307	38,627	101,934
Working age (14–59 years)	204,644	141,145	345,789
Total	340,718	253,026	593,744

Source: ERA R-10-10-101, l. 4.

In the first half of the 1950s, the lack of males and the labor shortage remained an urgent problem in the countryside (see Table 9). The number of children up to the age of six allows us to draw some conclusions about the birthrate. Approximately 9,000 to 10,000 children were born annually in the countryside; thus the birthrate was not lower than in towns. Yet in the prewar period, according to the share of population, many more children were born in the countryside than in towns. We should thus expect a real decline of the rural birthrate.

Table 9: Age and Gender Structure of the Rural Population, 1951–1956 (on January 1, in thousands)

Age group	1951 Female	1951 Male	1953 Female	1953 Male	1956 Female	1956 Male
Up to 6 years	29.0	29.4	29.2	29.4	27.6	28.5
7–15 years	44.0	45.2	41.3	42.4	37.7	39.2
16–54 years (female) 16–59 years (male)	150.6	113.8	146.5	105.2	140.6	111.5
55 years and older (female) 60 years and older (male)	80.2	35.0	82.6	35.0	84.6	35.3
Total	303.8	223.2	292.8	212.0	290.5	214.5

Source: ERA: R-10-10-101, l. 66–67.

The distribution of the rural population into individual households in the period from 1950 to 1956 indicates several tendencies (see Table 10). The number of members of kolkhoz households increased until 1952; by that time, collectivization was largely finished. In 1950, the number of members of households of independent peasants and craftsmen was 41 percent of the figure for kolkhoz households. However, this share declined to 9 percent in the following year and to 4 percent in 1952. But even by 1956, independent farmers and craftsmen had not disappeared completely. The number of workers, employees, and craftsmen in cooperative enterprises increased steadily, while the total rural population declined by nearly 9 percent from 1950 to 1956, similar to the decline from 1947 to 1950.

Table 10: Distribution of Rural Inhabitants in Households, 1950–1956 (on January 1, in thousands)

Type of household	**1950**	**1951**	**1952**	**1953**	**1954**	**1955**	**1956**
Kolkhoz household	295,406	355,451	359,203	353,388	334,483	329,496	317,074
Of which: works in state or cooperative institutions	10,926	13,359	14,916	15,027	17,845	17,816	17,319
Workers, craftsmen (in cooperatives), employees	119,507	125,391	132,873	138,261	148,090	150,775	164,229
Independent peasants and craftsmen	122,020	33,024	14,485	5,199	3,452	2,818	2,178
Simple households	3,153	3,637	3,603	3,870	5,536	6,071	6,675
Temporarily in the countryside	11,480	9,524	9,764	10,868	11,683	12,767	14,786
Total	**551,566**	**527,027**	**519,928**	**511,586**	**503,244**	**501,927**	**504,942**
Of which: works in state or cooperative institutions	66,061	69,269	74,795	80,539	87,927	89,639	94,134

Source: ERA R-10-10-101, l. 47–72.

Mortality, Birth Rate, and Marriages

The figures of registered births and deaths per 1,000 inhabitants probably correctly indicate the trends (see Table 11) and could be found in Soviet statistics, yet there are some doubts about their overall accuracy. The "normal" crude birth rate in Estonia was roughly 16 per 1,000. Surprisingly, it did not decline during the war. After the war it increased; by the mid-1950s it was higher than in the interwar period. Considering the lack of males and the standard of living, this comes as a surprise. Several factors obviously interacted: the unavailability of contraceptives, a catch-up effect after the war, the pro-natal family policy of Stalinism, and the reproductive behavior of the immigrants from the "old" USSR, where the birth rate was higher. For example, from 1958 to 1960 in Estonia, while the Estonian population had a natural growth of 6,100 people, the Russian-speaking population experienced a natural growth of 11,500 people, as they had more children per family.[413] This was despite the fact that, in Estonia at that time, there were four times as many Estonians as Russians. According to the figures, the natural population growth of Estonians was 0.2 percent annually and of Russian-speakers 1.5 percent.

The crude death rate, which in the 1930s was usually an annual 14–15 cases per 1,000 inhabitants, increased in connection with Sovietization. Victims of state violence and the war obviously were not included in the statistics; otherwise, the crude death rate would be double that of independent Estonia. Data for the German occupation seems to be too low; it is possible that not all deaths were registered. In the immediate postwar period, mortality peaked—a clear indicator of malnutrition and an extremely low standard of living. The crude death rate, which was one-half above the normal level, declined slowly by the end of the 1940s and, in the 1950s, officially fell below the prewar level.

There can be three basic reasons for dramatic increases in a population's mortality within a few years: a drastic decline of the standard of living, causing malnutrition or famine; a drastic decline in medical treatment; and/or deathly epidemic diseases. There is no information about the latter, but there is information on enormous problems with food supplies and of deficits in hygiene and medicine. Because of the mass production of new drugs like penicillin, the expansion of hospitals, and vaccination campaigns, the USSR was able to make considerable progress in the field of medicine, but whether this could reduce mortality to such a degree remains questionable. Even in 1956, the standard of

413 ERA R-10-43-159, l. 85.

living (to be dealt with in detail below) did not come close to the prewar level. It is possible that the data on mortality were manipulated in the 1950s, particularly since the low level of the late 1950s did not improve much in subsequent decades, despite medical progress and an increasing standard of living. Since detailed death tables for the Estonian SSR are still classified in Moscow for 1951 and afterward, we cannot determine the answer. It would be realistic to expect that the decline of mortality happened later. If we compare the table with a report from the State Planning Committee dated March 1948, it appears that the statistics have been manipulated. The crude death rates calculated by Gosplan for 1946 and 1947 were, respectively, 1.8 and 1.1 points higher than those listed below.[414] It is possible that the statistics were falsified by simply omitting the death of 2,600 citizens over two years.

In any case, for several years there was no natural population growth in Estonia. If those figures are correct, then the natural population growth from 1945 to 1956 totaled 40,000 people. As a conservative estimate, there were about 40,000 additional deaths in the 1940s, caused mainly by malnutrition, as well as by the lack of hygiene and medical treatment.[415] In the immediate postwar years, natural mortality was higher than before World War I.[416]

Table 11: Officially Registered Births, Deaths, and Natural Population Growth per 1,000 Inhabitants, 1938–1956

Year/Period	Births	Deaths	Natural demographic change
1938	16.3	14.6	+ 1.7
1939	16.3	15.1	+ 1.2
1940	16.4	17.0	– 0.6
1941–1944	16.1	15.0	+ 1.1
1945	17.3	23.9	– 6.6
1946	21.1	21.7	– 0.6

414 Planning Commission of the ESSR to Head of the Council of Ministers Arnold Veimer, March 17, 1948, ERA R-1-5-181, l. 17.

415 Mertelsmann, "Creating Malnutrition in an Agricultural Surplus Area."

416 See the data for 1901–1914 in Veimer, *Kompleksnoe razvitie*, p. 77.

Table 11: Continued

Year/Period	Births	Deaths	Natural demographic change
1947	22.9	21.7	+ 1.2
1948	21.2	17.1	+ 4.1
1949	21.4	16.4	+ 5.0
1950	18.7	14.6	+ 3.9
1951	18.8	13.9	+ 4.9
1952	18.9	14.1	+ 4.8
1953	17.8	12.8	+ 5.0
1954	18.4	12.3	+ 6.1
1955	18.2	11.9	+ 6.3
1956	17.1	11.1	+ 6.0

Not including victims of state terror and war. Data for the years 1950–1954 in the original crossed out.

Column 4 calculated according to columns 2 and 3.

Source: ERA R-10-43-155, l. 6.

A slightly different perspective on the changes in the birth and death rates over time is offered by the absolute numbers for the years from 1938 to 1944 (see Table 12). Perhaps the statisticians made a small mistake; nevertheless, the living conditions seemed better under German rule than in the subsequent three years under the Soviets. This might explain why the Estonian population viewed the German occupation as the lesser evil.

Table 12: Absolute Number of Births and Deaths, 1938 to the Second Quarter of 1944

Year/Quarter	Births	Deaths
1938	18,453	16,496
1939	18,475	17,101
1940	18,408	19,034

Table 12: Continued

Year/Quarter	Births	Deaths
1941	19,574	23,702
1942	18,993	20,097
1943	16,001	18,120
First quarter of 1944	3,881	7,056
Second quarter of 1944	3,587	6,193

Not including victims of state terror and war 1941–1944, based on the statistics of the German occupation.

Source: ERA R-10-43-155, l. 7.

Estonia prohibited abortion in 1934. When exceptions were made, they were mostly for medical reasons. Under Stalinism, the situation became more complicated due to the lack of contraceptives. This led, despite the ban, to a relatively large number of legal abortions and to an unknown number of illegal abortions; the latter were especially dangerous to the life and health of the women who had them. Directly after the war, the widespread rapes committed by Soviet soldiers were an additional factor causing women to seek to end pregnancies. A clue to the scale of abortions is offered by data from 1951–1952 (see Table 13). Concerning illegal abortions, only detected cases were reported. Officially, in Estonia one-quarter of all pregnancies were terminated outside a hospital; at least one-tenth happened illegally. The real figure must have been much higher. The Soviet Ministry of Health estimated that a termination of pregnancy was caused by abortion in 85 percent of the cases and by miscarriage in 15 percent of the cases.[417] In only half of the detected cases of illegal abortion during the first half of 1951 did legal proceedings follow.[418]

417 Chris Burton, "Minzdrav, Soviet Doctors, and the Policing of Reproduction in the Late Stalinist Years," *Russian History* 27 (2000), pp. 211, 214.

418 See Minister of Justice Strazd to Müürisepp, chairman of the Council of Ministers of the ESSR, August 17, 1951, ERA R-1-5-254, l. 262–263. One hundred sixty-five cases were opened and 142 people convicted, 107 accused women were subjected to a public reprimand and three to a fine, 18 helpers were imprisoned, and four received a suspended sentence.

Table 13: Number of Terminations of Pregnancy and Abortions, 1951 and the First Half of 1952

Termination of pregnancy outside a hospital		Illegal abortions (officially)	
1951	First half of 1952	1951	First half of 1952
6,964	3,614	693	360

Source: Chris Burton, "Minzdrav, Soviet Doctors, and the Policing of Reproduction in the Late Stalinist Years," *Russian History* 27 (2000), pp. 214.

The mortality of small children serves as a further indicator of the general development of natural mortality. Only in 1952 did it decline under the prewar level, and after then, it quickly declined further (see Table 14). The improvement of medical treatment and hygiene obviously played a central role, yet we can infer that until 1951, general mortality remained above the prewar level. The proportion of deaths in the countryside versus the town cannot be determined, since it is unknown how many ill children from rural areas were brought to urban hospitals and how many mothers no longer gave birth at home but did so in hospital.

Table 14: Total Number of Deaths among Small Children, 1937–1955

Year	Urban Up to 1 year	Urban 1–6 years	Rural Up to 1 year	Rural 1–6 years	Total Up to 1 year	Total 1–6 years
1937	367	142	1,282	464	1,649	604
1938	303	122	1,127	395	1,430	517
1947	1,280	318	1,478	576	2,758	894
1948	741	230	1,093	414	1,834	644
1949	822	249	972	276	1,794	525
1950	789	200	888	275	1,677	475
1951	844	198	736	276	1,580	474
1952	738	194	633	239	1,371	433
1953	569	150	482	182	1,051	332

Table 14: Continued

Year	Urban Up to 1 year	Urban 1–6 years	Rural Up to 1 year	Rural 1–6 years	Total Up to 1 year	Total 1–6 years
1954	581	129	455	117	1,036	246
1955	581	116	454	130	1,035	246

Source: ERA R-10-43-155, l. 38–39.

The number of marriages increased from 1945 to 1956, a trend that can be explained by the backlog in demand after the war and the increase of the population (see Table 15). A small decrease occurred after the forced collectivization and mass deportation in 1949, an indicator of fear of the future and despair. Overall, for this period, the divorce rate increased from 4 percent in comparison to marriages to nearly 10 percent.

Table 15: Marriages and Divorces, 1945–1956

Year	Marriages	Divorces
1945	6,605	277
1946	9,179	496
1947	11,192	650
1948	12,217	564
1949	10,810	378
1950	10,456	488
1951	10,103	578
1952	9,484	709
1953	11,083	669
1954	11,927	898
1955	12,238	1,155
1956	13,088	1,297

Source: ERA R-10-43-155, l. 8.

Life Expectancy

Life expectancy at birth is one of several demographic factors that reflects the level of development and standard of living of a given society. It depends on the provision of food, the quality of health care, hygienic conditions, everyday practices, medical knowledge, access to certain kinds of food, and other factors. Life expectancy is calculated by the age composition of those dying within a certain period, normally one year or one month. Life expectancy at birth refers to the average lifespan of a newborn baby, assuming that the conditions of life and the patterns of mortality remain stable. For historians, life expectancy becomes interesting if a dramatic change happens in a short amount of time.

Realistic data on life expectancy for Estonia is available for the period starting from the late tsarist era; the only real gap exists for the 1940s and 1950s. The official Soviet data cannot be trusted; they claim that life expectancy for the Soviet Union and Estonia in 1950 was 65 years.[419] During the interwar period, life expectancy had continuously increased in Estonia. By 1938/39 it reached 58.4 years,[420] only a few years less than in Western Europe.

The reason we know so little on life expectancy is that the relevant documents have not survived in Estonia. However, information on deaths, cause of death, and the age of the deceased was routinely collected. I know of only one source in Estonia from the Stalinist era: a death table for December 1940.[421] With the help of Donald Filtzer, I received copies of detailed death tables from the Russian State Archives of Economics for Tallinn in 1945;[422] the Estonian urban population in 1946, 1947, and 1950;[423] and the Estonian rural population in 1948, 1949, and 1950.[424] Later death tables remain classified.

---

419 Angus Maddison, *The World Economy: A Millenial Perspective* (Paris, 2001), p. 30; IMF Country Report No. 07/256, *Republic of Estonia: Selected Issues* (Washington, DC, 2007), p. 31.

420 Kuddo, Kirch, and Kirch, "Demographic Processes in Estonia," p. 45.

421 Age composition of the deceased in December 1940, ERA R-10-1-486, l. 4.

422 Overview of the deceased according to gender, age, and cause of death for 1945, Estonian SSR, town of Tallinn, RGAE f. 1562, o. 329, d. 1888, l. 63–64.

423 Overview of the deceased according to gender, age, and cause of death for 1946, Estonian SSR, urban population, RGAE f. 1562, o. 329, d. 2235, l. 30–40; for 1947, Estonian SSR, urban population, ibid., d. 2648, l. 3–4; for 1950, Estonian SSR, urban population, ibid., d. 4703, l. 378–379.

424 Overview of the deceased according to gender, age, and cause of death for 1948, Estonian SSR, rural population, RGAE f. 1562, o. 329, d. 3166, l. 57–58; for 1949, Estonian

With the exception of the information on December 1940, data coverage is very extensive. More than 80 individual causes of death are listed, according to gender and age. Soviet population statistics counted the civilian population, prisoners, and the military separately. Data on the civilian population was secret. Furthermore, data on prisoners and the military was highly classified; the available material excludes those two large groups. Under Stalinism, the published information on life expectancy was simply falsified. However, thanks to Vladimir Isupov, we at least have reliable data for Russia until World War II.[425] Those archival documents on Estonia are undoubtedly authentic, and there is no reason to doubt their accuracy or content. Of course, they might contain some inaccuracies, but the overall picture seems quite realistic. Since the age of the deceased is often expressed in categories such as three to four years, 30–39 years, or 70 and older, my calculations of life expectancy are only approximations and can be made only with reference to a few particular years. However, more precise information is not available in the archives.

During the first peak of mortality in the winter of 1940–1941 mentioned above, mortality increased in December 1940 by 76 percent over the previous December.[426] However, mortality among the elderly more than doubled, and because of this, life expectancy calculated using the available data remained stable, at 59.6 years.[427]

For 1945, data has survived only for Tallinn. Because of the high infant mortality, life expectancy was only 45.9 years.[428] The figure was similar to the French colonies in North Africa or to South America. The war, German occupation, the Stalinist restructuring of the economy, long-lasting malnutrition, and economic exploitation put Tallinn on the same level as the so-called Third World. Infectious diseases dominated among the causes of death; those diseases could be deadly for people suffering from years of malnutrition. Bad hygienic conditions in overcrowded flats and dormitories, which were insufficiently heated or, in some cases, always damp, also exacerbated the spread of such diseases.

SSR, rural population, ibid., d. 3814, l. 53–54; for 1950, Estonian SSR, rural population, ibid., d. 4703, l. 338–339.

425 Isupov, *Demograficheskie katastrofy*.

426 ERA R-10-1-486, l. 1.

427 Calculated according to: age composition of the deceased in December 1940, ERA R-10-1-486, l. 4.

428 Calculated according to: overview of the deceased according to gender, age, and cause of death for 1945, Estonian SSR, town of Tallinn, RGAE f. 1562, o. 329, d. 1888, l. 63–64.

The following years saw no improvement. The famine of 1946–1947 in western parts of the Soviet Union (western Russia, Ukraine, and Moldavia)[429] influenced Estonia indirectly. Unfortunately, we do not have separate statistics for the rural population. However, in the towns, life expectancy was 45.8 years in 1946, and in 1947, it was only 42.5 years. Between men and women, there was a clear five-year difference in life expectancy; in 1947, for example, it was 40.7 years for males and 45.8 years for females.[430]

A slightly different picture emerges in the countryside. The supply of food was better, people could produce their own soap, nearly everyone had access to a sauna, there was enough firewood, and overall, there was less destruction than in the towns. In 1948, rural life expectancy was 51.8 years,[431] nearly 10 years more than urban residents in 1947. The forced collectivization of agriculture is central in Estonian collective memory. Here, we might wonder whether collectivization is also reflected in life expectancy. In 1949, rural life expectancy was 52.8 years, and in 1950, it was 54.9 years.[432] This result comes as a surprise; an increase in life expectancy is quite unexpected, given the negative impact of collectivization. Obviously there was a long-term trend of recovery from war and the immediate postwar crisis, and collectivization could not change this. In addition, collectivization might have helped the weaker strata of rural society to secure subsistence.

In the towns, conditions improved, but slower than might be expected. In 1950, life expectancy, at 47.6 years, was still seven years below the level in the countryside.[433] This means living conditions in the countryside were far better

---

429 Zima, *Golod v SSSR*; Michael Ellmann, "The 1947 Soviet Famine and the Entitlement Approach to Famines," *Cambridge Journal of Economics* 24 (2000), pp. 603–630; Nicholas Ganson, *The Soviet Famine of 1946–1947 in Global and Historical Perspective* (Houndsmills, 2009).

430 Calculated according to: overview on the deceased according to gender, age, and cause of death for 1946, Estonian SSR, urban population, RGAE f. 1562, o. 329, d. 2235, l. 30–40; for 1947, Estonian SSR, urban population, ibid., d. 2648, l. 3–4.

431 Calculated according to: overview on the deceased according to gender, age, and cause of death for 1948, Estonian SSR, rural population, RGAE f. 1562, o. 329, d. 3166, l. 57–58.

432 Calculated according to: overview on the deceased according to gender, age, and cause of death for 1949, Estonian SSR, rural population, RGAE f. 1562, o. 329, d. 3844, l. 53–54; for 1950, d. 4703, l. 338–339.

433 Calculated according to: overview on the deceased according to gender, age, and cause of death for 1950, Estonian SSR, urban population, RGAE f. 1562, o. 329, d. 4703, l. 378–379.

than in the towns. Unfortunately, we do not have data for later years, but it seems likely that the prewar life expectancy of 58 years was only reached by the mid-1950s or even later. The official figure of 65 years for 1950 was 12–13 years higher than the reality. How does all this fit with the crude death rate falling below the prewar level by the early 1950s? The main explanation lies in the composition of the population. Enormous population losses were compensated for by hunger refugees, immigrants, returning citizens, evacuees, former prisoners, and prisoners of war. The vast majority settled down in towns. Those people and their children had a higher risk of dying early than those who stayed in Estonia. In addition, the age composition of the population changed. More births, in combination with increased infant and child mortality, leads to a shorter statistical life expectancy. Nevertheless, the crude death rate and life expectancy serve as clear indicators of how harsh and short life was under Stalinist rule in Estonia.

The Ethnic Composition of the Population and Migration

The censuses of 1934, 1941, and 1959 also covered the ethnic composition of the population (see Table 16). As in other statistics, these censuses excluded the members of the German occupation forces in 1941 and of the Soviet army in 1959. The category of ethnicity was based not on one's mother tongue but on self-identification. The Estonian share of the population continuously decreased, while the Russian share steadily increased. Taking into account that the territory Estonia lost to Russia in 1945 was inhabited mostly by Russians, we can estimate a total in-migration to Estonia of approximately 200,000 Russian speakers. The Baltic Germans had left the country between 1939 and 1941; the few who remained were deported in 1945. The 700 Germans in 1959 were basically Russian Germans. The Finns arrived after the war to escape discrimination and ethnic cleansing in the adjacent Leningrad oblast. Between 1946 and 1948, similar measures of cleansing also occurred in Estonia.[434] Among the Jews in Estonia in 1959, the majority were Russian Jews who had migrated there; perhaps one-fifth were returning Estonian Jews.

434 See Riina Reinvelt, *Ingeri elud ja lood: Kultuurianalüütiline eluloouurimus* (Tartu, 2002).

Table 16: Ethnic Composition of the Population, 1934–1959

	1934		1941		1959	
	Thous.	**%**	**Thous.**	**%**	**Thous.**	**%**
Estonians	993	88.2	908	89.3	893	74.6
Russians	92.7	8.2	72.8	7.2	240	20.0
Germans	16.3	1.5	-	-	0.7	0.1
Swedes	7.6	0.7	6.5	0.6	-	-
Jews	4.4	0.4	-	-	5.4	0.5
Finns	1.9	0.2	1.6	0.2	16.7	1.4

Source: Ene Tiit, "Eesti rahvastik ja selle probleemid," *Akadeemia* 5 (1993), p. 2118.

Not all Estonians mentioned in the statistics originated from Estonia: approximately 76,000 ethnic Estonians living in Russia and other parts of the USSR had migrated to Estonia by the end of the 1950s.[435] Before World War I, many Estonians had settled in Russia and other parts of the empire—whether in the large towns, in Siberia, or in the Caucasus. In some cases, their children or grandchildren spoke little or no Estonian. During the Great Terror of the 1930s in the USSR, this minority had been targeted, like Finns, Latvians, Poles, and Germans, as members of an "enemy nation" in special campaigns and intensely persecuted.[436] As a result, instruction in the mother tongue at school ended. Starting in 1940, Moscow used Estonians who had already been living in the Soviet Union to support the process of Sovietization in their "historic homeland." In January 1946, such Estonians constituted one-fifth of the members of the ECP.[437]

Immigration compensated for the population losses over 10 years, one important prerequisite for postwar reconstruction. Between 1946 and 1949, Russian net immigration alone was about 20,000 per year; in the five years after that, it was roughly 10,000 per year.[438] Since the level of education in the Soviet Union

435 Tiit, "Eesti rahvastik ja selle probleemid," p. 1849.

436 See Terry Martin, *The Affirmative Action Empire: Nations and Nationalism in the Soviet Union, 1923–1939* (Ithaca and London, 2001), pp. 335–341.

437 Hill Kulu, *Eestlaste tagasiränne 1940–1989* (Tartu, 1997), pp. 132–133, 140.

438 Tiit Tammaru, *Venelased Eestis: Ränne ja kohanemine* (Tallinn, 1999), p. 15.

was lower than in Estonia, the loss of human capital could not be compensated for. Apart from some experts and specialists such as medical doctors, scholars, engineers or technicians, immigration involved mostly unskilled labor. The rapid influx of Russian-speakers led to ethnic tensions and was deeply resented by the Estonian-speaking majority.[439] Moscow too was aware of these anti-Russian and anti-Soviet feelings.[440]

Immigration peaked in the second half of the 1940s.[441] The scale of war damage in Estonia was lower than in German-occupied territories of Russia, Belarus, or Ukraine, and the continued existence of private farms ensured a certain level of food supply. During the famine in western parts of the USSR, in which more than one million people died,[442] approximately five million fled from the affected regions.[443] In addition to hunger refugees and beggars searching for food, there were demobilized soldiers, repatriated *Ostarbeiter* (former forced workers in Nazi Germany from Eastern Europe), runaway peasants from kolkhozes, the inhabitants of burned-down villages, and returning evacuees. They shared the search for a better life; today one would call them "economic migrants." Thus it was stated in the CC Bureau of the ECP that 58 percent of those arriving did not have work or a place to live and that "the incoming element was responsible for a large share of crime."[444]

The Soviet Union always created the impression that it was managing internal migration logically and systematically. Because of this, there was a passport and registration system, and numerous places, such as large cities, the border zone, capitals of republics, or military bases were closed or restricted. The collectivized peasants did not possess a passport in the Stalinist era, except in the Baltic republics, and officially, they had to get the permission of the kolkhoz in order to leave it. To move to another town, they needed the appropriate documents and proof of a job and a place of residence. However, those papers could be obtained through contacts, bribes, a sham marriage, or on the black market. Although prices and wages were state-regulated and similar throughout the entire

439 See Olaf Mertelsmann, "How the Russians Turned into the Image of the 'National Enemy' of the Estonians," *Pro Ethnologia* (2005), no. 19, pp. 43–58.

440 See Zubkova, "Fenomen 'mestnogo natsionalizma,'" p. 92.

441 On the immigration in the postwar period, especially in northeastern Estonia, see Mertelsmann, "Die Herausbildung des Sonderstatus."

442 See Zima, *Golod v SSSR*.

443 Geoffrey Hosking, *Russia and the Russians: From Earliest Times to 2001* (London, 2002), p. 526.

444 Meeting of the CC Bureau of the ECP, March 19, 1947, ERAF 1-4-480, l. 230.

Soviet Union, there was still a major incentive for migration, because the supply of food, other goods, and living space, or the general infrastructure could vary considerably from one region to another. Additionally, cultural offerings, educational opportunities, and the attractiveness of jobs differed. The policy of a managed migration was not carried out successfully.[445]

In addition to the standard Soviet system of passports and registration, entering Estonia was subjected until 1946 to further restrictions.[446] Checks were regularly conducted at train stations and in trains. In addition, there were checks at the republican border. These measures were intended to discourage beggars, homeless people, and hunger refugees. In the first five months of 1947, in Tallinn alone 4,630 "suspicious elements without passport" were arrested for "filtration and expulsion."[447] There was an official immigration quota for labor, and an entry permit had to be applied for by an enterprise that wanted to hire workers from outside the republic. According to the Administration for Labor Reserves, Estonian enterprises applied for the immigration of 5,046 people from 1946 to 1948.[448] Some of the immigrants were designated to work in Estonia; others were especially hired. However, the vast majority of the immigrants who arrived in the Stalinist era came at their own initiative in a search for a better life. The documentation in Estonian archives tells a similar story as the migrants themselves.[449] The influx of migrants compensated for the population losses. Some migrants were able to make a career as "more reliable" Soviet citizens and were privileged, while others took the jobs that locals avoided, like mining oil shale. The preferred channel of migration was the large building sites in the northeast. They were always in need of labor. Once the construction enterprises had arranged

445 Cynthia Buckley, "The Myth of Managed Migration: Migration Control and Market in the Soviet Period," *Slavic Review* 54 (1995), pp. 896–916.

446 Minister of the Interior Resev to Karotamm, December 23, 1947, ERAF 1-5-36, l. 103.

447 Report of the Department for Serious Crimes, Ministry of the Interior, July 7, 1947, ERAF 1-5-36, l. 64–65.

448 Report on the activities of the administration of the labor reserves until 1948, ERA 1-47-29, l. 142. Individual enterprises might have been exempted from the obligation of permissions.

449 During an interview project in August 2003, a total of 100 life story interviews were collected in Narva, whose overwhelmingly Russian-speaking population consists mostly of immigrants and their descendants. The vast majority said that they or their ancestors immigrated on their own initiative and not in the framework of any state program.

the necessary documents and housing and the migrants got settled, many moved after several months to other sectors of the economy or other towns.[450]

450 Kala, Juursoo, "Nõukogude Eesti töölisklass," pp. 252–253.

4 The Standard of Living

Contemporary witnesses' statements on the development of the living standard in Estonia resembled one another, yet personal experiences differed from family to family. At the end of the 1930s, the standard of living was relatively high; however, the political takeover in Tallinn led to a remarkable decline. During and immediately after the war, the standard of living was lowest in the towns. Malnourishment was widespread. After the end of rationing in December 1947, the standard of living increased slowly, yet steadily; however, it remained relatively low. Those who had no personal contacts in the countryside struggled for survival until 1950.[451]

The peasants faced privations during and after the war, but they usually did not go hungry. As they could grow their own food, they fared better than any other segment of the population. Contemporaries called the situation satisfactory.[452] In the countryside, the standard of living declined after collectivization, and only after the death of Stalin did a real increase occur.[453] Immigrants from the "old" republics explained their move by saying that living conditions were far better in Estonia than in their home region.[454] What the locals considered a crisis situation was, for some immigrants, a salvation from utter destitution.

We would expect to find that the Stalinist restructuring caused living conditions in Estonia to converge with those in the rest of the Soviet Union. When using the sources, one needs to check whether the memories of contemporaries are confirmed by archival documents. Until 1941 and then again beginning in 1950, the documentation is quite good, but for the war and postwar period, a great deal of quantitative data is missing. Developments during the German occupation can be dealt with only briefly. In a command economy, different prices applied parallel for the same item; until December 1947 much of the population got supplies via ration cards; and a few goods were distributed directly. Thus information on nominal incomes is only of limited use. The food rationing cards,

---

451 Aino (born 1921), expert in economics, ERM-KV 984, l. 343: "From 1941 to 1950, the main thing in private life was: I am struggling for survival, for food. [...] I did not really starve, but I never felt fully fed."

452 See, for example, ERM-KV 900, l. 20; 904, l. 173.

453 For example, interview with Jaan Liiv (born 1928), then an agronomist, on August 19, 2004, in Verijärve.

454 Interview project in Narva in August 2003.

with their graduated rations, served as a way for the given regime in power to set priorities and to distinguish between important and unimportant activities. Some enterprises offered their workforce additional supplies via special shops or extra rations. Furthermore, until the money reform at the end of 1947, there was inflation; thereafter started deflation, meaning that the official prices declined from year to year. Even as money continued to circulate, alcohol and tobacco were used as alternative currencies. Since by far the largest share of income was used for food, food consumption—insofar as it was documented—appears to be a relatively good indicator of the development of the standard of living. The aforementioned development of natural mortality likewise indicates an extremely low standard of living in the 1940s.

The Starting Position: The Standard of Living at the End of the 1930s

Data on the monthly income of Tallinn workers' families in 1938 (see Table 17) allow for a comparison with the situation of Estonian workers in the 1950s. The amount of income indicates that typically, one household had two working members.

Table 17: Monthly Income of Workers' Families in Tallinn in 1938, in Kroons

75 or less	8.7%
76–100	24.3%
101–125	34.4%
126-150	21.4%
151–175	7.3%
More than 175	3.9%
Average	121 kroons

Source: Arvo Horm, *Eesti elatusstandard* (Tartu, 1940), p. 24.

The nominal wages in Estonian industry in 1939 (see Table 18) might also be used for comparison with the latter situation. Large enterprises paid substantially higher wages and salaries, and women generally earned less than men. Technical personnel like engineers and technicians had a clear income advantage over workers; in large enterprises the employees earned more than the laborers, but in small enterprises they earned less than the laborers. The support staff, such as unskilled cleaners, had the lowest income. Women were able to reach the Estonian average only in exceptional cases, while workers in large enterprises were clearly above this threshold. In addition, it must be noted that at the time, even an enterprise employing 20 people was defined as "large." Today it would be categorized as a small or medium-sized enterprise.

Table 18: Nominal Monthly Incomes in Estonian Industry in 1939, in Kroons

	Large enterprises		**Medium-sized enterprises**	
	Males	**Females**	**Males**	**Females**
Workers	96.87	58.99	80.91	49.59
Employees	106.90	71.30	71.90	48.10
Technical personnel	130.20	76.50	99.60	-
Supporting staff	59.60	37.20	46.00	27.50

Large enterprises are those with a workforce of more than 20. Medium-sized enterprises are those with a workforce of 5–19.

Source: R. Sõrmus, "Palgaolud tööstuses," *Eesti Statistika* 1940, pp. 269, 285–286.

According to Soviet sources, the average wage in industry was 72 kroons per month, with an income tax of 3 percent.[455] Employees of large enterprises and civil servants earned more; in the service sector and in agriculture, one would expect to find lower incomes, since the GDP per employed person in both of those sectors was much lower than in industry.[456] Given that farm workers could earn 40 kroons per month and got free room and board, and given that at the end of the 1930s Estonia had not only full employment but also a labor shortage, we might expect that the income differences between industry and agriculture were not severe. Concerning food consumption, we would expect the peasants to follow more or less the same pattern as urban workers.

If we go by currency conversion alone, then Estonian wages and salaries were only half as much as in Western Europe. Yet it should be considered that Estonia

455 Hendrik Allik, "Eesti töölisklassi elatustase kodanlikul ajal ja praegu," *Eesti Kommunist* no. 10 (1956), p. 19.

456 See the calculations in Jaak Valge, "Uue majanduse lätteil," pp. 2466, 2485, 2714.

had one of the highest employment rates in Europe, and the cost of living was far lower than in Western Europe. The Statistical Office of Latvia even claimed in 1935 that the real incomes of workers in Latvia and Estonia were higher than in several Western European countries.[457] The real wages in Estonia might have been approximately two-thirds of the Western European level; the ratio was thus slightly higher than today. Estonia was engaged in a catch-up modernization, and especially in the second half of the 1930s, the economic boom was broadly experienced throughout the society. The structure of expenditure changed more quickly than it did in Finland or Sweden, and by 1937, only 40 percent of expenditure was for food.[458] This might explain why the era of independence was idealized in later memories.

A 1938 Estonian budget survey compares the income of workers with their daily consumption of calories, protein, and fat (see Table 19). It should be noted that even the lowest income group had a relatively high calorie intake. Protein and fat was consumed sufficiently as well. As income increased, the food situation improved, and the average worker was able to eat a diet rich in calories, protein, and fat.

Table 19: Intake of Calories, Protein, and Fat in Estonian Workers' Households in 1938

Per capita income in kroons	Daily calorie intake	Protein in gr	Fat in gr
25 and less	2,935	86	74
26–35	3,189	95	82
36–45	3,305	101	92
46–55	3,527	105	102
56–65	3,705	115	109
66 and more	3,405	112	120
Average	3,405	102	94

Source: Riigi Statistika Keskbüroo, *I majandusloendus Eestis: Büdžetiuurimus*, booklet 4 (Tallinn, 1940), p. 78.

457 Central Statistical Bureau of Latvia, *The Baltic States before the Second World War: Brief Collection of Statistical Data* (Riga, 2002), pp. 14–15.

458 Timo Toivonen, "Classes, Countries and Consumption Between the World Wars: A Comparison of the Structure of Expenditure in Estonia, Finland and Sweden in the 1920s and 1930s," *Acta Sociologia* 35 (1992), pp. 224–225, 231.

A comparison with the diet of civil servants in the framework of the same budget survey also indicates a rich and nutritious diet (see Table 20). The higher-earning civil servants obviously subsisted on a diet that the population considered optimal. As inhabitants of an agrarian country, the Estonians ate better than many Western Europeans, including, for instance, the Germans.[459] From today's perspective, the consumption of fruits and vegetables was less than optimal, but this was apparently caused by the high prices for fresh fruits in winter and the traditional Estonian diet.

Table 20: Food Consumption of the Households of Workers and Civil Servants, 1938, per Capita in Kg

	Workers per year	Workers per month	Civil servants per year	Civil servants per month
Vegetables	59.4	5.0	64.5	5.4
Fruits	38.4	3.2	53.2	4.4
Bread, etc.	175.7	14.6	178.9	14.9
Potatoes	159.2	13.3	180.7	15.1
Fish	27.5	2.3	37.0	3.1
Meat	63.3	5.3	61.5	5.1
Milk and milk products	227	18.9	253	21
Sugar	29.8	2.5	35.8	3.0

Source: Riigi Statistika Keskbüroo, *I majandusloendus Eestis: Büdžetiuurimus*, pp. 83–86.

Developments in the 1940s

The outbreak of war in September 1939 influenced Estonia, too; the decline of international trade led to a small decrease in real incomes and the scarcity of some imported goods. The stationing of Soviet troops in 1939 slightly compensated for this, because Soviet construction orders revived the regional labor markets

459 See *Statistisches Jahrbuch für das Deutsche Reich 1938* (Berlin, 1938), pp. 382–385, 307*–310*.

and the Red Army bought mostly on the Estonian market. To ensure a proper comparison with later prices, we have listed here the prices for food in May 1940 (see Table 21). Given that the average income was roughly 70 kroons per month, the price level did not increase much after the outbreak of war, and a change in eating habits was not necessary. Even Soviet statisticians estimated the decline of real income to be only a few percent (see Chapter 1).

Table 21: Market or Retail Prices in May 1940 in Kroons per Kg

Rye flour	0.18	Potatoes	0.07
Wheat flour	0.27	Pork	1.08
White bread	0.45	Beef	1.15
Rye bread	0.21	Ham	2.40
Butter	2.15	Rice	0.65
Margarine	0.90	Sugar	0.60

Source: *Eesti Statistika* 1940, p. 320.

As detailed in Chapter 1, the Stalinist restructuring of the economy led to a roughly one-half decline of real incomes. This fact is not mentioned in most of the descriptions by contemporaries, since the misery of the subsequent war and postwar years overshadowed the memory of the declining standard of living during the first Soviet year. The increased natural mortality alone clearly indicates the economic catastrophe wrought by Sovietization. Eventually, the majority of complaints from the population up to May 1941 related to the supply situation.

The German attack on the Soviet Union exacerbated the situation. War damage and broken transport lines impaired trade. Additionally, the German occupiers prohibited several market economy activities, including most sales of agrarian products on peasant markets. The black market and personal relations saved many urban dwellers from hunger as food rationing was introduced and only skimpy rations were provided.

To better understand the supply situation, it must be stressed once more that Estonia was an agrarian country. Most urban residents had roots in the countryside or had relatives there. In times of need, factory workers or office employees could help with the harvest for a few weeks and thus get through shortages.

Many were helped by their relatives. What would have led to a famine in a purely industrial region could be reacted to more flexibly in an agrarian country.

Many basic consumables all but disappeared from trade. Replacing clothing was extremely difficult. In the occupied Soviet territories, the Germans introduced rationing for the entire non-agrarian population. Approximately 450,000 people received ration cards in Estonia—nearly everyone not living on a farm. Meanwhile, in other places, the Germans distributed cards only to those working. While in occupied Russia, Belarus, or Ukraine, segments of the population faced the threat of starvation, in the Baltic states a certain basic supply existed, even if at a much lower level than for the Germans. William Moskoff mentions that daily food rations in Estonia in September 1942 amounted to 1,069 calories, but in this figure, he does not include the annual potato ration he mentions. According to Moskoff, residents of Tallinn faced hunger in 1943.[460] Alvin Isberg indicates a daily ration of 1,275 calories in October 1941, which is close to Moskoff's figure.[461] Hans Umbreit is more precise: according to him, normal rations consisted of 1,305 calories in 1942–1943 and 1,420 calories in 1944. Thus the rations were higher than in occupied France.[462]

The official German rations were obviously smaller than in the occupied Soviet hinterland.[463] Nevertheless, those hunger rations did not lead to a sudden increase of natural mortality; on the contrary, mortality was lower than the Soviet figures. This could be due to inaccurate statistics but also to the fact that most urban residents were seeking opportunities to supplement their diet, whether from their own gardens, the black market, or relatives in the countryside. Thus the situation in the occupied Baltic states republics differed little from that in German-occupied Western Europe. In the life stories, those who lived through the German occupation remember it as a time of low standards of living—but not famine. The continued existence of private farms guaranteed a certain minimum of supplies. The peasants experienced the smallest losses in food supplies; many of them were able to continue their old eating habits and consumed a rich diet. Generally speaking, the standard of living was still lower than during the

---

460 William Moskoff, *The Bread of Affliction: The Food Supply in the USSR During World War II* (Cambridge, 1990), pp. 52ff.

461 Isberg, *Zu den Bedingungen*, p. 62.

462 Hans Umbreit, "Die deutsche Herrschaft in den 'germanischen' Ländern 1942–1945," in Kroener, Müller, and Umbreit (eds), *Organisation und Mobilierung des deutschen Machtbereichs*, second part, p. 226.

463 See the data in Moskoff, *The Bread of Affliction*, pp. 52, 139.

first Soviet year. Due to the lack of sources, no precise estimates can be made. The spread of tuberculosis indicates the decline in the standard of living. While in 1941, 4 percent of the population was infected, by 1944, the hospitals were reporting an infection rate of 7 percent.[464]

The Red Army's reoccupation of Estonia in 1944 caused more destruction and transport disruptions. However, the authorities tolerated the peasant markets to a certain degree, which eased the population's search for food. A report of the Ministry of Trade of the ESSR stated: "During the years of the German fascist occupation, trade on the market was absent from the Estonian SSR. The peasants and workers were forbidden to sell their goods on the market, and because of this, market trade stopped completely. After the liberation of the territory of the Estonian SSR, markets and kiosks started to be rebuilt." By January 1, 1945, there were 36 markets in the country; by July 1, 1948, the number had increased to 65.[465] Thus sometimes the Soviets even rebuilt and reopened markets.

The communists permitted markets not out of a preference for petty trade but out of practical considerations. Without private trade, supplies for the population could not be secured. The sales stock of state trade in 1947, for instance, was approximately 2 kg of meat, 3 kg of fish, 2 kg of fat, and six liters of milk per inhabitant annually.[466] As in other parts of the Soviet Union, Estonia had to allow private trade to ensure the survival of the population.

The peasants were initially able to profit from this policy; they were finally allowed to sell their products again freely, without having to worry about being accused of black marketing. Their standard of living began to decline with the significant tax increases that started in 1947, which were intended to pave the way for collectivization, and often reached the lowest level after collectivization. In the towns the situation was somewhat different; after a phase of stabilization after the end of fighting, the famine in the western parts of the USSR influenced the situation in Estonia, too. Thus Oskar Sepre, an official responsible for the planning of the economy, stated in June 1947: "This scarcity of food prevailing now—in 1946 there was a bad grain harvest, we have seen that the situation in 1946 was not as bad, the prices were not as high—this is food scarcity."[467] In

464 People's Commissar for Health Care Hion on the Fifth Plenum of the CC of the ECP, December 1–2, 1944, ERAF 1-4-107, l. 132–133.

465 Report of the People's Commissariat of Trade, October 9, 1948, ERAF 1-47-30, l. 70–71.

466 Calculated according to the statistical overview, ibid., l. 66–67.

467 Sepre on a seminar for the secretaries of parish party organizations, June 2–8, 1947, ERAF 1-4-497, l. 38.

addition to the bad harvest, hunger refugees from the western part of the Soviet Union, known as the "bag people," drove the prices high. In the summer of 1947, Estonia's standard of living fell to its lowest level in the 20th century.

In comparison to the German occupation, the number of recipients of bread rations, which were indeed slightly higher than under the Germans, decreased by roughly 100,000 people to 348,000 by March 1947.[468] Even before this, the rations actually distributed had been smaller than those officially announced; bread rations were about 8 percent smaller, and in the following year, they were 6 percent smaller. Meat and fat also became more scarce.[469] A March 1947 report from the small town of Rakvere describes the dramatic situation there: On each market day, 1,500 to 2,000 "bag people" and "speculators" arrived from the east, willing to pay any price for food. Since December, the market price for bread had increased from 20–25 rubles to 50–60 rubles. Approximately 1,600 people were removed from the list of recipients of rations. But even the recipients did not receive the full rations. Even the amassing of stocks of grain seeds was endangered.[470]

Food rationing ended in December 1947, and thereafter, the supply situation in the towns continuously improved. However, it must be noted that urban real incomes in the second half of the 1940s amounted to one-third or even less of those in the pre-Soviet era. Due to the lack of precise data, this is a rough estimate. The fluctuations of nominal wages and salaries over time are known, but it is impossible to construct a cost-of-living index.

When the cost of living in a command economy is compared to that of a market economy, the fixed prices of state trade are usually contrasted to the fluctuating prices of a market. Yet the command economy included markets whose price levels were consistently higher than those in state retail trade. Those markets presented a good opportunity to compensate for the constant shortages in state trade. Since it is unknown how much the population really bought on the market, a direct comparison of the cost of living is always based on estimates. Tallinn market prices in 1948–1949 (see Table 23) were two or three times higher than state trade prices, depending on the product, and they were 10 to 30 times

468 Report on bread rationing for the Secretary at the CC of the VKP(b), Kuznetsov, March 22, 1947, ERAF 1-5-77, l. 26.

469 Coverage of the ration cards by goods, statistical overview, ERAF 1-5-1, l. 47.

470 Janson, first secretary of the party committee of the ECP in Virumaa, to Karotamm, March 19, 1947, ERAF 1-5-36, l. 40.

higher than before the war. Still, they were below the level of February or March 1947, when hunger refugees drove the prices up (see Table 22).

Table 22: Market Prices in Tallinn in Rubles per Kg in the Winter of 1947

Product	February 1, 1947	February 15, 1947	March 1, 1947	March 15, 1947
Bread	14–18	14–15	18–22.50	20–20.50
Pork	50–110	50–125	50–145	70–150
Beef	25–55	25–55	35–70	50–70
Milk (liter)	9–12	10–12	10–15	14–15
Oil/fat	130–140	130–145	135–165	150–165
Potatoes	9–12	10–12	10–15	11–12
Cabbage	8–10	8–12	10–15	14–15

Source: Report on bread rationing for the secretary at the CC of the VKP(b), Kuznetsov, March 22, 1947, ERAF 1-5-77, l. 30.

Table 23: Market Prices in Tallinn in Rubles per Kg, August 1948–August 1949

Product	August 5, 1948	March 1, 1949	April 1, 1949	May 14, 1949	June 1, 1949	July 1, 1949	August 1, 1949
Wheat flour	3	3.50–4	3–4	4–4.50	4–5	3-4	5–6
Pork	25–50	20–40	20–40	20–40	20–40	18–35	18–35
Beef	15–25	11–30	12–30	10–28	12–30	12–28	10–30
Milk (liter)	4	4	3.50	3–4	2–2.50	2.50–3	2.50
Butter	55	45	40–45	44–48	40–45	38–45	38–45
Potatoes	1.25–1.50	1.50–2	1.25–1.50	0.80–1	0.60–0.80	0.70–1	1–1.20

Source: Statistical overview, ERA R-13-2-231, l. 1–18.

After the war, the Soviet Union established a network of "commercial shops" where goods could be obtained at a higher price (see Table 24). Normal retail stores offered little else but rationed products, and they did not even stock enough to supply all ration card-holders with the rations they were officially entitled to. Thus the urban population had to buy on the market and in the "commercial" shops just to survive. Given that wages and salaries were 400 to 700 rubles per month, the "commercial" prices were unaffordable.

Table 24: Prices of Rationed Goods and "Commercial Prices" in the USSR in Rubles, 1946

	Ration price, September 15, 1946	**"Commercial price," September 15, 1946**	**Ration price, September 16, 1946**	**"Commercial price," September 16, 1946**
Dark bread, kg	1.10	10	3.40	7.50
Potatoes, kg	0.90	27	0.90	24
Beef, kg	14	140	30	90
Pork, kg	14		30	
Cheese, kg	32.50	215	70	170
Ten eggs		100		50
Sugar, kg	5.50	170	15	70
Milk, liter	3.50	40	8	20
Vodka, liter	120	130		120
Cigarettes (25)	6	30		27
Soap, kg	3.10	60	13	54
Pair of woolen socks	5	62	8.25	45

Source: Donald Filtzer, "The Standard of Living of Soviet Industrial Workers in the Immediate Postwar Period, 1945–1948," *Europe-Asia Studies* 51 (1999), p. 1021.

The Statistical Office of the Soviet Union compiled data on the structure of expenditure of Soviet workers in the 1940s (see Table 25) indicating the large percentage of income spent on food. Yet the information is misleading. Expenditures for food, alcohol, and tobacco were underestimated, while those for other goods were overestimated. We can estimate realistically that these products constituted at least 70 percent of the total. Vassilii Popov states that the share of food expenditure of workers and employees in 1950 was 79 percent.[471] Janet Chapman has calculated that in the cost-of-living index of the USSR, the share of food in 1940 and from 1948 to 1954 was between 54 and 60 percent.[472]

Table 25: Monthly Structure of Expenses of Soviet Workers, 1940 and 1947–1948

	1940	**1947**	**1948**
Total expenses in rubles per person	184.7	463.7	398.5
Food	57.4%	62.8%	52.5%
Alcohol and tobacco	3.8%	2.8%	2.9%
Other goods	14.9%	12.8%	18.6%

Source: Information of the Central Statistical Office of the USSR about the budget of workers in 1948, in Elena Zubkova et al. (eds.), *Sovetskaia zhizn' 1945–1953* (Moscow, 2003), p. 93.

The Situation until the Mid-1950s

As mentioned above, the situation in the towns normalized slowly. From 1952 to 1956, a comprehensive budget survey was conducted of workers' families (see Table 26). This offers the opportunity for certain comparisons with the 1938 budget survey and with the income of collectivized peasants (see below). While the average household size on kolkhozes was 3.4 persons, among workers it was 2.5 persons. Many workers' households evidently consisted only of one member or included no children or other family members. Workers' per-capita income was twice as high as that for peasants on the collective farm. The relatively low increase until 1956 should not be misinterpreted; the real income increase was higher due to the shrinking state prices. However, even in the mid-1950s, the real income of Tallinn workers' households was only half that of 1938, because the

471 Popov, *Ekonomicheskaia politika*, p. 65.
472 Chapman, *Real Wages in Soviet Russia*, p. 70.

ruble prices were, on average, 20 times higher than the previous prices in kroons. The state prices for food, clothing, and shoes were, according to the calculations of communist politician Hendrik Allik, only 12 times as high in 1955, while rent and utility prices doubled.[473] Thus Allik disregarded the fact that many items were completely lacking in state trade, and others were only available at markets at a higher price. Taking into account how many products workers actually bought on the market, a 20-fold increase of prices and thus the halving of real incomes seems to be realistic.

Table 26: Family Size and Family Income of Workers, 1952–1956

Year	Family size	Total income in rubles	Income per family member
1952	2.50	1,334	533.6
1953	2.45	1,380	563.3
1954	2.41	1,396	579.3
1955	2.35	1,397	594.5
1956	2.41	1,484	614.5

Column 4 calculated according to columns 2 and 3.

Source: Budget study 1952–1956, ERA R-10-43-57, l. 1, 4.

The average incomes in September of 1945, 1950, and 1955 (see Table 27) should not be confused with net incomes. From the average income figures, we must deduct the 9 percent income tax, the 6 percent tax on the childless, and government bonds, which had to be purchased "voluntarily" in an amount equivalent to one month's wage per year. Thus net incomes after taxation were 17–23 percent smaller. In independent Estonia, direct taxation of wages was much lower.

In the course of 10 years, nominal incomes doubled in industry; in trade and gastronomy, they increased by two-thirds; and in health care and administration, they increased by one-half. Education, research, and culture saw an increase of only 40 percent. This development indicates a "proletarianization" and a de-emphasis of certain fields, especially those that were increasingly hiring women, such as medicine and education, while industry was preferred clearly.

473 Allik, "Eesti töölisklassi elatustase," p. 12.

In independent Estonia, for those in full-time positions, incomes in health care, state administration, education, research, and culture were much higher than in industry. However, in 1955, an industrial worker earned more than a physician or a teacher. The development of real incomes is hard to reconstruct, since in 1945 there was rationing, and trade commonly consisted of bartering. Prices continuously decreased from 1948 to 1955 in state trade and on the market; the number of goods on offer increased steadily. The real wage index of Soviet industrial workers illustrates this development (see Table 28). A comparison of the income levels of 1939 and 1955 can only be estimated. The purchasing power of one kroon was equal to 20 rubles, yet many goods were not available at all. According to this, the real incomes in industry declined by one-half. In other sectors, the decrease was 60 percent or more. In this context, it seems justified to speak of a "proletarianization," especially of the educated strata of society. However, in a system of ubiquitous *blat'*, meaning exchanges of favors, some occupational groups had access to additional sources of income, premiums, and privileges that were not indicated in the statistics. Those who worked in trade, for instance, could provide friends, relatives, and acquaintances with scarce goods and take advantage of their position under other circumstances. Black-market activities were also possible. In state administration there was an army of low-ranking civil servants, though those who had decision-making authority could be offered bribes or other advantages, including privileges. The state health care was free of charge, yet getting the required treatment was not always easy. Bribes were used in this context, too, and it was then that the custom of giving physicians gifts was introduced in Estonia, a custom that survived until several years after the collapse of communism. Some physicians also practiced privately.

Table 27: Average Gross Income in September in Rubles

	1945	**1950**	**1955**
Industry	397	714	819
Trade and catering	336	511	569
Education, science, and culture	483	691	688
Health	376	475	512
Administration	488	649	757

Source: Veimer, *Kompleksnoe razvitie*, p. 328.

The index of real wages of Soviet industrial workers (see Table 28) cannot be compared with an index of real wages in a market economy, yet it indicates general tendencies. In 1946, real wages plunged to their lowest level as a result of the famine; in 1949 they reached the prewar level and thereafter increased steadily. Since the average income in Estonia before Sovietization was well above that of the "old" republics, the level of the period of independence was not reached until the 1960s. How difficult the living conditions in the towns were in the first half of the 1950s is illustrated by the spread of dysentery, an infectious disease associated with poverty and caused by malnutrition in combination with bad hygienic conditions. From 1951 to 1953, approximately 3,000 cases were registered annually. More than one-third of these were small children up to the age of two years.[474]

Table 28: Index of Real Wages of Soviet Industrial Workers, 1940–1953

1940	**100**
Before September 16, 1946	28.7
Before December 16, 1947	39.1
1948	82.7
1949	100.3
1950	124.7
1951	141.1
1952	153.4
1953	180

Calculated on the basis of Moscow's cost of living index.

Source: Filtzer, "The Standard of Living," p. 1015.

In 1952, as part of a budget survey, 316 households of collectivized peasants were studied (see Table 29). To facilitate comparability, the statisticians converted the income in kind—roughly three-fourths of the total—into rubles, a procedure that introduced a large uncertainty factor. Excluding animal fodder, expenses

474 Velichko, deputy minister for state control, to Müürisepp, chairman of the Council of Ministers, July 20, 1953, ERAF 1-126-40, l. 13; statistical overview, ibid., l. 35.

per household (consisting of an average 3.4 members[475]) were found to be 10,500 rubles per year, or 875 rubles per month. Three-quarters of expenditures were for food, since the private plots of the peasants were not enough for subsistence. If we assume there were two working members in the household, then kolkhoz peasants earned only a little more than half of the income of industrial workers. In this respect, the peasants were the big losers of the Stalinist reconstruction; their real incomes declined to one-third or one-fourth of the prewar level. Understandably, estimates based on average values do not reflect the reality of individual families. A former family of rural workers lost less than the former owners of a large farm. The latter often became victims of political persecution and social discrimination.

Table 29: Structure of the Private Consumption of a Kolkhoz Household in the First Quarter of 1952

	Expenditure in rubles and in kind	**Percentage of total expenditure**	**Monthly expenditure per person**
Food	2,001.6	76.2	196.2
Other goods	239.4	9.1	23.5
Utility costs, heating	169.4	6.4	16.6
Other	217.1	8.3	21.3
Total	2,627.5	100	257,6

Column 4 calculated according to columns 2 and 3.

According to the document, only one-quarter of expenditure was in money, and the remainder, which was in kind, was converted into rubles.

Source: Budget study of kolkhoz households 1952, ERAF 1-114-57, l. 16.

The prices paid by Estonian collectivized peasants in 1952 are average figures (see Table 30). They were above the prices of state trade and below market prices; thus other sources were used, since state trade could not come close to covering demand.

475 Budget study 1952, ERAF 1-114-57, l. 8.

Table 30: Average Food Prices for Collectivized Peasants in 1952, in Rubles per Kg

Simple flour	2.04	Mutton	17
Barley meal	3.11	Pork	22.46
Wheat flour	5.74	Bacon	20
Pearl barley	5.18	Egg (1)	1.07
Potatoes	0.84	Honey	27.15
Beans	4.77	Milk (liter)	1.81
Vegetables	4.57	Cooking oil (liter)	31.18
Fresh fish	4.27	Sugar	10.80
Beef	7.59		

Source: Budget study of kolkhoz households 1952, ERAF 1-114-57, l. 21.

The food consumption of Estonian and Russian collectivized peasants in 1952 (see Table 31) indicates how impoverished the food producers had become. The higher consumption of potatoes and grain in Russia might be explained if animal fodder is factored in to the calculation. Apart from vegetables and cabbage, Estonian peasants were obviously better fed than Russian ones, especially when it came to meat, fish, eggs, and milk. However, the figures might still be overstated. The diet of Estonian peasants before the war was at least as good as that of workers, since as producers, they had direct access to food. Thus their diet became much worse because of collectivization. Their calorie intake was high, yet indicators of very poor nutrition cannot be overlooked. They consumed much less protein and fat, and many clearly suffered from a lack of vitamins and minerals. Concerning the food situation, the aforementioned decline of mortality below the prewar level looks somehow unrealistic or may perhaps have been caused by greatly improved medical treatment.

Table 31: Food Consumption of Kolkhoz Peasants in the First Half of 1952 in Estonia and Russia per Capita in Kg

	Estonia	**Russia**
Bread and flour	11.0	14.3*
Pearl barley, etc.	1.6	0.6
Potatoes	18.1	26.7*
Vegetables and cabbage	1.6	7.7
Fruits	0.1	0.2
Animal fat	0.4	0.2
Meat	3.4	2.6
Fish	0.7	0.1
Milk and milk products	13.1	8.3
Eggs (number of)	8.0	1.5
Sugar	0.4	0.5

* Partly fed to animals.

Sources: Budget study of kolkhoz households 1952, ERAF 1-114-57, l. 38; Russia calculated based on Verbitskaia, *Rossiiskoe krest'ianstvo*, pp. 153–156.

The food consumption of Estonian workers' families was thoroughly investigated in the framework of a budget study (see Table 32). Naturally, the data need to be viewed critically. Strikingly, the workers were fed better than collectivized peasants, especially in terms of fruits and vegetables, fish, and sugar. Consumption of milk and meat was a bit lower, but the diet was healthier. This diet covered the need for calories, but protein, fat, vitamins, and minerals were insufficient. The food situation became much worse than it had been in 1938. As with the peasants, among the workers one would not expect a decline of mortality because of nutrition.

We see that in Estonia there was less consumption of vegetables and fruits than the Soviet average (see Table 33), obviously due to the climate. At the same time, the consumption of fish and meat was twice as high, and for milk and dairy products, it was 50 percent higher. Thus the food situation of Estonian workers

Table 32: Monthly Food Consumption of Estonian Workers' Families, 1952–1956, per Capita in Kg

Year	**Flour**	**Gray bread**	**Dark bread**	**Pearl barley, etc.**	**Noodles**	**Pota-toes**	**Vege-tables and cabbage**	**Fresh fruits**	**Dried fruits**
1952	0.83	6.09	9.0	0.9	0.6	12.4	3.1	0.7	0.1
1953	1.3	5.7	8.8	0.9	0.6	12.2	4.5	1.2	0.1
1954	1.3	5.6	7.9	0.8	0.6	10.8	4.2	1.9	0.1
1955	1.4	5.2	8.6	1.0	0.6	11.2	4.5	1.6	0.1
1956	1.2	5.2	8.6	1.0	0.5	12.0	4.5	1.9	0.1
	Milk (liters)	Milk pro-ducts	Eggs (num-ber)	Ani-mal fat	Veg. fat	Meat	Sausage	Fish	Sugar
1952	10.2	0.3	7.8	0.7	0.3	2.4	0.6	1.3	1.4
1953	10.5	0.4	9.2	0.8	0.4	2.4	0.9	1.4	1.9
1954	11.0	0.4	10.6	0.9	0.4	2.5	1.1	1.4	2.0
1955	11.3	0.4	9.9	1.1	0.4	2.5	1.1	1.4	1.5
1956	12.8	0.5	9.9	1.1	0.4	2.6	1.2	1.4	1.7

All data rounded to the nearest 100 g.

Source: Budget survey 1952–1956, ERA R-10-43-57, l. 19–20.

was still better than the Soviet average, which was one reason why immigration continued.

Table 33: Monthly Food Consumption of Soviet Workers' Families in the Third Quarter of 1952 in Kg per Capita

Flour	**Gray bread**	**Dark bread**	**Pearl barley, etc.**	**Noodles**	**Potatoes**	**Vegetables and cabbage**	**Fresh fruits**	**Dried fruits**
1.1	10.2	7.4	0.8	0.6	9.8	9.4	2.0	0.1
Milk (liters)	Milk products	Eggs (number)	Animal fat	Veg. fat	Meat and sausage	Fish	Sugar	
6.9	0.3	7.2	0.3	0.5	1.7	0.8	1.5	

Source: Calculated according to Table 3.1 in Filtzer, *Soviet Workers and Late Stalinism*, p. 90.

The sources of food for Estonian workers are interesting (see Table 34). Besides bread and grain products, they provided themselves with food mostly from the market or from private sources (a private garden, relatives in the countryside, etc.). Because the staff of sovkhozes was entitled to private plots, similarly to the kolkhoz peasants, and were counted as workers, this may explain the scale of private sources. In addition, many workers possessed their own garden or had relatives, friends, or acquaintances in the countryside. The importance of state trade increased over time, yet in the case of the mentioned goods it rarely exceeded 20 percent, and in some cases it was practically irrelevant. In the market, the prices were often higher than in retail trade. Therefore, we can conclude that during the evaluation period, the turnover of private trade clearly exceeded that of state trade, since food was by far the largest category of expenditure in family budgets.

In addition to the conversion of prices, looking at food consumption helps us to estimate how far the standard of living declined in Estonia due to the Stalinist restructuring. As early as the 1950s, Aleksander Kaelas tried to calculate average incomes in terms of their purchasing power in goods (see Table 35). A worker's average monthly salary could buy more than 80 kilos of pork in 1938, yet it could buy only 27 kilos of pork in 1955. It must be kept in mind that for the year 1955, Kaelas used only the state retail prices, when in fact, in an economy of shortages

Table 34: Sources of Food of Estonian Workers' Families, 1952–1956, in Kg per Month

Year	**Potatoes**			**Vegetables**			**Fresh Fruits**		
	State trade	Market	**Private source**	State trade	Market	**Private source**	State trade	Market	**Private source**
1952	0.5	8.9	7.9	0.5	2.1	0.5	0.1	0.5	0.1
1953	0.3	7.1	9.2	1.0	2.7	1.4	0.1	1.0	0.2
1954	0.2	6.7	12.3	1.1	2.4	0.6	0.2	1.4	0.3
1955	0.5	5.7	10.4	1.3	2.0	0.7	0.3	1.1	0.4
1956	0.7	6.2	16.6	1.6	1.8	0.6	0.4	1.1	0.6
	Milk (liters)			Eggs (number)			Meat		
1952	1.3	7.5	2.2	0.5	6.5	0.2	0.1	2.0	0.3
1953	1.2	6.8	3.5	0.5	7.4	0.3	0.2	1.5	0.3
1954	1.2	7.4	4.0	1.0	7.7	0.7	0.3	1.5	0.6
1955	1.5	7.8	3.6	1.8	5.6	1.2	0.6	1.0	0.4
1956	3.6	6.7	3.5	3.6	4.6	0.8	1.1	0.8	0.4

All data rounded to the nearest 100 g.

Source: Budget study 1952–1956, ERA R-10-43-57, l. 25–26.

such as the Soviet one, many products could be obtained only at higher prices. He could also not take into account the decline in quality. In reality, the situation in 1955 was even worse.

Table 35: Monthly Average Income, 1939 and 1955, in Goods

	1939	**1955**
Rye bread	398	220
Pork, kg	84	27
Butter, kg	38	18
Sugar, kg	170	55
Potatoes, kg	1,592	956
Men's shoes (leather)	7	1.8
Suits for gentlemen (high quality)	1.5	0.5

Source: Kaelas, Das sowjetisch besetzte Estland, pp. 101–102.

Nevertheless—though the standard of living was much lower than in the 1930s—in the 1950s the life of urban dwellers slowly, yet noticeably, improved. After the deprivation of the 1940s, it was finally possible to consider buying something other than food. The clothing selection expanded, and gradually, more durable consumer products like bicycles or radios were bought.

The Comparison to the Situation in the Rest of the Soviet Union

Life stories of contemporaries mention repeatedly that the standard of living in Estonia was still higher than in the rest of the USSR, with the exception of Latvia. Stephen Wheatcroft has calculated how many calories were available on a daily basis in the Russian Empire and the Soviet Union (see Table 36), and he does not insist on high accuracy. Nevertheless, the figures contain a revelation: the citizens ate better under the last tsar than they did under Lenin or Stalin. Indeed, in addition to the large famines, sporadic regional famines were common. From 1916 to 1949, there were only three years without regional famines. Only starting in 1949 was the food situation more or less secure.[476] Under Khrushchev the pre-World War I level was restored. Hence the situation in Estonia was relatively good.

Table 36: Availability of Food in the USSR and in Tsarist Russia

Time period/year	Daily available calories per inhabitant
1900–1913	2,964
1921–1922	2,425
1928	2,804
1933	2,459
1940	2,707
1950	2,759
1960	2,978

The calculation is based on production data.

Source: Stephen G. Wheatcroft, "The Great Leap Upwards," *Slavic Review* 58 (1999), p. 51.

A Soviet archival source breaking down food consumption delivers a similar picture (see Table 37). Even in the late Stalinist era, the peasants were not eating better than they were under the tsar. It must be taken into account that people's consumption of some sorts of food was probably less than indicated, since grain and potatoes were also used as fodder.

Table 37: Monthly Food Consumption of Peasants in Tsarist Russia and in the Soviet Union, 1905–1953, in Kg

	1905–1913	1923/24	1928/29	1936	1940	1950	1952	First half of 1953
Bread and cereals	26.5	24.9	21.0	9.8	22.5	20.5	21.7	22.1

476 Hessler, "Postwar Normalisation," pp. 445–446.

Table 37: Continued

	1905–1913	**1923/24**	**1928/29**	**1936**	**1940**	**1950**	**1952**	**First half of 1953**
Pearl barley, etc.	1.8	2.0	2.1	1.6	1.2	0.8	0.8	0.9
Potatoes	10.9	13.2	13.6	19.9	11.4	23.7	18.7	17.8
Vegetables and cabbage	4.2	4.1	5.9	5.5	6.0	5.0	4.9	3.6
Fruits			1.0	0.5	0.5	0.8	0.6	0.2
Milk and milk products converted into milk	–	11.8	14.3	11.4	13.5	15.1	14.2	12.7
Fat	0.2	0.2	0.3	0.2	0.3	0.1	0.3	0.5
Eggs (number)	1.3	2.7	3.3	3.2	4.3	3.3	4.8	7.3
Meat and meat products	1.5	1.0	1.5	1.2	1.4	1.2	1.2	1.5
Sugar and confectionery	0.3	0.1	0.2	0.3	0.2	0.3	0.4	0.5
Number of researched family budgets	4,622	5,364	2,725	9,876	20,801	1,255	29,000	29,000

Source: Statistical overview of the Central Statistical Office of the USSR, October 5, 1953, in Zubkova et al. (eds.), *Sovetskaia zhizn'*, pp. 95–96.

Slightly different data is presented in a study about various occupation groups in 1953 in the USSR (see Table 38). However, Estonian workers fared much better than they did.

Table 38: Monthly Food Consumption of Different Households in the Soviet Union, 1953, in Kg per Person

	Workers	Technical staff of industry	Employees of industry	Collectivized peasants
Bread and cereals	11.9	10.7	10.6	15.1
Pearl barley	0.8	0.8	0.8	0.8
Noodles	0.6	0.6	0.6	0.1
Potatoes	10.6	9.8	9.9	17.8
Vegetables and cabbage	6.3	6.7	6.4	6.4
Fruits	1.2	1.6	1.5	0.9
Milk (liters)	5.3	6.1	5.6	11.4
Milk products	0.3	0.5	0.4	0.4
Fat	1.1	1.1	1.1	0.5
Eggs (number)	7.2	10.5	9.0	6.1
Meat and meat products	2.7	3.3	2.9	1.5
Fish	0.8	0.9	0.8	0.2
Sugar	1.7	1.8	1.8	0.4
Confectionery	0.8	0.9	0.9	0.2

Source: Report of the Central Statistical Office of the USSR for Malenkov, March 5, 1954, in: Zubkova et al. (eds.), *Sovetskaia zhizn'*, p. 102.

When we compare the actual and the then-recommended consumption of individual foodstuffs in 1954 in the USSR (see Table 39), it becomes clear that the food supply did not even match the Soviets' own official requirements. The indicated figures suggested, to some degree, a flawed diet and a lack of vitamins. In addition, fish and meat consumption, in my opinion, was overstated.

Table 39: Daily, Respectively Annual, Consumption and the Nutritionally Recommended Consumption in the USSR in 1954

	Recommended consumption	**Real consumption**	**Real consumption as a percentage of the recommended value**
Daily: Protein in gr	105	78	74
Fat	99	57	58
Carbohydrates	415	480	116
Calories	3,053	2,814	92
Vitamin A in mg	3.27	1.635	50
Vitamin B1	1.9	2.006	108
Vitamin B2	2	1.55	78
Vitamin C	54	33	61
Vitamin PP	16.2	17.9	110
Yearly: Vegetables and cabbage in kg	141	66	47
Fruits	98	13	13
Fish	18.6	8,9	48
Meat	65	32	49

Source: Report on the food situation of the population, October 3, 1955, in Zubkova et al. (eds.), *Sovetskaia zhizn'*, p. 127.

The comparison of calorie intake per inhabitant of different Soviet republics puts Estonia in first place (see Table 40). However, the consumption data in the cited report on the food situation of the Soviet population[477] are clearly inflated and do not correspond to the budget surveys. The actual calorie intake might have been 5–10 percent lower, depending on the republic. After we reduce the figures this way, it becomes clear that in a couple of Soviet republics, the food situation was Third World-level, despite the fact that those living in climatically warmer regions like Central Asia needed fewer calories than those in Northern Europe. Furthermore, it must be considered that most grown-ups did physical labor and clearly needed more than 3,000 calories.

Table 40: Per Capita Calorie Intake for Each Soviet Republic in 1954

Estonian SSR	**3,081**
Latvian SSR	3,059
Lithuanian SSR	2,960
Georgian SSR	2,912
Russian SFSR	2,834
Belorussian SSR	2,770
Azerbaijan SSR	2,762
Ukrainian SSR	2,727
Kazakh SSR	2,721
Turkmen SSR	2,666
Tajik SSR	2,666
Uzbek SSR	2,646
Moldavian SSR	2,621
Kirghiz SSR	2,615
Armenian SSR	2,594

Source: Report on the food situation of the population, October 3, 1955, in Zubkova et al. (eds.), *Sovetskaia zhizn'*, p. 129.

The Question of Living Space

The war had caused the destruction of living space, though less than was officially announced (see Chapter 2). However, the size of the available flats also says something about the standard of living, since communist propaganda focused on the low rents and utility bills. In 1940 there was 15.5 m^2 of living space per urban dweller; this figure declined in 1945 to 12 m^2, in 1950 to 9.3 m^2, and in

477 Report on the food situation of the population, October 3, 1955, in Elena Zubkova et al. (eds.), *Sovetskaia zhizn' 1945–1953* (Moscow, 2003), pp. 129–130.

1955 to 8.8 m^2.[478] Behind those figures were many people forced to live in communal apartments, dormitories, or barracks. Only by the end of the 1970s was the prewar level of living space per capita restored.

Postwar Stalinism in Estonia had other targets than building flats. Between 1946 and 1954, only 2 million m^2 of living space were constructed; of this, nearly 350,000 m^2 was built privately.[479] Under Stalinism, 9 m^2 was a norm, and 6 m^2 was a minimum. Despite this, between 1940 and 1950 each Soviet urban dweller had only about 4 m^2 of living space.[480] In that sense, the inhabitants of Estonia could feel privileged despite the cramped quarters at home. Yet even in Estonia, one region was in crisis. Ida-Virumaa had been hit harder by the war than any other Estonian region; the town of Narva had been almost completely destroyed, and especially after the war, a "large building site of socialism" was erected there. In March 1948, each inhabitant of Narva had, on average, only 1.77 m^2 of living space at his disposal.[481] The cramped housing situation in barracks and dormitories, the lack of soap, and substandard nutrition and clothing facilitated the spread of infectious diseases and vermin in the USSR.[482]

The Reasons for the Low Standard of Living

There were several reasons for the fall in the standard of living in Estonia. The main reasons were war and destruction, the expense of the Cold War, Stalinist reconstruction, and the economic policy of the regime. Given the large amount of cultivated land per capita, hunger and widespread malnutrition can only be interpreted as a failure of the state. The low procurement prices discouraged producers from selling more food. Regulations preventing market activity and a policy of exploitation like that under the Germans aggravated the situation.

Since collectivization and industrialization began in the USSR in 1929, the share of private consumption of the national income was kept artificially low to

---

478 Misiunas and Taagepera, *The Baltic States*, p. 364.

479 Jüri Kõre, Mare Ainsaar, and Magnus Hendrikson, "Eluasemepoliitika Eestis 1918–1995," *Akadeemia* 8 (1996), pp. 2142–2143.

480 Duskin, *Stalinist Reconstruction*, p. 146, note 76. Filtzer, *Soviet Workers and Late Stalinism*, p. 92, gives figures of 5.2 m^2 in 1940 and 4.7 m^2 in 1950.

481 Karotamm to Pozdniak, administration for the control of Party organs at the CC of the VKP(b), March 29, 1948, ERAF 1-7-98, l. 194.

482 Filtzer, "The Standard of Living," p. 1028. See also Donald Filtzer, *The Hazards of Urban Life in Late Stalinist Russia: Health, Hygiene, and Living Standards, 1943–1953* (Cambridge, 2010).

finance Stalin's ambitious plans of industrialization and later of arms and naturally also the war and the Cold War. According to the calculations of Abram Bergson, in the Stalinist era the share of private consumption of the national income was only about one-half. In 1944, it was even as low as one-third.[483]

Low procurement prices and high sales prices for food—the largest item of expenditure for the population—generated huge profits for the state. Table 41 indicates how high the turnover tax was even immediately after the death of Stalin. The state was financed to a considerable degree by the extremely low prices paid for forced procurement from the agrarian producers, which were then sold with a substantial turnover tax or other such surcharge. A high tax on alcohol, tobacco, or luxury goods might be justified, but excessive taxes on products of daily use really amounted to state exploitation of the citizens.

Table 41: Turnover Tax on Selected Products, April 1, 1953

	Price in rubles	Taxes in percent		Price	Taxes
Vodka (liter)	40	89	Salt	0.40	54
Beer	4.40	74	Black tea	84	20
Margarine (kg)	14.80	40	Cigarettes (25)	2.60	76
Sugar	9.40	75	Pobeda wristwatch	342	71
Beef	10.97	70	Men's boots	222	45
Pork	16.86	69	Sewing machines	583	58
Cold cuts	16.70	65	Matches	1	56
Sausages	13.30	48	Socks	4.25	49
Noodles	4.30	62	Soap (400 gr)	2.25	31
Rye bread	1.35	56	Kerosene (liter)	1.05	70

Source: Report of the Central Statistical Office of the USSR for Malenkov, March 8, 1953, in; Zubkova et al. (eds.), *Sovetskaia zhizn'*, pp. 525–526.

483 Bergson, *The Real National Income*, p. 277.

Despite the propaganda, prices in the USSR were not stable; the state could always increase them to receive more revenue. The fluctuations of prices of state retail trade hint at the inflationary and later deflationary tendencies (see Table 42). Still, it must be kept in mind that even in 1941, the Soviet price level had not been established in Estonia, and private trade was not covered by the data.

Table 42: Price Index of State and Cooperative Trade, 1940 and 1950–1956, in the USSR

Year	**Index**
1940	100
1950	186
1951	170
1952	161
1953	146
1954	138
1955	138
1956	138

Source: TsSU SSSR, *Narodnoe khoziastvo SSSR v 1956 godu*, p. 232.

The low standard of living in the 1940s and 1950s in Estonia and elsewhere in the Soviet Union demonstrated the inefficiency of the command economy, yet it was also the result of an intended state policy. The inhabitants of Estonia were lucky to be spared the deprivations of the Soviet experiment from 1917 to 1940. Even in the aftermath of the war, they suffered less economic hardship than those living in other Soviet republics. Nevertheless, the problems of everyday life definitively demonstrated the defects of the system. Whether Stalin's calculated risk—speeding up economic growth through extreme austerity—worked out in the long run remains highly questionable. People who are fed badly are not very productive at work. The notoriously low work morale, the rampant absenteeism, the frequent changing of jobs, and the inadequate work performance were closely related to the low standard of living of those who were hired.

5 Agriculture and Forced Collectivization

Estonian agriculture developed in the 1930s using a peasant-oriented strategy based on the Scandinavian, especially the Danish model, whereby the yields remained remarkably lower than in Denmark. Agriculture was the most important sector of the economy. Due to the low population density, there was ample land, and production was diversified, encompassing potatoes and grain and animal husbandry. The loss of the Russian market was compensated by exports, mainly to Germany and Great Britain. Those exports were supported by the state and the self-organization of peasants in co-operatives. Fertilizer had to be imported, and the level of mechanization was relatively low. The peasants were oriented towards the market, even when the role of the state in agriculture was steadily increasing.[484]

A contemporary analysis identified some problems: the lack of credit left capital stock too small. There was a shortage of breeding stock and of agricultural workers, and the prices for agricultural goods were relatively low.[485] The shortage of mechanical equipment, mostly tractors, had to be compensated for by horses and human labor. Because of this, agriculture tied up more labor than necessary. In addition to the lack of capital, this situation was caused by the small size of many farms. Back then in Estonia, only for farms of 20 to 30 hectares was the purchase and use of agricultural machinery clearly cost-effective.[486] Estonia and Latvia, along with the Netherlands and Denmark, were among the largest agricultural producers in Europe per capita.[487] However, both Baltic countries needed more workers. Some crofts were barely able to survive in subsistence farming.

From the Beginning of Sovietization to the Forced Collectivization

With the political takeover in Tallinn, the circumstances for the peasants changed fundamentally. Due to the sealing of the borders, lucrative exports ceased.

484 See Kõll, *Peasants on the World Market.*

485 E. Walter, *Estland, Lettland und Litauen: Das Gesicht der baltischen Staaten* (Berlin, 1939), p. 74.

486 Allen, *Farm to Factory*, p. 77.

487 See Central Statistical Office of Latvia, *The Baltic States*, pp. 29ff.

Fertilizer could no longer be imported; nor could concentrated feed, spare parts, or new machines. The lack of fertilizer and machinery would hamper Estonian agriculture until the end of the 1950s and undermine yield-increasing and labor-saving measures. The state, whether it was the Soviet Union or the Third Reich, dictated the purchasing prices and kept them artificially low—in some cases, below production costs. At the same time, shortages started, creating a situation in which the peasants could barely buy anything with their money. The population losses of the 1940s led to a labor shortage, which increased after collectivization as many people moved to the towns.

On many farms, the owners kept an exact account of income and expenses, as had been required since the 1940s. Furthermore, the peasants were market-oriented; in fact, with the help of the co-operatives, they had even placed their goods on the world market. Thus they generally reacted in an economically rational way. Under such overall conditions, the best solution was to reduce output and fulfill only the minimum requirements for procurement norms; to produce for one's own needs; and to search for lucrative, perhaps illegal niche activities. Retreating to a subsistence economy, falsifying the fulfillment of norms, and taking recourse to the black market or the peasant market was how the farmers ensured their existence. In this process, they did not provide what the state demanded but instead pursued their own interests. Under the rapidly changing circumstances, this seemed to be the best strategy. Usually, peasants tend to engage in long-term planning; however, the state ruled out that possibility, so they switched to short-term planning. This included making no long-term investments.

The first measure to hit the peasant was a land reform in the fall of 1940. The authorities justified this land reform and the one after the war by saying, among other things, that they would strengthen small farmsteads at the expense of large farms. Officially, no one mentioned that, as a result, the supply of food might worsen. However, data on agriculture in independent Estonia indicated a certain tendency (see Table 43) that was also observed elsewhere. The smaller a farmstead is, the fewer products are marketed, and the larger the share of the output is used by the producers. Obviously, this was also caused by the lower productivity of very small farms. The agrarian reform thus resulted in a decline in food supplies and in output.

Table 43: Share of Market Production Exceeding One's Own Consumption, Calculated in Kroons

	1937/38	1925/26–1937/38
Small farms	11.2%	7.9%
Normal-size farms	19.1%	7.9%
Above-average farms	21.4%	14.9%
Large farms	32.0%	25.9%

Source: Kaur, *Wirtschaftsstruktur*, p. 38.

The system of forced procurement for peasants was introduced in April 1941; the scale depended on the farm size. The prices paid were extremely low, though, (see Table 44) and did not even cover the production costs. They were between one-fifth and one-tenth of the sums the peasants had received for their products in independent Estonia. In that sense it seems wrong to speak about forced procurement; this was a tax paid in kind and compensated for by some worthless rubles. This system existed throughout the entire period covered by this book. The 1941 prices changed little after the war; in real terms, they even declined because of inflation.[488]

Table 44: Purchasing Prices for Forced Procurement in Rubles per Tsentner, May 9, 1941

Wheat	16.40
Rye	11.10
Potatoes	5.50
Beef, fat	42
Beef, normal	34
Beef, lean	27
Mutton, normal	30

488 See the price lists and an example of a purchasing power calculation, ERA R-1-9-8, l. 8–9, 28.

Table 44: Continued

Pork, fat	118
Pork, medium-fat	107
Pork, lean	83

1 tsentner = 100 kg

Source: ERA R-1-9-8, l. 8–9.

As a result of the first Soviet year, the capacity of Estonian agriculture was reduced substantially (see Chapter 1). The war led to some damage and loss of livestock. Moreover, many farms were deserted, because the owners had fled or died, or had been mobilized or deported. Other farms were headed for years by women or remained operational with the help of farmhands. During the German occupation, agricultural output declined to a low level, where it would remain in the postwar years (see below). The land reform was often reversed de facto, but not de jure. The procurement prices were fixed at 60 percent of the level of East Prussia for compulsory deliveries.[489] Their value was at least two or three times higher than under the Soviets. The "brown" commissars replaced the "red" ones, but the German administration was stretched so thin that the peasants in the village dealt with representatives of authorities of the Estonian Self-Administration. It sought to produce as much from the land as possible, at the lowest possible prices, to supply the front, the occupying troops, and in individual cases, even Germany with food. Fundamentally, there was a great similarity between the German and Soviet agrarian policies. Contemporaries remembered that during the German occupation, some means were used to stimulate the output of large farms.[490] During this time, the peasants developed a very important business: producing moonshine for their own consumption and the black market.

The invasion of the Red Army did not substantially change the framework. Initially, the procurement norms remained at the same level as during the German occupation;[491] later, they were raised substantially. The prices of forced

489 Misiunas and Taagepera, *The Baltic States*, p. 54.

490 For example, Karl (born 1929), ERM-KV 912, l. 48–49.

491 Amount of the delivery norms, meeting of the CC Bureau of the ECP, September 11, 1944, ERAF 1-4-114, l. 159–168; see also the diary of peasant Gustav Põldmaa (1885–1964), ERM-KV 899, l. 150.

procurement remained far below production costs. A peasant named Gustav Põldmaa noted about the forced procurement of his "norm cow": "I received 131 rubles and 92 kopeks. A bottle of three-quarters of a liter of Soviet vodka costs 76 rubles. The cow was so cheap that I could not even get two bottles of 40-percent-alcohol state vodka for it."[492] He could have bought three liters of moonshine for the same sum.

In addition to the purchasing norms, the peasants were, in practice, also taxed in kind; they had to maintain rural roads and deliver timber. The peasants had been requested to perform those duties earlier, but not at that scale. Between 1945 and 1947, peasants cut between 80 and 93 percent of the wood in state forestry, and they took care of 85 to 97 percent of the transport. On an average workday, they cut 1.6 to 2.3 solid cubic meters of timber and transported between 1.6 and 2.5 cubic meters of it,[493] of course without using any modern technology. The amount of this additional work, done with practically no compensation, was calculated according to the farm size. In some cases, it was 50 or more than 100 cubic meters—an extraordinary additional burden, especially for single women, the elderly, and the ill. Põldmaa wrote: "I received the strict order to transport 10 solid cubic meters of timber from the forest. If I do not obey the order, a trip to Siberia awaits me. Forced labor!"[494] Those who did not fulfill these and other norms or did not pay their taxes were usually threatened with imprisonment. In one county, 697 farms did not fulfill the procurement norms, and the CC of the ECP criticized the fact that penalties were imposed in only 21 cases.[495]

Initially, the receipt of the contributions on the spot happened sometimes rather chaotically. There was a transport shortage, the purchase agents did not always issue certificates of delivery, and the accounting was inaccurate.[496] The partly reversed land reform started anew in fall 1944, to the disappointment of many peasants, and lasted until 1947. It targeted farms of more than 20 to 30 hectares of land, and the holdings of so-called "enemies of the people," "collaborators," and people who fled the country.[497] Yet some of the land reform happened only on paper, since a couple of farmsteads received land only on

---

492 ERM-KV 899, l. 186.

493 Report on the development of forestry until 1948, ERA 1-47-29, l. 105, 107.

494 Entry in March 1946, ERM-KV 899, l. 189.

495 Meeting of the CC Bureau of the ECP, February 7 and 13–16, 1945, ERAF 1-4-165, l. 61.

496 Viru and Järva counties were accused of this: meeting of the CC Bureau of the ECP, November 29, 1944, ERAF 1-4-126, l. 31–32, 34.

497 Kahk and Tarvel, *An Economic History of the Baltic Countries*, p. 121.

paper and the old property structure endured. An audit found that 1,450 new farmsteads—approximately 6 percent of all farms—were fictitious.[498] The real figure was obviously higher.

Whereas the peasants evaluated the re-establishment of markets positively. Comrade Toomel, a peasant himself, said at a propaganda meeting for peasant in 1945: "I would like to deliver the best wishes of the inhabitants of the parish of Haljala, because the Soviet Estonian government enables free trade, since during the German occupation there was only barter trade. Regarding the towns, when we see the market of our capital, we catch sight of life, and this life builds up values, because every peasant can now walk freely to the market and, together with the craftsman and the urban worker, bring the work of his hands to this market—and this advances life."[499]

Agricultural taxes and forced procurement were essential control elements of agrarian policies in this period. They provided the state with revenues and helped to enforce state policies. Alongside this, there was an attempt, aided by parish-level agriculture commissioners —to call them "specialists" would be an exaggeration—to implement production plans and to monitor the peasants. However, the department heads for agriculture of the executive committees of parishes (their official title) possessed no high esteem or assertiveness as we learn from life stories. This was no wonder: in 1947 two-thirds of them had finished only elementary school. Moreover, 95 percent had been in their position less than a year and "lacked any knowledge about agriculture."[500]

Taxes and norms remained key policy tools. The agricultural taxes from 1944 to 1948 are indicated in the following table in rubles (see Table 45), yet they were overwhelmingly paid in kind. As a comparison, industrial workers' monthly wages were between 400 and 700 rubles. Until 1946, the total sum of taxes remained nearly constant; the sum tripled in 1947 and quadrupled in 1948. New farmers, who had received land through the land reform, were initially exempted from those taxes, but later they, too, had to pay. Obviously, not all farms paid the tax, which led to many court trials and convictions. The 1947 tax increase was intended to prepare the collectivization of agriculture; this was especially hard on the so-called "kulaks." Their tax burden in 1947 was already equivalent to the

498 Report on the work of the CC of the ECP, 1947, ERA 1-5-2, l. 12.

499 Comrade Toomel on the republican meeting of the agricultural workforce of the ESSR, January 17–19, 1945, ERAF 1-4-239, l. 16.

500 Kuzmin on the 18th Plenum of the CC of the ECP, July 29–30, 1947, ERAF 1-4-392, l. 119.

annual wage of an industrial worker. In 1948, it was equivalent to two annual wages—a ruinous tax rate. The number of "kulak farms" declined substantially in 1948, as those affected gave up farming or had their status as a "kulak" withdrawn. Other farms were also hit by the tax increase.

Table 45: Agricultural Taxes, 1944–1948, in Rubles

Year	Taxation sum in millions	Kulak tax	Included farms in thous.	Tax-paying farms in thous.	Kulak farms	Average tax per farm	Kulak tax per farm
1944	62.1		117	81		760	
1945	61.4		145	72		845	
1946	69.6		145	97		717	
1947	173	36.7	145	106	4,100	1,332	8,953
1948	275.8	48.9	144	127	2,743	1,815	17,813

Source: ERAF 1-47-49, l. 110.

Yet the figures mentioned above were still too low. According to a September 1947 circular letter by First Party Secretary Karotamm and Nikolai Puusepp, deputy chairman of the Council of Ministers, the tax burden was considerably higher.[501] Per hectare of arable land, the average tax was 600 rubles in 1946 and 1,300 rubles in 1947. A cow was subject to tax of 500 rubles in 1946 and 1,200 rubles in 1947. A horse was subject to 500 rubles of tax in 1946 and 600 rubles in 1947. The figures for 1947 surpassed even the kulak tax of this year. It might be that this tax was mainly paid in kind and that the two sources simply used different prices for the conversion into rubles.

Since the peasants did not pay the expected taxes, an explanation had to be taken from the arsenal of communist ideology. Thus the Estonian Central Committee decided at the beginning of January 1947 that there was a class war in the villages.[502] Oskar Sepre, an official responsible for planning, said: "The peasants

501 Circular letter to the Chairmen of Executive Committees and of party secretaries of the counties, September 3, 1947, ERAF 1-5-74, l. 134.

502 Meeting of the CC Bureau of the ECP, January 4, 1947, ERAF 1-4-480, l. 8.

understand it as being to sow only for themselves and not for the government. This means that they want to cultivate less land, keep fewer cows, etc."[503] In reality, this was a logical outcome of the state pricing policy. The following dialogue hints at the solution of the problem and at disagreements in the leadership:

> Leonov: The peasants have good opportunities to hide something from us. This is a law for kolkhozes.
> Vdovin: There are special instructions for the Baltic republics.
> Leonov: Faulty and incorrect ones. They are inadequate.
> Vdovin: This is a lack of motivation.
> Leonov: You are all being deceived.[504]

The decision to implement collectivization in the newly annexed western territories of the USSR was made in Moscow in spring 1947. At first, collectivization was to be conducted "voluntarily" with the help of economic pressure in the form of taxes and purchase norms, assisted by the example of some model kolkhozes. The first step was the so-called "de-kulakization";[505] this process lasted for two years. Initially, those classified as kulaks simply needed to pay higher taxes. (They had the right to appeal the decision, and rural authorities were overburdened by adjudicating who was a kulak and who was not.) However, in March 1949, being labeled a kulak meant being on the deportation list. Arnold Veimer, chairman of the Council of Ministers, was still speaking in 1948 about "the liquidation of kulaks as a class through financial measures," meaning taxes.[506] Taxation was intended to drive the peasants into kolkhozes. Taxes were based not on real but on potential income.[507] Rein Taagepera indicates agricultural taxes of 173 million rubles for 1947 and 275.8 million rubles for 1948, including converted deliveries in kind.[508] The situation of many farmsteads grew worse due to the ban on hiring workers. Single women, the ill, or the elderly risked being denounced as "exploiters" or ending up on the kulak list just for hiring a farmhand.

In spring 1947, the party dealt with the model kolkhozes to be established. During the talks about the collective farm statutes, it was clear to those involved that the small piece of individual farmland (usually 0.5 hectares) would become

503 Ibid.
504 Ibid., l. 8–9.
505 See Anu Mai Kõll, "Tender Wolves: Identification and Persecution of Kulaks in Viljandimaa, 1940–1949," in Mertelsmann, *The Sovietization of the Baltic States*, pp. 127–149.
506 Meeting of the CC Bureau of the ECP, August 25–26, 1948, ERAF 1-4-656, l. 185.
507 Taagepera, "Soviet Collectivization of Estonian Agriculture: The Taxation Phase."
508 Ibid., p. 267.

a second source of income.[509] Yet the peasants did not want to be collectivized. The hunger refugees of the previous years had told others a great deal about the horrors of the kolkhoz system, and some peasants had seen Soviet kolkhozes firsthand as soldiers during the war. The few existing kolkhozes were not allowed to give membership to "collaborators" with the Germans and kulaks. Economically, they did not develop well, and they could not serve as a model for the peasants. At the beginning of 1948, some peasants came forward, willing to be collectivized, yet the party leadership knew that the main reason these peasants volunteered was that they faced tax debts. The few existing kolkhozes needed to be supported.[510]

Nikolai Karotamm got to the heart of the matter: "The peasants on the market say it is better to become a member of the kolkhoz; this means there is no workforce, but there it will be easier. Probably some think that they will not work on the kolkhoz—let the others do the work, but I will live on their expenses."[511] With those words he identified a central problem of collective economic units that were larger than an extended family. New Institutional Economics describes this as the problem of free-riding.[512] A collective farm consisting of ordinary human beings not united by strong family ties or religious or ideological convictions cannot function properly, because in the long run, some members will always cheat others.

But the kolkhoz of the Stalin period had other problems, too. The members had to give most of their animals, often part of their buildings, and nearly all of their land, except for (typically) half a hectare of individual farmland, to the kolkhoz. The collective farm followed a production plan given by the state, and the members had to work a certain number of norm days on the kolkhoz. The income of the kolkhoz consisted of the price paid for forced procurement by the state and sales on the collective farm market. The earnings had to cover operation costs, a certain sum had to be invested, and only the remaining money was distributed among the members, according to the number of norm days each worked. Basically, the kolkhoz followed the principle of the command economy, it received orders from the state and the party, and within his kolkhoz, the chairman could exercise one-man rule. Because in the Stalinist era the little

509 Meeting of the county secretaries of the ECP, May 30, 1947, ERAF 1-4-496, l. 4.
510 Veimer on the meeting of the CC Bureau of the ECP, January 10 and 12, 1948, ERAF 1-4-651, l. 9ff.
511 Ibid., l. 30–31.
512 See North, *Institutions, Institutional Change*, pp. 13, 21.

that the state paid for forced procurement did not even cover the costs, kolkhoz members received only very small sums in money or in kind, if at all. Thus work on the kolkhoz did not pay off, and the collectivized peasants concentrated instead on their private plots.

Since efforts to convince the peasants to join the kolkhozes "voluntarily" were not successful, the state used violence. A mass deportation of kulaks, "collaborators," helpers of anti-Soviet partisans, and others, including their family members, was planned for March 1949; the decision had been made in Moscow in January. The idea was that fear would convince the Baltic peasants to join collective farms. Karotamm spoke in February 1949 about collectivizing 25–30 percent of all farms that same year.[513] In reality, by October, 78 percent were collectivized.[514] However, information in the literature differs concerning the speed and the degree of collectivization. Nevertheless, the party leadership was surprised by the scale and the speed of the development. Collectivization was prepared badly. For example, the new kolkhozes did not have enough blank forms, and only in June was a decision made to send enough clerks to the collective farms to make the complicated calculations.[515]

Collectivization in the Baltic republics was not much different from the model of the "old" Soviet republics, insofar as, in both cases, there was considerable improvisation. Yet in the Baltic republics, one mass deportation was sufficient, and no extensive bloodshed was needed.[516] Collectivization here required less time. Still, it must be asked: why did collectivization happen? Soviet kolkhozes did not prove economically sound. Yet in the long term there was no exception for newly acquired Soviet territories. The final consolidation of power in the countryside could only occur through collectivization.[517] In the USSR, the kolkhozes fulfilled their main purpose: they supplied the state with food, mainly bread grain, at low prices. Because of the collectivization, the Soviet state could obtain vast

513 Meeting of party activists, February 8, 1949, ERAF 1-4-878, l. 5.

514 Liivik, "ECP Kekskomitee rahvamajanduse valitsemisel," p. 226.

515 Meeting of the CC Bureau of the ECP, June 15, 1949, ERAF 1-4-770, l. 25–26.

516 On the collectivization in the USSR, see Sheila Fitzpatrick, *Stalin's Peasants: Resistance and Survival in the Russian Village after Collectivization* (New York and Oxford, 1994); Ivnitskii, *Kollektivizatsiia i raskulachivanie*; Merl, *Bauern unter Stalin*; Lynne Viola, *Peasant Rebels under Stalin: Collectivization and the Culture of Peasant Resistance* (New York and Oxford, 1996).

517 David Feest, "Terror und Gewalt auf dem estnischen Dorf," *Osteuropa* 50 (2000), p. 660. See also David Feest, *Zwangskollektivierung im Baltikum*.

quantities of grain, more than ever before, at a low cost.[518] Because of this, the state accepted the low productivity. The profit from reselling grain and other food, whether to Soviet customers or abroad, served, in a sort of "primitive socialist accumulation," to finance industrialization, defense, and other projects, at the peasants' expense.[519] Only with collectivization could Stalin force the peasants to sell their products in large numbers at prices the state dictated.

In Estonia the main target was not grain but the products of animal husbandry—milk, eggs, and meat. Until the mid-1950s the value of the kolkhozes' crop products was typically twice the value of their animal products. Yet starting in 1952, state procurement of animal products clearly exceeded those of crop products.[520] In the first year after collectivization, in 1950, the amount of delivered agricultural goods for the state, after a low level in 1949, had returned more or less to the 1948 level.[521] Two years later, the amount of purchased animal products had allegedly already doubled.[522] While the deliveries of crop products stagnated or declined, the first target had been reached. Similarly to the collectivization in the rest of the Soviet Union, it was not the total output of agriculture that was important but the size of the forcibly procured part. Even in 1948, before the collectivization, a substantial share of animal products was being exported to other Soviet republics.[523] For the period after collectivization, we do not have precise data. However, from the budget survey mentioned in Chapter 4, we know that in 1952, Estonian workers' households bought, per person, six eggs, 15 liters of milk, and 800 g of meat in state trade.[524] Thus we can assume that most of the animal products delivered to the state in Estonia were either exported—Leningrad and Moscow being the most obvious destinations—or

518 Apart from the years 1942 and 1943, the state had between two and four times the amount of grain as it did on average in 1921–1928. See Vassilii Popov, "Khleb kak ob"ekt gosudarstvennoi politiki v SSSR v 1940-e gody," *Otechestvennaia istoriia* 9 (2000), no. 2, p. 51.

519 Allen, *Farm to Factory*, pp. 57–58; Gregory, *The Political Economy of Stalinism*, pp. 30–31.

520 Based on prices of 1951, Rubin, "Varumishinnad," p. 355.

521 Report on procurement by the state, 1948–1950, ERA 1-72-6, l. 68ff.

522 Käbin on the Eighth Plenum of the CC of the ECP, October 8–9, 1953, ERAF 1-4-1470, l. 54.

523 Approximately one-fifth of products of animal husbandry bought by the state, see data for 1944–1948, overview of exports and imports, December 9, 1948, ERAF 1-47-29, l. 195–196.

524 ERA R-10-43-57, l. 26.

consumed by the Soviet army inside Estonia. The small local elite could not have eaten all those animal products themselves.

Apart from the kolkhozes, there was a second form of state-run agricultural production, the sovkhozes. They were practically state-owned manors. They had emerged in Estonia from existing state-owned manors, their number increased over time, and they specialized more in animal husbandry than the kolkhozes did. Since they earned higher prices for their output, they generally did better economically than kolkhozes. However, they were less productive than private farms. According to a 1947 report of the Estonian Ministry for Sovkhozes, the best sovkhozes had a productivity per worker of a four-hectare farm, and the weakest had the productivity of a two-hectare farm,[525] thus of an unprofitable part-time farm.

Based on nationalized horses and machinery, Horse- and Machine-Lending Stations were established, and later, the machine park was complemented with Soviet production. Additionally, Machine-Tractor Stations (MTS) were established. These institutions were set up to lend, first to the peasants and then to the kolkhozes, machines, horses, and tractors at a profit, to generate additional income for the state budget. In their life stories, contemporaries called this exploitation. In February 1945, the Lending Stations did not have an orderly bookkeeping or work plans.[526] Moreover, their later importance was not as large as some believe. In 1949, MTS tractors were plowing only 5 percent of the cultivated area.[527] In the 1940s, many machines were still in the hands of various agricultural co-operatives, which mushroomed shortly after the war. For example, in 1947, such co-operatives had more than 100,000 members,[528] thus representing two-thirds of all farms.

After Collectivization

Opposite to a widespread assumption, collectivization did not lead directly to a decline of agricultural output; this development is described extensively below. In the first two years, agricultural production remained stable and thereafter decreased dramatically. The worst years were 1951–1954, when the harvest was

525 Output per workforce, report of the minister, 15th Plenum of the CC of the ECP, March 3–4, 1947, ERAF 1-4-384, l. 45. The data was recalculated by me to apply to a private farm.

526 Meeting of the CC Bureau of the ECP, March 3 and 5, 1945, ERAF 1-4-164, l. 38.

527 Second Plenum of the CC of the ECP, March 3–5, 1949, ERAF 1-4-679, l. 75.

528 Report on the work of the CC of the ECP, 1947, ERA 1-5-2, l. 14.

small, the collectivized peasants fought with each other, and the animals died of hunger.[529]

Why did output decline so much, and what accounts for the timing of the decline? In many life stories, the authors report that the collectivized peasants continued to work as usual unless they realized that work on the kolkhoz did not pay off. Then they reduced their work effort there, which was barely paid for anyway, and concentrated on their private plots. This explanation is textbook economic theory, is correct in my opinion, and provides the main reasons for the decline. According to Soviet statistics from 1950, the average wage per norm day on Estonian kolkhozes was 2.3 kg of grain, 1.6 kg of potatoes, and 1.68 rubles. Two years later, it was 1.0 kg of grain, 0.7 kg of potatoes, and 1.14 rubles.[530] Incomes varied considerably between kolkhozes; some did not pay anything at all, and several different average figures can be found. Yet those incomes offered no incentive for work. In addition to feeding their family, collectivized peasants had to feed their privately kept animals. The figures mentioned above were only a small fraction of wages in industry. Even in the "good" year of 1950, a worker laboring for one norm day on the kolkhoz earned less than an unskilled worker would before the war doing one hour of work. The private plot or "soul land" (in Estonian: *hingemaa*, because it kept the souls alive) turned into a place of refuge, but even the revenue from those plots was heavily taxed. Gustav Põldmaa calculated that in 1952, for his 236.9 norm days on the kolkhoz, he received 118 kg of grain and 47 rubles. Because of his age, he was exempted from most of the taxes for his private plot, but he still had to deliver 165 liters of milk, pay 228.43 rubles in tax, buy government bonds for 250 rubles, and pay 77.16 rubles for the compulsory insurance.[531] In other words, one year of work on the kolkhoz earned him so little that he was able to cover only slightly more than one-third of his taxes and other obligations for his private plot. The peasant Gunnar Kaasik (born in 1929) found that after collectivization, he had to pay taxes on his private plot amounting to 80 percent of what he had previously paid on his entire farm. Additionally, he was forced to transport 87 m^2 meters of timber.[532]

The delay in the decline of output was caused by the fact that the "old," productive way of working was replaced by the Soviet style only slowly. It took time for

529 Leila (born 1928), ERM-KV 910, l. 70.

530 Statistical overview of the development of Soviet kolkhozes, 1956, ERAF 1-302-1, l. 267, 300.

531 ERM-KV 899, l. 327, 344.

532 ERM-KV 911, l. 163.

the peasants to react to the reduction of their incomes on the collective farm, as the incomes were calculated only once a year. Yet the initial changes were evident immediately. "One can instantly see where a collectivized peasant is working and where an individual peasant is working. If somebody is sitting on the sowing machine or on the fence smoking, that is the kolkhoz member," reported a comrade from Tartu County to the Central Committee in Tallinn, two months after the beginning of collectivization.[533] In November 1949, Jaan Roos noted in his diary a scene commonly witnessed until the end of the Soviet era: "Everywhere, the grain lies unthreshed in the open air and rots and decays. On the one hand, it is eaten by mice and rats, and on the other hand, the autumn weather does its part."[534] In 1954, 15.4 percent of the collectivized peasants did not even fulfill their compulsory number of work days, and 2.9 percent did not show up at all.[535] The harvest was not brought in on time or was partly rotted, and work was no longer carried out in a reliable manner.

Apart from the poor wages, there were a couple of other reasons for agriculture's decline in performance. The victims of the mass deportation were mostly farmers. During the process of collectivization, it was better to sell or slaughter animals or horses than to give them up for nothing to the kolkhoz. Starting in 1940, the capital stock of agriculture, tangible assets like machinery and buildings, continuously shrank. The lack of agricultural machinery was first remarked on after the war. An amazed Jaan Roos noted in his diary on August 2, 1947, that on that day he saw, for the first time in decades, a peasant cutting rye with a scythe.[536] The lack of spare parts, the termination of foreign trade, and the virtual cessation of new purchases of equipment led to a de-mechanization of agriculture. Work previously done by machines increasingly became manual work. The technical regression reached its nadir in the first half of the 1950s; collectivization sped up this development.

Before the war, Estonia had 1,818 Western-built tractors.[537] In 1951, there were reportedly 2,181 tractors, mostly Soviet ones, in MTSs.[538] Soviet technology was substandard, as if "intended to torture human beings. Most of the

---

533 Meeting of the CC Bureau of the ECP, May 18, 1948, ERAF 1-4-872, l. 158.

534 Jaan Roos, *Läbi punase öö* III (Tartu, 2001), p. 305.

535 Statistical overview on the kolkhozes, ERA R-1-5-406, l. 11.

536 Roos, *Läbi punase öö,* II, p. 119.

537 Report by the People's Commissariat of Agriculture on the situation before June 21, 1940, ERAF 1-1-265, l. 62.

538 Statistical information on agriculture 1952, ERA R1-114-57, l. 22.

workday was spent repairing tractors and agricultural machinery, not engaged in productive labor," a contemporary remembered.[539] How many tractors were working is unknown; because of the lack of spare parts, some tractors were cannibalized to keep the others running. To solve this problem, republican industrial enterprises, such as those from the oil shale industry, were asked to produce spare parts for tractors.[540] In 1958, when the MTS system was dismantled and its technical equipment transferred to the kolkhozes, 2,070 tractors and a workforce of 15,000 were recorded.[541] Not until the late 1950s at the earliest did the available tractors provide more draft power than the available horses. However, many Soviet machines, such as combine harvesters, were unsuitable for Estonian soil. In January 1956 the stockpile of unusable technical agricultural equipment was officially valued at 13 million rubles.[542]

After the communist takeover, the peasants did not earn a reasonable amount, and there was a shortage of building materials; thus there was not enough investment into buildings. The abandonment of farms caused by flight, deportation, or moving to a town caused the loss of many more buildings than war damage did. Until the mid-1950s, the kolkhozes did not have the financial means to preserve all the existing buildings. In addition, the vast majority of the agricultural buildings were made of wood, which needed repairs more often than brick buildings did. Precise data is not available, yet we can assume that the total size of agricultural buildings declined constantly throughout the period under study.

Apart from the shrinking capital stock and the low pay, with a resulting decline in work morale, the reduction of workforce in agriculture mentioned in Chapter 3 was another decisive factor in the decline of output. The workforce was disproportionately female and old. The few young males in the countryside headed for other, more lucrative fields, like work on an MTS. Moreover, it would be wrong to believe that collectivized peasants conducted only agricultural labor. In 1949, the draft for the distribution of workdays for model kolkhozes anticipated that 17 percent of the work would be administrative.[543] According to a March 1957 report in the newspaper *Rahva Hääl* (People's Voice), 22.3 percent of all norm days on the kolkhozes were spent in administration.[544] In the Soviet

539 Einar (born 1927), ERM-KV 988, l. 68–69.

540 Fourth Plenum of the CC of the ECP, March 12–13, 1951, ERAF 1-4-1116, l. 26.

541 Liivik, "ECP Keskkomitee rahvamajanduse valitsemisel," p. 234.

542 Ninth Plenum of the CC of the ECP, ERAF 1-4-1930, l. 87.

543 Second Plenum of the CC of the ECP, March 3–5, 1949, ERAF 1-4-679, l. 72.

544 Quoted from Kaelas, *Das sowjetisch besetzte Estland*, p. 85.

Union, those jobs were done mostly by middle-aged males because they required relatively little work and netted relatively high incomes.[545] In other words, the main labor on the kolkhoz was largely conducted by the weaker members of the collective farm—women and the elderly. The exodus of workers into administration is a good example of the aforementioned problem of free-riding.

The catastrophe started in 1952. Due to a decline in fodder production, animals starved to death in a couple of kolkhozes. Another contributing factor was the party's demand that animal husbandry be accelerated. The animals were so weak that they could not stand up on their own. A veterinarian remembers that such cases appeared regularly until 1958.[546] Others confirm this. To compensate for the lack of fodder, the authorities sent schoolchildren to collect twigs in the forest in the winter of 1953/54.[547] The twigs were ground up and used as fodder. Reports of the dying animals and those desperate measures even reached the West.[548] In the Väike-Maarja district, within just three months in 1953, the number of cattle declined by one-fifth; approximately 15 percent perished in this year as a result of hunger or bad treatment. The milk yield per cow decreased to one liter per cow daily. On one kolkhoz it happened that the cows were no longer milked daily.[549] What the peasants thought when their former cattle died can easily be imagined.

The peasants viewed the collectivization as a "second serfdom" and reacted accordingly. David Moon has pointed out that the situation collectivized Soviet peasants faced was actually worse than serfdom. Serfdom had been imposed on an existing agricultural order. But during collectivization, the peasants lost most of their land, their belongings, and the freedom to make their own decisions. Few noblemen dictated to their serfs exactly what to sow and how to till the land, as the chairman of the kolkhoz, the party, and the planning institutions did. With collectivization, the traditional peasant society practically disappeared.[550] It seems appropriate to describe the state policy as a "policy of looting."[551]

---

545 Stephan Merl, *Sozialer Aufstieg im sowjetischen Kolchossystem der 30er Jahre?* (Berlin, 1990), pp. 254–255.

546 Elmar (born 1926), employed in the veterinary office, EKM-EKLA 350-861, l. 11.

547 Maali, born 1923, teacher, ERM-KV 987, l. 186.

548 Hellmuth Weiss, "Die baltischen Staaten," in Birke and Neumann (eds.), *Die Sowjetisierung Ost-Mitteleuropas*, p. 55.

549 Meeting of the CC Bureau of the ECP, January 21, 1954, ERAF 1-4-1722, l. 49.

550 David Moon, *The Russian Peasantry 1600–1930: The World the Peasants Made* (London and New York, 1999), p. 363.

551 Dietrich Beyrau, "Nationalsozialistisches Regime und Stalin-System: Ein riskanter Vergleich," *Osteuropa* 50 (2000), p. 720.

The situation improved somewhat only after Moscow decided on a change in agrarian policy in September 1953. The state procurement prices were to increase continuously until 1958.[552] It took some time before positive results were felt. In 1955, the Estonian party leadership admitted, behind closed doors, that agricultural output had declined drastically.[553]

The Development of Agrarian Output

The official data on the output of animal husbandry in 1945–1956 (see Table 46) represented a substantial decrease from 1940. Indeed, at some points, the output was lower than it had been in 1913. The lowest point was in the immediate postwar period; in the long term, collectivization seemed to have no negative consequences on this output. During the postwar years, the weight at slaughter continuously declined from 1944 to 1948 for the cases registered by the state. Pigs' weight declined from 117 to 88.5 kg, while cattle's weight declined from 233 to 84.8 kg (in part because later, mainly calves were slaughtered). In 1944, 22.9 percent of slaughtered cattle had received less food than average; by 1948, the figure had increased to 41.2 percent.[554] After collectivization, many farm animals not only suffered from malnutrition but virtually starved to death. The data in the table appear to be relatively realistic until 1950. However, after that year, the figures were obviously manipulated, as proven by a comparison with the number of farm animals and the available information on milk yield per cow.

Table 46: Official Information on the Production of Animal Husbandry, 1913, 1940, and 1945–1956

Year	Weight at slaughter in thous. tons	Milk in thous. tons	Eggs in millions
1913	60	415	67
1940	72.1	781	133.6
1945	30.4	393	31.4

552 Rubin, "Varumishinnad," p. 349. On the change in agrarian policy under Khrushchev, see E. Zelenin, "Agrarnaja politika N. S. Khrushcheva i sel'skoe khoziaistvo strany," *Otechestvennaia istoriia* 9 (2000), no. 1, pp. 76–93.

553 Meeting with writers, March 9, 1955, ERAF 1-4-1918, l. 4ff.

554 Report of the Food Ministry, October 11, 1948, ERAF 1-47-30, l. 84.

Table 46: Continued

Year	Weight at slaughter in thous. tons	Milk in thous. tons	Eggs in millions
1946	32.9	397	39.5
1947	37.3	405	54
1948	43.4	477	76.6
1949	49.1	505	108.7
1950	54.1	508	121.7
1951	56.3	523	115.5
1952	58	573	132.5
1953	54.3	552	150.9
1954	60.3	588	159.5
1955	61.6	558	146.7
1956	63.4	621	156.3

Source: ERA R-10-43-110, l. 1–2.

In Estonia there was a system to check milk output per cow (see Table 47); these checks were cut back over time. Only selected cattle were checked; the figures do not offer an average for the entire country. The average was always lower. The decline of milk output directly after the war might be explained mainly by the fact that the fodder supply bottomed out in 1946/47.

Table 47: Annual Milk Production of Checked Cows, 1940/41–1947/48

Year	Milk yield per cow in kg	Number of checked cows
1940/41	2,924	62,823
1944/45	2,350	15,147
1945/46	2,257	16,906
1946/47	2,187	18,744
1947/48 (preliminary)	2,311	21,416

Source: ERAF 1-47-49, l. 69.

The information on the milk yield per cow of the Ühisjõud ("United Force") Kolkhoz (see Table 48) should be treated with caution, since this was a model kolkhoz; the data would not have found their way into the press otherwise. However, it is important that the collectivization led to a substantial decrease. The lowest point was reached in 1954, when even this model kolkhoz reported only half the yield as before the war. The reasons were lack of fodder and the negligent work habits of the discouraged collectivized peasants. In other words, people living on an insufficient diet will not put much effort into unpaid work.

Table 48: Annual Milk Production in Ühisjõud Kolkhoz

Year	**Milk yield per cow in kg**
1950	2,214
1951	1,654
1952	1,906
1953	1,668
1954	1,299

Source: *Rahva Hääl*, March 19, 1955.

The number of livestock in Estonia (see Table 49) declined as early as the first Soviet year. This decrease of approximately one-third dwarfed the one-tenth decline during the German occupation. The next count, by the end of 1944, registered an all-time low as a result of combat, as well as animal slaughtering by peasants and occupiers. Livestock recovered slowly until the end of the 1940s. As a result of collectivization, pig breeding increased slightly, and the keeping of goats and sheep declined. In comparison to July 1, 1939, in 1956 there were only two-thirds as many cattle and pigs, 57 percent as many milk cows, and one-third as many sheep and goats. The number of horses declined from 210,000 in 1939 to 120,000 in 1956.[555] Given the bad fodder situation and the decline of milk output, one has to expect a nearly one-half decrease of animal husbandry. Concerning the accuracy of the figures for animal husbandry, a caveat must be made: from the beginning of the command economy, the data was not very exact. Private owners

555 Number of horses: 1939, see Chapter 1; 1956, see information for the CC of the CPSU 1956, ERAF 1-211-5, l. 16.

tried to avoid a complete count of their animals, in order to avoid being liable for additional deliveries. Kolkhozes, sovkhozes, and state institutions, by contrast, tended to provide higher figures in order to be seen in a better light.

Table 49: Livestock Numbers in Thousands, 1939–1956

Year	Cattle	of this, milk cows	Pigs	Sheep and goats
July 1, 1939	675.4	458.9	425.9	657.9
1940	597	419	371	488
January 1, 1941	504.8	382.4	290.4	316.1
1943	460	-	274	258
End of 1944	336	193	169	206
1945	401	226	196	264
1946	410	234	201	250
1947	436	248	237	264
1948	445	259	232	268
1949	437	279	269	272
1950	450	294	279	287
1951	462	283	297	274
1952	484	275	313	279
1953	488	269	300	254
1954	448	258	308	242
1955	447	267	313	253
1956	435	263	276	241

Sources: 1939 and 1941, ERAF 1-47-49, l. 61; 1940, 1943, and 1944, ERA R-6-16-1, l. 8, 14; R-10-43-133, l. 1–22.

Compared to the "old" republics (see Table 50), in Estonia there was originally clearly many more livestock, an indicator of more intensive use; higher yields, which meant sufficient fodder; and higher incomes. Moreover, the food supplies of the population were better, and surplus production could be exported. A direct result of the introduction of the Soviet system was a decrease of livestock.

Table 50: Average Livestock Husbandry in the USSR in Thousands, Converted to the Number of Inhabitants of Estonia on January 1, 1938–1940

Year	Cattle	Pigs	Sheep and goats
1938	339	171	444
1939	357	168	539
1940	319	152	511

Source: Calculated according to Table 20 in Davies, Harrison, and Wheatcroft (eds.), *The Economic Transformation*, p. 289.

Based on the existing information on livestock and milk output, the following estimate attempts to reconstruct milk and meat production trends from 1951 to 1956 (see Table 51). Uncertainties surrounding the existing statistics make it impossible to come up with a more precise estimate. In my opinion, the official data for milk and meat production are not realistic because of the fodder situation and the decrease of livestock and milk output. In certain cases, the official data is overstated by up to 30 percent. A downward revision of this data more accurately represents the consumption detailed in budget surveys and the surviving figures on state procurement meant mostly for shipment to Russia. The number of products purchased by the state could be manipulated only a little bit, while overstating other, more-difficult-to-control data was easier, since superior institutions might not realize this. Those who falsified their data were seen in a better light, and the superiors wanted to believe in the higher figures.

Table 51: Estimate of Milk and Meat Production, 1951–1956

Year	Estimated weight at slaughter in thous. tons	Estimated milk production in thous. tons
1951	50	450
1952	48	440

Table 51: Continued

Year	Estimated weight at slaughter in thous. tons	Estimated milk production in thous. tons
1953	45	375
1954	40	300
1955	45	350
1956	40	375

As a basis for this estimate, the number of animals and an estimated milk production per cow was used.

The output not only of animal husbandry but also of land cultivation declined. The changes in the structure of field use until 1955 (see Table 52) indicate that the share of technical crops and of grain farming declined substantially, while the cultivation of animal fodder increased. This made the value of the harvest per hectare considerably smaller. In any case, the amount of cultivated land had already declined. Only the relatively profitable cultivation of potatoes and vegetables increased, mostly on the private plots.

Table 52: Structure of Field Use, 1940–1955, in Percent

	1940	1950	1955
Animal fodder	25.6	28.8	40.5
Cereals	61.2	55.7	45.0
Potatoes and vegetables	9.3	12.9	13.0
Technical crops	3.9	2.6	1.5

Source: E. Vint, "Põllumajanduse areng Nõukogude Eestis," *Nõukogude Eesti majandus*, p. 79.

In the Soviet Union, wheat was the most important crop, yet the yields per hectare remained low and fell to their lowest point in the 1940s (see Table 53). In Estonia the yields were definitely higher until 1951.

Table 53: Yields per Hectare of Wheat in the Soviet Union, 1935–1950

Year	Tsentner per ha	Year	Tsentner per ha
1935	7.5	1943	4.2
1936	5.8	1944	6.0
1937	9.4	1945	5.6
1938	7.4	1946	4.6
1939	7.4	1947	7.3
1940	8.6	1948	6.7
1941	7.3	1949	6.9
1942	4.4	1950	7.9

Source: 1935–1939: Table 23 in Davies, Harrison, and Wheatcroft (eds.), *The Economic Transformation*, p. 291; 1940–1950: Popov, *Ekonomicheskaia politika*, p. 166.

Data on grain harvests in Estonia from 1940 to 1956 (see Table 54) might contain some inaccuracies. In particular, how much land was actually being cultivated cannot be determined definitively. Still, the tendency is clear. The harvest declined. Two factors have to be considered: yields per hectare vary depending on the weather, and thus usually long-term time spans of five years were compared; and under the climatic conditions of the Baltic republics, roughly two tsentners per hectare were needed as seed for the following year (1 tsentner = 100 kg).[556] This explains the difference between the gross harvest and the net harvest. When the yield per hectare declines from 11.5 tsentners per hectare to 6.5 tsentners, only 4.5 tsentners are available for consumption instead of 9.5 tsentners. With yields below five tsentners per hectare, the USSR was threatened by famine.

Until 1951, the yields per hectare in Estonia remained mostly stable. Then in 1952–1956, they declined dramatically to an average of 6.6 tsentners. Thus the net yield per hectare decreased from 8.5 to 4.6 tsentners. The low yields also explain the decrease of grain farming; this was not planned but was dictated by the shortage of seeds. The net harvest from 1945 to 1950 was already smaller than before the war. Since grain requires more labor than animal fodder, the amount

556 Pranas Zunde, *Die Landwirtschaft Sowjetlitauen* (Marburg, 1962), p. 33.

of cultivated land decreased in 1951, and thereafter, it declined further. The size of the grain harvest was determined by three main factors: human workforce, fertilizer, and the weather. It is unlikely, and unreported in the sources, that poor weather conditions in four consecutive summers, from 1952 to 1956, reduced the harvest. Artificial fertilizer was in extremely short supply, and the shrinking number of farm animals, now used mainly on the private plots, led to a lack of natural fertilizer. All this caused a decline in the available animal fodder, leading to a further decrease of natural fertilizer. In addition, after two years of practically unpaid work, the collectivized peasants were unwilling to make the necessary effort, again leading to a decline of output.

Apart from the increase in consumption of unpretentious potatoes, which served as a sort of sheet anchor for agriculture and the population,[557] a 60 percent decline of plant production since the prewar period seems like a realistic estimate, based on the official statistics.

Table 54: Official Information on the Grain Harvest in Estonia and the Estimated Net Yield, 1940 and 1945–1956

Year	Grain harvest in thous. tons (gross)	Grain harvest in thous. tons (net)	Yield per ha in tsentner
1940	654	540	11.5
1945	370	287	8.9
1946	412	309	9.6
1947	613	505	11.9
1948	528	433	9.8
1949	560	469	11.9
1950	522	432	11.5
1951	451	359	10.1
1952	329	239	7.2
1953	276	191	6.1

557 The average potato harvest from 1946 to 1955 was, according to official data, roughly one million tons per year. ERA R-10-43-133, l. 1.

Table 54: Continued

Year	Grain harvest in thous. tons (gross)	Grain harvest in thous. tons (net)	Yield per ha in tsentner
1954	281	211	6.6
1955	228	161	6.7
1956	288	222	8.7

Column 3: Calculated grain harvest (net) = grain harvest (gross) less seeds.

Source: ERA R-10-43-124, l. 3, 77–78.

It seems possible that crop production declined even more than mentioned above. Apart from the fact that a larger share of the harvest rotted due to improper processing and storage than occurred under market conditions, the size of the harvest was also related to the area of cultivated land. In an October 1949 letter to Malenkov, Karotamm complained about the Ministry of Agriculture. The ministry calculated the area of cultivated land according to the reports of the parishes in spring, while the Statistical Administration computed the same figures before harvest with the help of a network of observers. From 1945 to 1947, the Statistical Administration came out with lower figures than the ministry; the difference was between 7 and 20 percent (the latter percentage amounted to 160,000 hectares). Karotamm himself believed the Statistical Administration.[558] Of course, the larger figures for the area of cultivated land were used in the official statistics. In the CC Bureau, Hendrik Allik indicated in 1947 that the sown area was larger in 1945 than in 1946.[559] In 1945 the sown area was 696,000 hectares, according to a later time series by the Statistical Office, while the Statistical Administration declared it to be 788,000 hectares, and the Ministry of Agriculture even said it was 845,000 hectares.[560] Given the low procurement prices and the lack of horses and workers, the smallest figure appears to be the most realistic.

In 1940, Estonia had a sown area of 918,000 hectares, part of which had recently been cultivated with state support. Following the calculations of the data for the harvests, there were 887,000 hectares of arable land in 1952 and 853,000 hectares in 1954.[561] Due to a border change in Russia's favor, Estonia

558 Letter, October 26, 1949, ERAF 1-14-113, l. 71ff.

559 Meeting of the CC Bureau of the ECP, January 4, 1947, ERAF 1-4-480, l. 9.

560 ERA R-10-43-124, l. 3; Karotamm to Malenkov, October 26, 1949, ERAF 1-14-113, l. 71–72.

561 ERA R-10-43-124, l. 3.

lost 5 percent of its agricultural land in 1945. As mentioned above, the number of horses decreased drastically, and tractors did not play an important role. How could it be that plowing and working on the arable land declined by only a few percent when there were practically no tractors, the number of horses was reduced by almost one-half, and the workforce shrank by one-third? In other words, the data on the use of arable land that formed the basis for the calculation of the harvest were grossly overstated. Again, in this case, the figures were manipulated. The falsification of data might not have been centrally organized, but at every level, something was added. When the size of arable land was 7, 10, or even 20 percent smaller, then the harvest figures had to be reduced accordingly. This applies to the time before and after collectivization.

One report on the work of Gosplan for the members of the CC Bureau contains data on the actual sown area from 1946 to 1950 (see Table 55). Those figures are the lowest, yet they appear to be the most realistic. Using them to calculate the size of the grain harvest, we find that the harvest in this period was between 10 and 15 percent lower than in the official statistics. The possibility that the later-corrected yields per hectare were fictitious cannot be evaluated here.[562] Various discrepancies can be found in the sources. Any of the leading politicians who understood something about agriculture must have known that the data reported to Moscow was highly incorrect.

Table 55: Actual Sown Area, 1946–1950

Year	Area in thous. ha
1946	643
1947	746
1948	773
1949	725
1950	746

Source: Documents for the protocol of the meeting of the CC Bureau of the ECP, September 28, 1950, ERAF 1-4-1045, l. 17.

562 Ants Ruusmann thinks that the corrected statistical series of the yield per hectare was realistic in the postwar period. Evald Laasi believes the figures were too high. Ruusmann, "Eesti agraarajaloo allikad," p. 83.

In this context, not all Soviet statistics on agricultural production can be checked critically, since the available sources do not allow for this. Even in Soviet times, the decline of agricultural output could not be disguised.[563] However, the scale of the decrease was obviously higher than admitted. As long as private farms predominated, output during and after the war presumably fell by one-third of what it had been before the war. After collectivization, output declined further, down to perhaps 40 percent of the level of 1939. When we try to calculate the national income, the question arises which prices to use. Part of the production had to be sold at fixed prices, while another share went to the market. One proper method of calculation would be according to world market prices. Yet the Estonian peasants had no longer had access to the world market, and we do not know exactly what part of the production statistics was made up. Because of this, I have refrained from further estimates.

The Stalinist restructuring led to enormous losses in agriculture. There was no lack of attempts to address the problems, such as merging kolkhozes, increasing procurement prices, and the rather stupid idea to grow corn in Estonia, which kolkhoz chairmen passively resisted, according to the party.[564] However, the main reason for the inefficiency of agriculture could not be eliminated. That was the misguided structure of Soviet agriculture, based on the command economy and the collective farm.

The Structure of Agriculture in the Mid-1950s

The distribution of agricultural usable area on January 1, 1956 (see Table 56), gives us a picture of the structure of the primary sector. The largest area was used by kolkhozes, one-tenth was used by sovkhozes, 2.7 percent were private plots, and 1.9 percent was the land of agricultural and state institutions and enterprises. The last group could include agricultural test stations, but the majority of the land was used for another aim. To improve the food supply of their own personnel, many industrial enterprises and state authorities owned "supporting agricultural enterprises" (in Estonian, *abimajand*), an indicator of the low efficiency of trade and the poor division of labor in the economy. Although private plots covered only a tiny space, their economic importance was enormous. Only on these plots could one speak of intensive agriculture being done, and they represented an important source of income for nearly 150,000 families. Roughly

563 See Arnold Purre, *Soviet Farming Failure Hits Estonia* (Stockholm, 1964).

564 Meeting of the CC Bureau of the ECP, March 15 and 24, 1955, ERAF 1-4-1847, l. 57.

every second inhabitant of Estonia was supplied with food from private plots. Late-Stalinist-era society was still deeply agrarian, because countless other families supplemented their diet with the help of private gardens. In some places in Western Europe at that time, allotments were also widespread, especially among workers' families, but they never reached the importance they possessed in a command economy.

Table 56: Agricultural Land on November 1, 1956

User	Area in ha
Kolkhozes with 118,226 households	2.45 million
89 sovkhozes	0.29 million
436 agricultural establishments of companies and institutions	54,500
1,246 individual farms and small producers	4,000
Private plots of the collectivized peasants (116,236 households)	63,260
Other garden land (31,021 households)	11,940

Source: Overview on the use of land, ERA R-6-18-162, l. 1–3.

The scholarly literature has addressed the importance of private production in Estonian agriculture, yet source material on this subject has been unavailable.[565] The budget surveys already suggested the enormous role of kolkhoz markets and private plots for general food supplies; this could also be found in the calculation of national income according to Soviet methods (see Table 57). According to this, just 38 percent of agrarian output came from the state-controlled sector of kolkhozes and sovkhozes; the remaining part was produced privately. Taking into account the land distribution (see above), the sovkhozes were obviously more productive than the kolkhozes. The main reason was the higher prices the sovkhozes received for their products. It must be noted that Soviet plan prices undervalued grain production, the domain of the kolkhozes, and overvalued the animal products of private plots and sovkhozes. Nevertheless, it could be said that private agricultural production generated a large percentage of quality

565 Järvesoo, "Privatunternehmen in der sowjetestnischen Landwirtschaft."

food—maybe even the majority. The highest productivity was achieved by the few remaining independent private farms. According to Soviet data, on 0.14 percent of cultivated land, with 0.5 percent of people employed, they generated 1.3 percent of agricultural output. This data from a Soviet source supports the estimate by O. Verbitskaia that, in Russia, three-fourths of the value of agrarian products came from private plots.[566] An official Soviet study on the importance of private gardens and plots concluded that 51 percent of plant production and 62 percent of animal production in the USSR in 1950 happened privately.[567] Given those figures, the inefficiency of kolkhozes and sovkhozes becomes clear; they represented a massive waste of resources. However, the private plots could not exist alone but only in a symbiosis with kolkhozes and sovkhozes. From there fodder, machinery, and seeds were procured.

Table 57: Agricultural Gross and Net Production in 1955 in Million Rubles and in Consecutive Plan Prices of 1955

	Gross production	**Net production**
Garden land of kolkhoz peasants	1,297.6	899.1
Kolkhozes	1,184.4	447.6
Garden land of workers and employees	427.9	308.5
State enterprises and sovkhozes	346.4	113.8
Individual peasants and independent craftsmen	24.6	19.2

Net production (*chistaia produktsiia*) = gross production (*valovaia produktsiia*) less costs.

Source: Calculation of the national income of the Estonian SSR for 1955, ERA R-10-19-1, l. 8.

Yet not only the kolkhoz economy was inefficient. The private plot might have been the main source of income for many families, but if they devoted much of their work time to their own half-hectare private plot, while there was a considerable amount of other work to do, this also represented a large waste of resources. The principles of distribution of labor, specialization, and mechanization were not applied to the private plots. The communists criticized the fact that there

566 Verbickaia, *Rossiiskoe krest'ianstvo*, p. 75.

567 Quoted from Pikhoia, *Sovetskii Soius*, p. 19.

was so much free labor in the countryside, but this was caused by their own policies. As long as an economy of shortages persisted, it made more sense for many people to work on the kolkhoz and the private plot instead of in a more productive factory. If the aforementioned estimates are roughly correct, then per capita productivity in Estonian agriculture reached its lowest point at the beginning of the 1950s, after collectivization limited the country's economic development.

At first glance, it is hard to understand why Soviet leaders did not completely abandon the policy of collectivized and state-run agriculture, given that it was so unproductive and led to a decline in output. Even with the exaggerated statistics, the basic truth was known to Stalin and his associates, and any layperson could have drawn the right conclusions. Literature sometimes attributes the policy to ideology. Another, more important reason was the control of production. In a mostly nationalized agriculture, the USSR was able to receive much more tax in kind than it would if it were taxing millions of private farms individually. The largest source of income of the state budget was turnover tax. In Estonia, 66 percent of turnover tax in the first half of 1951, and 63 percent of turnover tax in the first months of 1956, originated from the sale of food, alcohol, and tobacco. While the propaganda spoke of industrialization, the regime financed itself mostly by purchasing the products of food producers at extremely low prices and selling them to the population at high prices. We should not forget that collectivization supported the consolidation of power of the regime.

Table 58: Turnover Tax Receipts in 1951 and 1956

Source of income	**Jan.–June 1951 Turnover tax in million rubles**	**Jan.–June 1951 Share of the tax in percent**	**Jan.–Oct. 1956 Turnover tax in million rubles**	**Jan.–Oct. 1956 Share in percent**
Alcohol	165	19.4	381	24.6
Cereal processing	173	20.0	294	19.0
Sugar	61	7.1	126	8.2
Tobacco	42	4.9	60	3.8
Other food	131	15	124	7.9

Table 58: Continued

Source of income	Jan.–June 1951 Turnover tax in million rubles	Jan.–June 1951 Share of the tax in percent	Jan.–Oct. 1956 Turnover tax in million rubles	Jan.–Oct. 1956 Share in percent
Clothing and shoes	113	13	359	23.2
Other products of industry	181	20.8	212	13.7

Source: Compiled and calculated based on ERA R-4-9-247, l. 18.

After the death of Stalin, a shift in agricultural policy was inevitable and was finally announced in 1955 by the CC of the CPSU. The procurement norms decreased and prices increased; a declared aim was to raise the incomes of the collectivized peasantry. The mechanization of agriculture was to continue, and more fertilizer, construction materials, and credits were to be made available. The kolkhozes were to be strengthened with the aim of increasing agricultural production.[568] Some years later, the Machine-Tractor Stations were disbanded. In the long run, Soviet agriculture was turned from an exploited sector into a subsidized sector, without solving the basic problem of low productivity.

568 In Moscow the final decision for a change in agricultural policy was made at the beginning of 1955. In Estonia this was announced at the Sixth Plenum of the CC of the ECP, June 29–30, 1955, ERAF 1-4-1831, l. 6–7.

6 Industry[569]

Stalinism is generally associated with the industrialization of the Soviet Union. In the Baltic republics, too, industrial output skyrocketed—on paper (see Table 59). Often industrial growth is regarded as one of the few positive side effects of Stalinist rule. For many developing countries, this aspect of the Soviet economic model seemed very attractive at one time. At first glance, the figures on industrial growth in the Baltics sound miraculous. However, a closer look raises doubts concerning the accuracy of the data. Was the starting point really so low and growth really so large? True, the Baltic republics had to overcome the aftermath of war and destruction. Still, if the data were correct, the German, Italian, or Japanese economic miracles of the postwar period would pale in comparison to the Baltic industrial miracle.

Table 59: Official Index of Gross Industrial Production in Prices of 1926/27

Year	Estonia	Latvia	Lithuania
1940	1.0	1.0	1.0
1945	0.73	0.47	0.4
1950	3.42	3.03	1.91
1955	6.7	5.85	4.9

Source: Misiunas and Taagepera, *The Baltic States*, p. 361.

However, even early on, there were doubts about the accuracy of the growth figures. Estonian exile historians assumed that for the base year, 1940, only the last five months were used so that the later growth would seem that much more impressive.[570] However, that would still mean that output more than doubled from 1940 to 1955 and increased by nearly 10 times from 1945 to 1955.

The annual double-digit growth of Estonian industrial output is truly impressive (see Table 60). Directly after the war, this might have been plausible, as

569 This chapter is mainly based on Mertelsmann, "Was There a Stalinist Industrialization?"

570 Järvesoo, "Die Wirtschaft Estlands," p. 15; Misiunas and Taagepera, *The Baltic States*, p. 361; Raun, *Estonia and the Estonians*, p. 176.

factories reopened that had been closed for a long time. However, a long-lasting growth at that speed—even if at a decreasing speed—appears to be a fantasy. Sometimes those unrealistic figures are quoted in scholarly works.[571]

Table 60: Official Annual Growth Rate of Estonian Gross Industrial Production in Prices of 1926/27

Year	Percent
1946	66
1947	37
1948	38
1949	21
1950	23
1951	21
1952	15
1953	11
1954	14
1955	21

Source: *ENSV ajalugu*, vol. 3 (Tallinn, 1971), p. 571.

The Industrial Policies of the Postwar Period

After the end of the war in Europe, the communists drew up the guidelines for the reconstruction of Estonian industry. The energy sector and the oil shale industry played an important role. Later, the production of construction materials, mechanical engineering, and metalwork had to be developed. Only after this was light industry supposed to be redeveloped.[572] Heavy industry dominated thus Stalinist planning; the role of the arms industry was extremely important. In 1953, the rulers were satisfied with the development of the energy sector and the oil shale industry and announced a further industrialization of the country.[573] The available data suggests a steady decline of the share of light industry in total production and an increase of the share of heavy industry, especially when comparing the 1930s with the 1950s.[574] Undoubtedly, the role of heavy industry grew,

571 For example, Tomson, *Eesti majandusajalugu*, p. 87.

572 Explanation of the plan for Estonia's national economy, May 16, 1945, ERAF 1-3-429, l. 1.

573 Report on the first years of the five-year plan, ERAF 1-1-126-33, l. 119.

574 For example, Kala and Juursoo, "Nõukogude Eesti töölisklass," p. 257.

yet a meaningful comparison was hampered by the simple fact that in the 1930s, market prices applied, while in the 1950s, prices were fixed by the state. The state valued the products of heavy industry more than those of light industry and fixed the prices accordingly. Because of this, Soviet data on the weighting of light and heavy industry needs a correction: light industry was more important than indicated, while heavy industry was less important.

Doubts Concerning the Growth Rate

The first doubts about the accuracy of the growth figures arise when examining the development of infrastructure, because the increased production would have needed an expansion of the transport network. Since Estonian industry specialized not in high technology but in goods like textiles or oil from oil shale processing, transport volumes and capacity should have grown in parallel with output. Before 1940, imports and exports had gone mostly by sea; but after the Soviet takeover, they went mostly overland, and thus transport shifted more to roads and railways. However, no new railway line was built. According to official information, between 1940 and 1955, the road network decreased by one-fifth. At the same time, asphalted roads increased by only one-half.[575] Employment in the sector of transport and communications grew from 24,000 in 1940 to 57,000 in 1955.[576] However, the question remains how raw materials and industrial products were transported, since their volume increased by more than six times.

Chapter 4 discusses how the standard of living decreased because of Stalinist restructuring. Undoubtedly, a large share of industrial products was consumed by the state, the military, and industrial enterprises. Yet given the growth rate, we might expect to find that private consumption of industrial products also increased. Because of the decline in real incomes, this could not have been the case. On the contrary, the population could not buy consumer goods on the same scale as in the 1930s.

Employment in Industry

The doubts concerning the growth rate increase when we explore industrial employment in depth. Officially, employment increased from 73,000 in 1940 to 127,000 in 1955.[577] But what does the data cover? The statistics of independent

575 TsSU ESSR, *Estonskaia SSR*, p. 105.

576 Ibid., p. 127.

577 Misiunas and Taagepera, *The Baltic States*, p. 361.

Estonia categorized industrial occupation in two different ways. At one time, a narrowly defined term was used, counting only the employment in large enterprises. According to the Estonian definition, then, a large enterprise had a workforce of at least 20. A broader definition also included smaller enterprises and handicraft enterprises. According to the 1934 census, the entire industrial sector, including craftsmen and small enterprises, employed 105,000 people,[578] while for 1940, a figure of 73,000 was given, which covered only large enterprises. Yet over time, the Soviets merged small enterprises and craftsmen into cooperatives and trusts. However, those merged enterprises fell now into the category of industry in the narrow sense, because they had a large workforce. The Soviet statistics compared apples and oranges to suggest an increase in industrial employment. According to Jaak Valge, by 1938, 19.8 percent of the workforce was employed in the secondary sector[579]—equivalent to about 130,000 people.

An internal statistical overview on the distribution of the employed according to sector made high industrial growth appear quite unrealistic (see Table 61), since for each job in industry, there were nearly two positions in agriculture and in the service sector. Information on the military and the security organs was not given. Additionally, the number of positions in industry was only slightly higher than in 1940.

Table 61: Information on Employment in Different Sectors, 1955

Sector	Employed in thous.
Agriculture and Forestry	205
Industry	123
Other	197
In education or vocational training (16 years and older)	38

Source: Statistical overview, ERA R-1-5-406, l. 5.

A distinctive feature of industrial enterprises during the Stalinist era in comparison to market economies of the time was the much higher share of employees.

578 Kaur, *Wirtschaftsstruktur und Wirtschaftspolitik*, p. 18; *Eesti arvudes 1920–1935* (Tallinn, 1937), p. 14.

579 Valge, "Uue majanduse lätteil," p. 2451.

The organizational problems of the command economy and the increased transaction costs created a greater need for bureaucracy. Large enterprises also assumed some social tasks, like the provision of kindergartens and clubs, and they had their own shops, another reason for the relatively high share of employees. In 1955, white-collar workers constituted 16 percent of employment in Soviet industry.[580] For 1940, John D. Barber and R. W. Davies even offer a figure of 33 percent.[581] On January 1, 1948, in Estonian industry, only 68 percent of the employed were workers.[582] For the reasons mentioned, the number of productive industrial laborers in the mid-1950s could not have been significantly higher than in the late 1930s.

The industrial workers of the postwar period typically had little job experience (see Table 62). Many were young and starting their first job or came directly from agriculture. The industrial world and its rules were initially strange to them. Great numbers of workers were inexperienced, a situation caused by the enormous human losses due to war and state terror, by the influx of women into industry, by the massive immigration of low-skilled people, and by the declining attractiveness of the agricultural sector. Given the workers' lack of experience, significant increases in productivity per worker could not be expected. Workers gained knowledge only slowly, especially because there were few courses or job-training measures. As a result, the qualifications of industrial workers in Estonia declined from 1947 to 1953.[583]

Table 62: Work Experience in Industry, 1947–1957, as a Percentage of the Employed

Year	Less than 1 year	1–3 years	3–5 years	5–10 years	10–15 years	15–25 years	More than 25 years
1947	53.3	29.7	6.2	4.9	2.1	2.5	1.3
1948	36.5	34.1	15.4	5.7	2.7	3.3	2.3
1950	31.9	36.5	15.5	11.3	1.8	1.8	1.2

580 TsSU SSSR, *Narodnoe khoziastvo SSSR v 1956 godu*, p. 50.

581 John D. Barber and R.W. Davies, "Employment and Industrial Labour," in Davies, Harrison, and Wheatcroft (eds.), *The Economic Transformation*, p. 90.

582 Statistical overview, ERAF 1-7-27, l. 45.

583 Pullat (ed.), *Istoriia rabochego klassa*, p. 207.

Table 62: Continued

Year	Less than 1 year	1–3 years	3–5 years	5–10 years	10–15 years	15–25 years	More than 25 years
1957	20.0	26.3	16.8	25.7	9.1	1.6	0.5

Source: Pullat (ed.), *Istoriia rabochego klassa*, p. 338.

The level of general education left much to be desired (see Table 63). The level of education could therefore be no reason for the growth of production. Before the war illiteracy was no typical problem among Estonian workers, yet by 1952 the industrial workforce comprised of 14 percent uneducated, mainly immigrants, among them many illiterates. Also the amount of people passing a "serious" vocational training of mostly two years declined from 2,350 annually by the end of the 1930s to 2,000 in the beginning of the 1950s.[584] Vocational schools suffered additionally from a lack of qualified teachers and instructors holding a master craftsman degreemasters and material resources. Many students in vocational training had not even finished the six years of elementary school.[585]

Table 63: General Education of Industrial Workers in 1952

Degree	In percent
Higher education or unfinished higher education	0.3
Specialized secondary education	1.1
Secondary school	3.4
Unfinished secondary school	21.2
Elementary school	60
Uneducated (*malogramotnyi*)	14

Source: Pullat (ed.), *Istoriia rabochego klassa*, p. 345.

584 Kala and Juursoo, "Nõukogude Eesti töölisklass," p. 254; A. Lepp, "Lõpetanute arv õppeasutustes," *Eesti Statistika* 1940, pp. 217–234.
585 Kala and Juursoo, "Nõukogude Eesti töölisklass," pp. 252–253.

Generally speaking, the situation of workers in the postwar period was difficult all over the Soviet Union. Despite labor laws mandating punishment if a worker was late three times or making a change of employer difficult, Estonian factories had no stable workforce after the war. The labor turnover rate in 1947, for example, averaged 74.2 percent. In the oil shale industry, it was a whopping 147.4 percent.[586] Thus the turnover rate was double the Soviet average,[587] an indicator of the relative weakness of the new regime in Estonia. Especially in the difficult postwar period, workers changed jobs in search of better living conditions. However, it was not only experience, education, and vocational training that was lacking; work morale was also low (see Table 64). Under normal conditions, a rate of absence caused by illnesses could be expected to reach roughly 5 percent. Yet the absence rate in 1947 was 12 percent, an indicator of great dissatisfaction, very low work morale, and extremely difficult living conditions. In addition, production regularly came to a halt. According to official data, in this way 15 percent of work time was lost. The degree of absenteeism clearly demonstrates that the draconian labor laws were not fully applied; otherwise, there would soon be no workers left. Another indicator of the low work morale was the common practice of drinking on the job. For example, at the Ilmarine Factory, some employees could not begin work "without 100 to 150 g of vodka."[588]

Table 64: Rate of Absenteeism and Production Stoppages in 1947

Month	Daily rate of absenteeism in percent	Stoppages in percent of work time
January	12.3	3.8
February	11.2	2.4
March	12.3	2.1
April	12.8	3.2
May	13.4	1.9

Information for republican enterprises.

Source: Statistical overview, ERA R-12-3-27, l. 11ff.

586 Report by Gosplan, December 4, 1948, ERAF 1-7-27, l. 33.
587 See figures for the Soviet Union in Filtzer, *Soviet Workers and Late Stalinism*, p. 167.
588 Meeting of the CC Bureau of the ECP, April 10, 1946, ERAF 1-4-359, l. 9.

The small real incomes and the low standard of living have been discussed above. They sapped workers' motivation and discipline and increased the labor turnover. Additionally, having to line up at state shops and to "hunt" for goods in short supply, often during work time, made life difficult. The question of urban living space was another problem; per capita, it had been halved.[589] Many workers had to live in primitive dormitories or in barracks erected for prisoners of war or even concentration-camp inmates. The Estonian Oil Shale Construction Trust offered its workers exactly 1.25 m^2 of living space per person.[590] The workers were living in the barracks of a former prison camp with three-story bunk beds. In the devastated city of Narva, earthen huts were also used.

None of the workers were truly free, but there were variations in the restrictions they faced. In May 1945 there were approximately 38,000 prisoners of war in Estonia[591] used in construction and industry. The extent to which other prisoners of the Soviet camp systems were used is unknown. However, for at least a while, the share of forced labor in industry and construction must have been larger than one-third. Thus forced labor was, on average, more prevalent in Estonia than in the rest of the USSR; for a time, it accounted for one-fifth of the industrial workforce.[592] Additionally, there were the labor battalions of the Soviet Army. However, forced labor was inefficient and the productivity of a prisoner much lower than that of a "free" laborer. In addition, personnel were needed to act as guards. Concerning the Soviet construction material industry, Donald Filtzer cites estimates stating that prisoners achieved only one-fifth or one-sixth of the usual productivity.[593] Finally, the widespread forced labor instead caused reconstruction to slow down.

Prisoners were released under the condition that they would work for a certain time in a prescribed enterprise.[594] Political prisoners could also be banished to work in oil shale mining. Youths were often mobilized by force. Counties and parishes had to send a certain number of youths to the labor reserve schools or factory schools, a sort of vocational school with a shortened program. After a short training, they were dispatched to factories or mines, where they were

---

589 See Misiunas and Taagepera, *The Baltic States*, p. 364.

590 Overview on working conditions, November 1, 1950, ERAF 1-4-1069, l. 4.

591 Deputy People's Commissar for Internal Affairs Ivanov to Karotamm, May 30, 1945, ERAF 1-3-438, l. 4.

592 Filtzer, *Soviet Workers and Late Stalinism*, p. 23.

593 Ibid., p. 26.

594 See, for example, Minister of the Interior Resev to Karotamm, December 23, 1947, ERAF 1-5-36, l. 103.

forced to work as mobilized people.[595] Since the wartime regulations applied until 1948, those who left the workplace could face three to 10 years of imprisonment in a work camp.[596] However, by May 1948 the majority of mobilized youths—59 percent—left their workplace in Ida-Virumaa.[597] Appalling living and work conditions were the reason. The regime had no way of holding these youths back. Another form of dependence was job placement with the help of *orgnabor*, which was responsible for the organized recruitment of labor. Newly hired workers had to sign a contract (usually for five years) and were subject to further limitations.[598] From 1945 to 1948, 17 percent of all new hires in Estonia were recruited in this way.[599]

However, the other workers were not free either, as the Soviet labor laws applied to them, too. Between 1940 and 1952, 3.9 million workers and employees in the Soviet Union were punished with imprisonment for illegally changing their job. Furthermore, 10.9 million were punished for unexcused absence with six months of corrective labor in their enterprise and a one-quarter reduction of their wages.[600] Other deeds were punished strictly, too, yet we do not have statistics for Estonia. It must be noted that only a fraction of the cases were really prosecuted. In the early 1950s, work conditions in industry normalized, pressure decreased, and the standard of living increased. However, this did not mean a restoration of prewar conditions. Industrial labor remained dirty, dangerous, physically demanding, and badly paid; thus work morale remained low. Since the workers had no representation of interest—the trade unions served as "transmission belts" of the state—and the regime lacked the legitimacy to motivate the workers psychologically, the work itself was badly organized, yet there was a chronic shortage of labor, and so productivity stayed low.

Various campaigns tried to address the demoralizing conditions. Like everywhere else in the Soviet Union, the regime attempted to improve performance through "socialist competition," Stakhanovist and shock workers (see Table 65). By 1949, more than 90 percent of Estonian workers were involved, according to a

---

595 For example, meeting of the CC Bureau of the ECP, June 23–28, 1948, ERAF 1-4-579, l. 22–26.

596 Filtzer, *Soviet Workers and Late Stalinism*, p. 35.

597 Meeting of the CC Bureau of the ECP, May 19, 1948, ERAF 1-4-654, l. 136.

598 Filtzer, *Soviet Workers and Late Stalinism*, pp. 31–32.

599 Report on the activities of the administration of the labor reserves until 1948, ERA 1-47-29, l. 142.

600 Filtzer, *Soviet Workers and Late Stalinism*, p. 163.

report for Malenkov,[601] yet the Stakhanovist movement and other measures did more to fulfill propaganda aims than real results. In life stories, those measures are rarely mentioned, and they were not reflected in output statistics. In fact, their effect was negative, because at peak times of competition, the machines were overloaded, and they wore out quicker.

Table 65: Number of Stakhanovist and Shock Workers in Estonia, 1946–1951

On January 1	Stakhanovist workers	Shock workers
1946	4,304	10,564
1947	9,201	14,698
1948	13,145	21,190
1949	16,014	23,379
1950	19,424	26,228
1951	23,270	32,081

Source: Leede, *Bor'ba partiinykh organizatsii*, p. 97.

However, not only the workers but also the management and leading personnel received insufficient education and training (see Table 66). Though the level of education and training improved, it remained alarmingly low. As one-third of the engineers possessed no subject-related preparation, not much could be expected of them. This situation was caused by the huge losses of human capital and the repeated purges directed against "bourgeois nationalists." There were not enough qualified "red" cadres to replace them, so instead, inexperienced graduates from university and colleges and personnel called "practitioners" had to be used. An example of problems with the management was the Punane Reet Factory in 1953. The factory could not fulfill the plan. According to the investigation report, irregular production, the low quality of products, and the generally bad organization of the plant were caused by a management that was undisciplined, incompetent, and had drinking problems.[602] The life stories include many accounts of the substandard management of enterprises.

601 Karotamm to Malenkov, December 31, 1949, ERAF 1-14-26, l. 10.
602 Meeting of the CC Bureau of the ECP, March 30, 1954, ERAF 1-4-1740, l. 28–29.

Table 66: Educational Level of the Management and the Higher-Ranking Employees in Industry in Percent

Position	**Higher education**		**Specialized secondary education**		**Without special education**	
	1947	1956	1947	1956	1947	1956
Directors	12.1	10.7	17.8	20.7	74.1	64.1
Management	20.4	25.0	19.8	23.6	59.8	51.4
Heads and deputy heads of department	4.7	10.9	19.8	23.6	69.6	76.1
Engineers	17.7	33.8	22.7	31.2	59.6	35.0
Technicians	1.0	3.6	30.0	43.2	69.0	53.2
Total	8.1	15.2	17.8	20.7	74.1	64.1

Information for November 1, 1947, and December 1, 1956.

Source: Veimer, *Kompleksnoe razvitie*, p. 317.

Investment

If the workers and the management do not serve to explain the proclaimed industrial growth, perhaps investment played an important role. With new machinery and better technology, productivity might be increased enormously. Officially, the capital stock of Estonian industry grew rapidly in the postwar period (see Table 67). But investment was measured by Soviet bookkeeping in current ruble prices. Especially during postwar inflation, this led to massive distortions.

Table 67: Official Capital Stock of Industry in Current Ruble Prices, 1945–1951

Year	**Million rubles**
1945	805
1946	1,070
1947	1,279

Table 67: Continued

Year	**Million rubles**
1948	1,579
1949	1,931
1950	2,236
1951	2,769

Source: Development of Estonian industry, ERAF 1-72-37, l. 146.

To check the plausibility of the investment statistics, we need to investigate the level of capital stock of industry before the war. We have precise data for 1936, when the capital stock was estimated to be 259 million kroons.[603] Moreover, in the subsequent years before the communist takeover, investment was higher than natural depreciation. As mentioned above, investment declined markedly after the beginning of Sovietization and could not ensure the maintenance of the capital stock. During the war the investment rate was negative; some factories closed, and war damage decreased the capital stock. At the end of fighting, about half of the capacity of industry was destroyed, because retreating German and Soviet troops blew up installations or took machinery and equipment with them. However, the figure of 805 million rubles presented in the table is clearly too low, particularly as a threefold increase of the capital stock from 1945 to 1951 is completely unrealistic. Since investment was given in current prices in Soviet statistics, a value of approximately three billion rubles for the capital stock might be seen as a rough approximation for 1945.

Archival documents as well as published data list a total investment of 3.5 billion rubles in Estonian industry by 1955.[604] Larger investment was foreseen in the plan, yet the investment plan for 1947 was fulfilled only by 67 percent and for 1951 by 82 percent.[605] Soviet data on investment and the development of the capital stock was distorted by three main problems. Annual depreciation was usually understated and amortization too low. Not all industrial investment actually went to industry. Military investment was often listed in the category of

603 Riigi Statistika Keskbüroo, *I majandusloendus Eestis: Tööstus*, p. 25.

604 *Eesti Nõukogude Entsüklopeedia*, vol. 2 (Tallinn, 1987), p. 322; for the years 1945 to 1951, ERAF 1-72-37, l. 146.

605 ERAF 1-5-2, l. 9; ERAF 1-58-1, l. 103.

industrial investment. For example, the investment plan for the Estonian SSR for the first half of 1946 was only fulfilled by 66 percent. Twenty-nine million rubles out of 124 million was used mainly for military construction.[606] Money to build flats or dormitories for workers, or to open factory shops or even hospitals or kindergartens, ended up in the statistics as investment in industry. For example, in 1951 the ESSR's Ministry of Light Industry used one-fifth of the budget of industrial investment for social and infrastructure measures.[607] Since the Soviets favored large industrial projects that took years or even a decade to start operation, a great deal of investment did not lead to any immediate results. For example, by 1951 about 670 million rubles already had been invested in unfinished projects,[608] nearly one-third of the total investment since the end of the war. When we add to these three factors the widespread theft of materials mentioned again and again in life stories and party documents, then the real investment in producing factories was at least one-third lower than officially announced.

Estonian industry indeed suffered from a lack of investment and money, even when individual branches, like the oil shale industry, had ample financial reserves. It is possible that by 1955, the capital stock of industry had recovered from the results of war, but in all likelihood, it had not. The production of construction materials was, at that time, a good indicator of real investment activity. According to the data on brick and concrete production, the prewar level was exceeded by 1949 (see Table 68); however, building activities had been artificially increased by the garrisoned troops of the Soviet army in the sense that bases and barracks needed to be built for them. Not only the capital stock lost during the war but also the buildings damaged in combat had to be restored. How could such a large alleged investment happen with so few construction materials? Import from other Soviet republics could not have accounted for it; between 1944 and 1948, the total value of construction material imported by Estonia was only 0.5 million rubles.[609]

606 Statistical overview, fulfillment of the investment plan of the Estonian SSR, first half of 1946, RGASPI f. 598, o. 1, d. 9, l. 117.

607 ERA R-9-3-318, l. 2.

608 Report on investment 1951, ERAF 1-58-1, l. 104.

609 Statistical overview by Gosplan, December 9, 1948, ERAF 1-47-29, l. 188–193.

Table 68: Production of Bricks and Cement, 1939–1940 and 1945–1951

Year	Bricks in millions	Cement in thous. tons
1939	57.4	73.6
1940	57.6	70.9
1945	19	45
1946	25	48
1947	37	70
1948	51	75
1949	68	91
1950	83	90
1951	100	94

Sources: 1939–1940, ERAF 1-47-49, l. 14; 1945–1951, ERAF 1-72-37, l. 145.

Another distinctive feature of the investment structure during the Stalinist era was that a relatively small share of investment was used for technology and machinery, while the lion's share was used for construction projects. Between 1944 and 1948, machinery valued at only 95 million rubles was imported,[610] mostly dismantled in Germany and Central Europe. An appropriate use for those machines could not always be found. Often spare parts and instructions were lacking. From 1951 to 1953, only 131 million rubles was invested in machinery and equipment,[611] less than one-tenth of total industrial investment. The reason for this development lay in the cynical calculation that technology was more expensive than human labor. Women and youths in particular proved to be cheap labor.[612] Stalinism counted on extensive rather than intensive development. As long as the incomes of the employed were kept artificially low, there was even a degree of logic to this kind of exploitation. In the long run, technological backwardness in many fields was consolidated.

---

610 Ibid.
611 Report on the first years of the Five-Year Plan, ERAF 1-1-126-33, l. 120.
612 Filtzer, *Soviet Workers and Late Stalinism*, p. 223.

The problematic structure of investment—little spent on technology or equipment, yet continuous efforts to build more buildings—was discussed in the CC Bureau of the ECP. Concerning the situation of the Estonian Oil Shale Enterprise, Vassilii Kossov stated: "This is the only business with such financial means. All those losses are caused only by the lack of equipment. They are building new buildings, but there is no equipment."[613]

While propaganda claimed that the Estonian industrial output in 1950 was 3.42 times as high as in 1940, a leading Estonian economist in the ESSR's branch of Gosplan, Juhan Janusson, gave a more realistic assessment. His opinion was quoted in the CC of the ECP as follows: "Output is lower than in 1940. The factories are outdated; there are few new machines and equipment. This means it is impossible to exceed the prewar level of Estonian production." Janusson was denounced as a "bourgeois" and "incompetent" economist. However, the head of the Estonian branch of Gosplan had to admit that investment was indeed extremely low.[614]

A report from 1951 on the development of industry stated that in the future, a switchover needed to be made to Soviet technology.[615] Thus in 1951, Estonian factories were still using mainly machinery and equipment from the prewar period. The Seventh Party Conference of the ECP in September 1952 made the decision to finish reconstruction and the conversion of individual sectors of industry by 1955.[616] If the party set this goal at the party conference, then obviously the new and expanded capacities were nonexistent. Some at the party conference expressed doubts as to whether this schedule could be kept. The director of the Kiviõli Oil Shale Enterprise, Dobrynin, warned, for example, that if investment were not increased, it would take eight to 10 years for his enterprise to finish reconstruction.[617] In 1955, too, the Central Committee of the ECP viewed the modernization backlog and the slow introduction of new technologies as essential problems. More than 500 units of equipment with new technology were waiting in Estonia to be installed; in one factory, 37 machines had been standing unused since 1950.[618]

---

613 Meeting of the CC Bureau of the ECP, January 14, 1952, ERAF 1-4-1434, l. 113.

614 Meeting of the CC Bureau of the ECP, September 28, 1950, ERAF 1-4-1093, l. 45.

615 ERAF 1-58-1, l. 182.

616 ERAF 1-4-1282, l. 38.

617 Ibid., l. 366.

618 Eighth Plenum of the CC of the ECP, November 29–30, 1955, ERAF 1-4-1836, l. 8-12.

The obvious underfunding of Estonian industry stood in sharp contrast to the fact that the Soviet Union invested a larger share of its national income than contemporary market economies did.[619] There are two possible explanations. The economic output generated per capita under Stalin was much smaller than in contemporary market economies, even compared to a less developed country like Estonia in the interwar period, and investment was carried out inefficiently. The fact that, after the end of the command economy, only a few factories were competitive and could survive indicated low efficiency. And of course, Soviet per capita GDP was low. The leading communists in Estonia saw no problem with underfunding and low investment in technology. The CC Bureau stated succinctly in January 1950: "Under the conditions of a socialist economy, it is possible to increase productivity sustainably without investing. For this we need the creativity of the employed to rationalize, to realize new inventions, and to elaborate work methods."[620]

Lines of Development

With the beginning of Sovietization in 1940, the Soviet model was followed; initially, however, it was very improvised. In October 1940 the Estonian Economic Council, which coordinated economic reconstruction, summed up its policy: "Considering the demand after [industrial] goods, our main target should be to increase prodution. It is not always possible to ensure an efficient way of producing the goods."[621] With this the path was set; cost-effectiveness criteria took a back seat to increasing the output volume. This volume was measured in rubles at fixed unchanged prices, and the fulfillment of the gross production plan in rubles became the main target of every industrial enterprise. Profit, however, did not play an important role in the thinking of industrial managers. For example, a couple of enterprises in the oil shale industry made "planned losses" for years and were subsidized by the state.[622]

---

619 See the estimates in Bergson, *The Real National Income*, p. 277.

620 Meeting, January 18, 1950, ERAF 1-4-912, l. 21.

621 ENSV Majandusnõukogu bülletänn no. 1 (October 8, 1940), ERA R-1206-1-8, l. 121.

622 In the oil shale enterprises of the responsible Estonian ministry, about 5,000 people worked. Those businesses sold the oil shale below production cost, and from January 1945 to September 1948, they received a total of 91.9 million rubles of subsidies, two-thirds of the wage expenses of the period. Calculated according to the report of the Ministry for Oil Shale and Chemical Industry of the ESSR for the period 1940–1948, ERAF 1-47-30, l. 127, 132.

As in the rest of the Soviet Union, in Estonia the Stalinist reconstruction of the economy brought with it the typical problems of Soviet industry. The goods were of low quality. Labor, materials, raw materials, and means of transport ran short.[623] Deliveries, especially from the more distant regions of the Soviet Union, took place irregularly, and only negotiations with higher-standing institutions could ensure supplies. Shortages were widespread, and the tendency toward autarky increased among regions, enterprises, and ministries.[624] The system functioned only because the shadow economy, illegal means of procurement, the use of middlemen, the *tolkachi* (literally *pushers*), *blat'*, the black market, and extraordinary degrees of improvisation kept it running.[625] Working conditions were bad; at times, in the oil shale region, they were even terrifying.[626] The production rhythm was irregular; the end of a planning period typically witnessed widespread "storming," a phenomenon noted (and criticized) even in the strictly censored newspapers.[627] A former miner explained: "There was a lot of action at the end of each month! Everyone was interested in plan fulfillment, the miners and the superiors! We even worked on Sundays."[628] An audit of the two Tallinn-based factories, Volta and Ilmarine, in the first quarter of 1955 established that between 10 and 20 percent of the monthly plan was fulfilled in the first 10 days of a month, between 16 and 22 percent in the next 10 days, and between 57 and 76 percent in the last 10 days.[629] How this depreciated the machinery and equipment can be easily imagined. Questions of discipline of the workers have already been covered above; this was also affected by the irregular rhythm of production.

Georgii Perov of the Estonian Bureau of the CC of the VKP(b), a sort of surveillance institution that Moscow used on the Estonian leadership, described Estonian industry in February 1946 as follows: "Our industry functions badly. There are stoppages of 10 to 15 days a month in industrial enterprises, the workflow is badly organized, wages are paid too late, and the workers earn only a little. The lack of laborers is unfortunate, but the existing workers are not used

623 See, for example, the report on the activities of the Ministry for Local Industry of the ESSR, October 7, 1948, ERAF 1-47-30, l. 26–35.

624 See meeting in the People's Commissariat for Light Industry, March 20, 1941, ERA R-12-1-31, l. 12–13.

625 See especially Berliner, *Factory and Manager in the USSR*.

626 Report of the Leningrad mining inspection, October 28, 1950, ERAF 1-46-40, l. 59–68.

627 *Sirp ja Vasar*, September 29, 1945.

628 Viktor (born 1927), employed in mining since 1950, EKM-EKLA 994, l. 195.

629 Meeting of the party activists of the republic on economic questions, July 28, 1955, ERAF 1-4-1915, l. 23.

in a reasonable way. I checked 11 enterprises; due to idling and absenteeism, 30 percent of working time is lost. Labor productivity is low. The wage system takes no interest in work performance. The people might have the impression that the state took over industry without asking them. And the state is unable to organize the workflow, the wage system, etc., correctly."[630] Perov's assignment was to check on and criticize the Estonian leadership, but in principle he draw a realistic picture of industry in the postwar period.

Planning did not run smoothly either, as indicated by data from the Põhjala Factory (see Table 69). Numerous plans that had to be followed were created often not in advance, but during the corresponding planning period or even after that period had ended. In this example, the documents on the intended increase of plan figures of the first quarter reached Põhjala only on the third day of the second quarter. The various plans were far from coordinated; in some cases, they were even contradictory. The plan was permanently changed. In the socialist planned economy there was, in practice, less planning with foresight than in market economies, and the continuous changes in the plans led to substantial losses. Especially during the Stalinist era, planning only added to the chaos. Some enterprises were subordinated to the republic, while others reported directly to a union ministry. Responsibilities could change in the course of few years.

Table 69: Planning at Põhjala Factory 1949/50

Date of drafting	Plan developed
October 13, 1949	Plan draft 1950
October 20	Plan for 1950
January 1, 1950	Plan for the first quarter
January 12	Work, wages, and salaries (first quarter)
January 27	Changes in the plans for gross production and costs
February 2	Changes in production plan
February 6	Production plan 1950
February 7	Work, wages, and salaries 1950

630 Tenth Plenum of the CC of the ECP, February 16–17, 1946, ERAF 1-4-250, l. 244.

Table 69: Continued

Date of drafting	Plan developed
February 15	Changes in work plan (first quarter)
March 7	Changes in the plan for wages and salaries (first quarter)
March 29	Plan for 1950
March 29	Changes in production plan (first quarter)
March 30	Changes of the plan targets for the first quarter, arrived April 3
April 3	Plan targets (second quarter)
April 8	Plan targets for individual products (second quarter)
April 15	Plan targets for work (second quarter)
April 18	Plan to develop new colors
April 23	Changes in the wage and salary budget (second quarter)
April 26	Changes in product plan (second quarter)

Source: ERAF 1-142-16, l. 221.

Since fixed prices were applied in the economy, they did not reflect costs, or the scarcity of resources, or the relationship between supply and demand. The prices served as an instrument of bookkeeping to measure plan fulfillment. As a result, considerable imbalances existed. Some fixed, unchanged prices were too high to demonstrate huge successes, like in the arms industry and heavy industry, and others were too low, like in the energy sector. It became virtually impossible to conduct a realistic cost-benefit calculation or to figure out whether a business was making profits or losses. The real costs of indvidual steps in production could not be determined correctly, since the materials used might be overpriced or highly subsidized. In fact, in a couple of cases, factories did not add value but actually destroyed it.[631] The longer such a system persists, the larger the share of real loss-makers grows, without the state even knowing it.

631 See Clifford G. Gaddy and Barry W. Ickes, *Russia's Virtual Economy* (Washington, DC, 2002), pp. 47ff.

One example of such a case was the oil shale industry in Estonia.[632] Oil shale served as a source of energy, whether through burning it or through electricity and gas production. It also provided the basic materials for a chemical industry that existed back before the war. Oil, lubricants, gasoline, and kerosene could be produced from oil shale, which was also used in the production of concrete. The Soviets followed a trend that had already started in independent Estonia before the war. This was a nice example of path dependence, meaning continuing along a path of economic development even when that path no longer makes sense economically. During independence, economic nationalism, ideas of self-sufficiency, and later, German interest in special fuels for the navy since the second half of the 1930s led to the development of the oil shale industry.
Estonian historian Jaak Valge has researched the history of state oil shale mining until 1940. Oil shale possesses a much lower fuel value than coal or oil, and after burning, it leaves behind considerably more ash and slag—about 60 percent of the volume. This leads to problems of disposal and air pollution. As a source of energy, Estonian oil shale was able to outcompete firewood in industry and to increase its market share at the expense of coal, but only because it was protected by import tarrifs. Only the international arms race shortly before the outbreak of World War II made the production of shale oil economically sound. It was only then that production costs fell below the world market price. The production of gasoline was economically unsound, and the enterprises made profits only because of high import duties and export subsidies.[633] Without state intervention and subsidies, the oil shale industry would never have developed in this way. In other words, in the 1930s, the Estonian consumer, by paying more for energy, and the state, by using subsidies financed through taxes, enabled a massive misallocation of investment capital. During the Soviet period, the value destruction was to continue on a larger scale.

From the end of the war to 1950, more than 40 percent of all industrial investment in Estonia was directed to the oil shale industry. Leningrad received gas extracted from oil shale in 1948, and Tallinn received it five years later.[634] The regime thus supported an asymmetric industrial development, since aside from Tallinn and Ida-Virumaa, there was little investment in other regions of the

632 See Rurik Holmberg, *Survival of the Unfit: Path Dependence and the Estonian Oil Shale Industry* (Linköping, 2008).

633 See Jaak Valge, "Riiklik põlevkivitööstuse majandustingimused ja -tulemused 1920. ja 1930. aastatel," *Akadeemia* 7 (1995), pp. 1712–1740, 1929–1949.

634 Kalev Kukk, "Industry," in Kahk, *World War II*, p. 64.

country. However, the massive expansion of the oil shale industry did not make much sense economically, because even according to Soviet bookkeeping methods, half of the enterprises of the Estonian Ministry for Oil Shale made losses in 1951.[635] The following data on the output per workday in mining are taken from an economic history of the Estonian SSR (see Table 70). Originally, this was intended to demonstrate the huge productivity of Estonia's miners. In fact, however, the data shows the opposite. Indeed, the output of oil shale per workday in Estonia was double that of coal in the Soviet Union. Yet the fuel value of oil shale is only a quarter of that of coal. We can conclude that mining one ton of oil shale in Estonia cost slightly less than half as much as mining one ton of coal in the USSR, since under the primitive conditions back then, wages were the largest cost factor. The low fuel value of oil shale is the reason. Other countries mined oil shale only on a small scale, even if they had sizable deposits of it. A large-scale oil shale industry is mostly economically unsound.

Table 70: Output in Mining in Tons per Workday, 1955

Coal **Soviet Union**	**1.43**
Great Britain	1.37
France	1.55
Canada	2.59
USA (1954)	7.3
South Africa	1.46
Oil shale Estonia	2.7

Source: I. Kaganovitš, "Materiaalse ja tehnilise baasi arenemine ja tööviljakuse tõus Eesti NSV põlevkivi kaevandavas tööstuses," *Nõukogude Eesti majandus*, p. 230.

Since the Estonian oil shale industry was able to develop in this way only due to protectionism and subsidies, its further expansion after the war made no sense economically, given that worldwide energy prices were low until 1973. This

635 Balance sheets of the enterprises of the ministry, ERA R-4-13-43, l. 18–23.

expansion can be explained only by the absence of a realistic cost-benefit calculation and by the Soviets' ideological belief in the importance of heavy industry.

Understanding Soviet Industrial Statistics

The reason for the seemingly vast growth of industrial output mentioned at the beginning of this chapter was the statistical methods used by the USSR. Since the first Five-Year Plan, Soviet gross production was measured in unchanged fixed prices of 1926/27. After 1950, state wholesale prices briefly served as a unit of measurement, and then in 1952, the standard returned to unchanged fixed prices. However, it was not important whether goods were really sold or produced for the scrap heap.[636] Setting high plan prices on one's own products made it easier to fulfill the gross production plan in rubles, the most important plan for all enterprises.

Using fixed prices leads to certain problems. Initially, this price needs to contain the costs of production, amortization, and a small profit. New products were usually valued according to their cost as of the time production started. However, pilot products are normally more expensive than later mass production.[637] In addition, over time, many industrial products become cheaper in real terms, especially when they are technologically aging. Wily managers often simulated innovation to receive a higher plan price for a nearly identical product. Mark Harrison estimates that inflation hidden in the unchanged prices of industrial goods amounted to 150 to 200 percent from 1928 to 1955.[638]

Another problem was that the prices fixed by the state did not reflect the scarcity of goods, the demand, or the production costs. In an economic system that operates with fixed prices, even a calculation of real costs turns to be impossible in the long run. Some prices are subsidized and therefore too low, while others are too high. The longer such a system persists, the further efficiency declines, because loss-making enterprises cannot be distinguished from profit-making enterprises. A factory might make losses for decades but is not closed and continues to destroy more value.

In the interest of better plan fulfillment, Soviet managers tried to produce goods that received a higher plan price. In addition, the prices set by the state could not be properly compared across branches. Estonian industry provides a

636 Nove, *Das sowjetische Wirtschaftssystem*, p. 116.
637 Harrison, "Prices, Planners and Producers," p. 1043.
638 Harrison, "Soviet Industrial Production," pp. 146, 153.

good example of those practices (see Table 71). The value of produced combs per worker in the Tartu Comb Factory was 90 times higher than that of the bricks from Türi. The seeming explosion in productivity of enterprises like Ehitustarve (construction materials) or Norma was simply caused by reorienting production towards products receiving a higher plan price. In individual cases, material production might have even decreased.

Table 71: Gross Output per Worker in Prices of 1926/27 in Selected Factories

Factory	1940	1947	Per capita output 1947 in percent of 1940
Red Kunda	4,040	5,692	141
Tallinn Brick factory	4,106	2,613	64
Türi Brick Factory in Türi	1,315	447	34
Silicate	7,321	3,132	43
Armatura	14,822	9,144	78
Ehitustarve	5,333	26,209	492
Technique	3,960	1,280	32
Torch	13,710	15,710	115
Vega	9,323	7,673	83
Urania	8,036	18,188	226
Metallmärk	7,660	41,172	538
Norma	2,576	12,623	490
Victory	1,835	5,465	298
Tav	2,966	12,985	437
Estonian Motor	29,457	14,745	50
Keila	3,962	9,426	238
Red Dawn	9,921	10,790	109
Marat	6,841	6,732	99

Table 71: Continued

Factory	**1940**	**1947**	**Per capita output 1947 in percent of 1940**
Bolshevik	2,888	3,465	120
Kemaks	6,091	13,375	220
People's Furniture	889	6,740	758
Tartu Comb Factory	55,005	40,338	74
Kalev	9,884	15,498	156
Leek	20,005	21,870	109
Tallinn brewery	15,451	14,719	95
Võru Industry	6,454	23,304	361
Tallinn Milk Plant	16,309	35,100	215

Source: Statistical overview, ERAF 1-47-38, l. 28–31.

The Estonian CC supported and used this technique of easier plan fulfillment, as did other Soviet republics. Whenever it had to be decided whether to fund the textile industry or the engineering industry, the money went to engineering, because with the same input, it delivered a higher output in terms of gross production in rubles.[639] High plan prices could send the wrong signals. This was a general problem for a seller's market, which mostly ignored the needs of consumers. This internal logic of the system led to the misallocation of capital, and economic realities and profitability were ignored. As a result, in Estonia the overall plans for gross production were fulfilled, yet the plans for certain products covering only a small part of the actual production range were not. For example, in 1953, the plan for certain products was fulfilled in only 55 percent of the cases.[640] This was also one reason for the permanent shortages. Even when the plan called for the manufacture of a certain number of bicycles or leather shoes, the fulfillment of the gross production plan was more important, because this was related to bonuses.

---

639 Meeting of the CC Bureau of the ECP, July 29, 1948, ERAF 1-4-656, l. 46.

640 Johannes Käbin, first party secretary, at the Ninth Plenum of the CC of the ECP, February 3, 1954, ERAF 1-4-1702, l. 10.

Another phenomenon occurring with the use of constant prices and indices is defined by the factor time. If—as in the Soviet cases—the price index is weighted according to the output of the base year (a Laspeyres index), the result differs from an index whose structure is oriented towards the output of the current year (a Paasche index). If an index is chosen whose base year was long ago, the increase in production seems larger than it actually is. This is known as the Gerschenkron effect.[641] Thus the Soviet statistics were unwittingly distorted and became subject to inflation because they were based on the long-ago base year of 1928.

At the time Estonia was annexed by the Soviet Union, the legal tender was the kroon. The unchanged Soviet prices from 1926/27 could not have been introduced for thousands of industrial goods in a short span of time. Because of this, until the end of 1940, the gross production of Estonian industry was measured in kroons in prices from 1939. Statisticians estimated the volume to be 275 million kroons.[642] This figure appears to be realistic, particularly as the Statistical Office still operated according to the old methods. Later on, prices calculated on the spot were used. There were many opportunities to get higher prices approved to simulate an increase of production. Only starting July 1, 1945, did the Soviet lists of unchanged, fixed prices of 1926/27 apply.[643] Still, clever managers could still get higher prices assigned to their goods if those goods were produced exclusively in Estonia and could not be found on the lists.

To be able to offer a proper estimate of industrial production, we need to find out which exchange rate the statisticians used to convert prices in kroons from 1939 into unchanged, fixed plan prices. If we look at the index of gross production until 1950 at unchanged prices[644] and compare the data with the output of 1940, we see that the official Soviet exchange rate is used: one kroon for 1.25 rubles. This procedure was also mentioned at a meeting of the People's Commissariat of Light Industry in January 1941.[645] The key question is whether this exchange rate was justified. What was the value of one kroon according to unchanged prices?

---

641 S.G. Wheatcroft and R.W. Davies, "The Crooked Mirror of Soviet Economic Statistics," in Davies, Harrison, and Wheatcroft (eds.), *The Economic Transformation*, pp. 31–32.

642 Documents for the speech of Karl Säre, first party secretary, January 1941, ERAF 1-4-49, l. 65; meeting in the People's Commissariat of Local Industry, January 15, 1941, ERA R-12-1-31, l. 58.

643 Meeting of the CC Bureau of the ECP, July 3, 1945, ERAF 1-4-231, l. 14–15.

644 Statistical overview, ERAF 1-72-37, l. 142.

645 ERA R-12-1-31, l. 58.

To give an exact answer is impossible. For this it would be necessary to compare and analyze countless price lists. However, an estimate seems possible. The food prices in Moscow stores were, for example 13 times higher than on the Tallinn market;[646] in this case it is not even taken into account that prices in the Moscow markets were still higher than in the Moscow shops. Goods in shortage or industrial products were even more expensive in the Soviet Union than in Estonia. The purchasing power of one kroon must have been 10–15 rubles before the communist takeover. This assessment was shared by contemporaries. At the time, the ratio of the ruble to the unchanged prices was an average 2.86 to one.[647] However, industrial goods received higher plan prices than food. Taking this into account, the exchange rate for Estonian industrial goods from 1939 prices to unchanged 1926/27 prices should have been not 1.25 but approximately 6. Therefore, the output of the base year 1940 was 4.8 times larger than Soviet statistics indicated. One could certainly argue with the estimate, but the tendency was definite. Estonian industrial production in 1940 was indicated as being much smaller than it really was. The aim of this seems clear: to assert the superiority of Soviet policies of industrialization in comparison to "backward" Estonia. However, in reality, Estonia was more industrialized than the USSR.

The accuracy of Soviet statistics was further affected by fraud and forgery. Since the dictator demanded quick, extraordinary, and often unrealistic successes, "massaging" one's own production figures was widespread at all levels. For example, to receive their bonuses, the Tallinn Furniture Factory reported that they had fulfilled their plan. When the books were audited, it was discovered that the recorded output for April 1949 was 54 percent higher than real output. The remaining goods existed only on paper. The management was corrupt, and local civil servants and party functionaries had been bribed with free furniture.[648]

Taking into consideration all the factors—falsified plan fulfillment, hidden inflation, the "unchanged" prices, the transition to more "lucrative" goods, the gross understatement of the base year, and the Gerschenkron effect—it is possible that industrial output in 1955 did not even reach the prewar level. Indeed, postwar reconstruction was not finished. Contemporaries asked one question often: We read in the newspapers of breathtaking growth, but where are all the

646 Tallinn prices in May 1940 in *Eesti Statistika* 1940, p. 320; Moscow prices in July 1940 in Zaleski, *Stalinist Planning*, pp. 688–691.

647 See Simonov, *Voenno-promyshlennyi kompleks*, p. 181.

648 Report for Karotamm, ERAF 1-38-1, l. 48–51.

industrial goods? The answer was easy—this growth did not exist; it was a statistical sleight-of-hand. After the war, factories fully reopened and industry grew, yet the prewar level was reached only in the second half of the 1950s. The population could not buy many industrial goods. For example, figures in 1955 show that in Estonian retail trade, 63 percent of turnover tax was paid for foodstuffs.[649]

The claim of a 6.7-fold increase in industrial production is absurd. Realistically, I estimate the output to still be slightly smaller in 1955 than before the war.

649 Calculated on basis of the fulfillment of the turnover tax plan in the first 10 months of 1955, ERA R-4-9-247, l. 18.

7 The Service Sector

When examining the service sector during the Stalinist era, we encounter a paradox. This sector grew enormously, yet we know very little about it. In research, the development of agriculture and the forced collectivization are dealt with extensively, as is industry. However, services are barely covered at all. One exception is the pioneering study by Julie Hessler, a social history of Soviet trade in 1917–1953.[650] However, neither the scholarly literature nor the primary sources provide much useful information on the tertiary sector. That is the reason why this chapter is shorter and more incomplete than the two previous ones.

This "gap" was caused by several factors. The ideologically generated fixation on material production—whether grain or machinery—obscured the part of the economy that was not producing "tangible" goods. The plans first measured the value of material products at unchanged prices and only then measured the fulfillment of the product plan. The service sector was not adequately covered in the plan, or in bookkeeping, or in official publications. For example, in 1956, 85.9 percent of the Estonian gross national income officially came from industry, agriculture, and construction, and only 14.1 percent was contributed by transport, communication, trade, and other services.[651] Since the socialist countries represented a "service desert," and the lack of customer-oriented services was sometimes even more severe than the shortage of goods of "material" supplies, the sector often disappears from view and was not tangible. Propaganda, which focused on industrialization and happy kolkhoz peasants, also did not touch on the topic much.

Yet this impression was misleading. Customer-oriented services were subject to shortages; however, some state-provided services became more widely available during the Stalinist era, such as medical treatment, education, culture, and sports. Because the command economy and the planning did not function efficiently, the number of those involved in adjusting the system increased steadily, including planners, accountants, administrators, *tolkachi*, and black-market traders.

In 1938, the tertiary sector accounted for 24.4 percent of employment in Estonia.[652] An analysis of employment in Estonia in the 1950s might shed some

650 Hessler, *A Social History of Soviet Trade.*

651 TsSU ESSR, *Estonskaia SSR*, p. 57.

652 Valge, "Uue majanduse lätteil," p. 2451.

light onto the development of the service sector. About the "labor reserves," the archives contain different data, some of which slightly contradict each other. The presented data from 1955 (see Table 72) might offer some orientation, yet the general trend of the figures is believable. In this case, the figures are taken from the plan. "Labor reserves" covered the working-age population, plus working youths and pensioners. In agriculture and forestry, 205,000 people worked. Yet under point f), "Employable population occupied with work at home and the private economy," there were more than just "housewives." Approximately 50,000 family members did not work on the kolkhoz or the sovkhoz or in any other enterprise, but they were mainly engaged with private plots. Category f) also covered people working in the service sector, such as private trade on the kolkhoz market, on the black market, or as clandestine workers. A realistic estimate for the distribution of workers per sector would be 250,000 employed in agriculture, 145,000 in industry and construction, and 230,000 in the service sector. The statistics do not provide separate information on the military and the security organs; hence these, too, were treated as part of the service sector. According to this, for each person employed in industry, there were nearly two people in agriculture and in services, a distribution similar to the situation throughout the Soviet Union back then. In 1950 in the USSR, there were 35.7 million employed in agriculture, 15.3 million in industry, and 30.1 million in other sectors.[653]

Table 72: Distribution of the "Labor Reserves" According to the Plan in Thousands in 1955

"Labor reserves" total	**702.1**
(a) Employment in state and cooperative institutions	356.3
of this: Industry	122.6
Construction	22.2
Transport and communications	44.9
Sovkhozes and forestry	50.2
State trade	25.2

653 See Angus Maddison, "Measuring the Performance of a Communist Command Economy: An Assessment of the CIA Estimates for the U.S.S.R.," *Review of Income and Wealth* 44 (1998), pp. 314.

Table 72: Continued

"Labor reserves" total	**702.1**
Education	25.2
Health	19.0
(b) *Artel's*	13.5
(c) Collectivized peasants	154.4
(d) Studying 16 years and older	38.0
(e) Individual peasants and independent craftsmen	0.9
(f) Employable population occupied with work at home and the private economy	139.0

Source: Statistical overview, ERA R-1-5-406, l. 5–6.

Thus, during the Stalinist reconstruction of Estonia's economy, an interesting development took place. The workforce in agriculture shrank. The number of people active in industry was, by the mid-1950s, similar to the prewar level. Only the service sector expanded rapidly; yet paradoxically, this sector received the least attention. The reasons for this are mentioned above.

How important the service sector really was for the Soviet national economy is illustrated by an estimate conducted by the CIA for the year 1950. Based on Soviet prices, 34.4 percent of the gross national product was generated by industry, 34.1 percent by agriculture, and 31.5 percent by other sectors, mainly services. If we apply not Soviet prices but corrected factor costs, the picture changes: 18.4 percent of gross national product came from industry, 40.6 percent from agriculture, and 41.0 percent from other sectors.[654] Naturally, this is only a rough estimate, but the academic literature (rightly) calls it one of the most reliable. Consequently, the productivity differences between the sectors were smaller than generally expected. However, the information cited above about gross production in Estonia is unrealistic in any case and implies that value added in industry was several times higher than in services.

If, from 1938 to 1955, employment in the service sector in Estonia did indeed increase from one-fourth to nearly two-fifths of the working population

654 Ibid., p. 315.

and productivity declined only a bit, then the tertiary sector was the only sector of the economy that saw real and significant growth. However, this was accomplished not by increasing productivity but by expanding the workforce.

The Restructuring of the Service Sector

The development of trade is the best documented, yet almost all of the records are only for the trade regulated by the state. Private trade and the black market remained largely undocumented; however, as indicated by the budget surveys from the 1950s and by many life stories, they were of extraordinary importance. Similarly, we know something about the increase of public services. From 1945 to 1955, for example, the number of medical personnel in the Soviet Union doubled.[655]

The speed with which public services expanded in Estonia is indicated by employment figures. (Statistics were not given for the self-employed, the military, and the security services.) From 1940 to 1955, employment in trade and catering doubled, and in transport and communications it grew by 80 percent. Property management and communal services grew by 40 percent. Employment in education, research, and culture increased by 140 percent; in state administration, banking and insurance, it increased by one-third; and in sports, health, and social affairs, it tripled.[656]

After the political takeover in 1940, transport and communications enterprises that were not already run by the state were nationalized. However, in the postwar period, private drivers of horse-drawn carriages and luggage porters still offered their services. Until the end of the Soviet period, vehicle drivers of state institutions and enterprises earned additional income by offering "private" transport services. Neglect reigned in the state sector. Aleksander Kaelas has noted complaints about bus transport: on occasion, the drivers were drunk, did not keep to the schedule, and/or pocketed the fares they collected.[657] Sports, the arts, education, and health care, along with property management and communal services, were placed under state control. Clubs and societies were dissolved or subjugated to state institutions.

Some of the "new" jobs were generated by the professionalization of hitherto voluntary activities. Sometimes this kind of employment could be considered

655 Mark G. Field, *Doctor and Patient in Soviet Russia* (Cambridge, MA, 1957), p. 25.
656 TsSU ESSR, *Estonskaia SSR*, p. 127–128.
657 Kaelas, *Das sowjetisch besetzte Estland*, p. 67.

hidden unemployment. For example, before the war, many villages and parishes had small libraries maintained by the church, teachers, or clubs, where volunteers sacrificed some hours of their leisure time. All those libraries were nationalized and reorganized; in other cases, libraries were newly founded. The goal was to establish a nationwide library system, with one full-time employee in each branch. By 1950, according to state statistics, there were a total of 727 libraries in the countryside, each with an average of 164 readers, 1,628 books in its collection, and 810 books borrowed per year.[658] This means that at each library, only about three books were borrowed per workday! What the party saw as cultural policy, was in reality a job-creation program. Because of censorship and the thinning out of the number of available books in Estonian, the offer became less attractive for readers than before. The "librarians" spent their time reading and doing gardening work, perhaps to stave off boredom. Another example of hidden unemployment was the Estonian Broadcasting Company: in 1941, 194 people worked for 104,000 registered radio listeners. This figure increased to 449 in October 1948. However, there were only 59,900 registered radio listeners left, amounting to one employee per 133 listeners.[659]

The fact that some public services became free did not always mean they improved, as illustrated by health care. In December 1940 the workers in Valga County complained about the situation: "Among the workers, resentment of and dissatisfaction with the new health care system can be noted. They argue that previously, medical attention was available more easily, more quickly, and for cheaper; now this is free of charge, but they have to pay for medicines, and these are more expensive than they used to be."[660] Over time, it became necessary to pay bribes and bring "gifts" in order to visit the right physician.[661] However, the expansion of health care in the 1950s led to a real improvement in medical treatment.

The expansion of education is definitely noteworthy: from 1940 to 1955/56, the number of students in secondary education and of secondary education diplomas doubled.[662] The fast-paced expansion had a price: because teachers

---

658 Report on the situation of the libraries in the countryside, A. Kellberg, secretary of the CC of the ECP, 1950, ERAF 1-46-94, Bl. 79–82.

659 Report of the Radio Committee, October 11, 1948, ERAF 1-47-35, l. 113.

660 Report on the situation in Valga County, December 8, 1940, ERAF 1-1-56, l. 16.

661 Donald A. Barr, "The Ethics of Soviet Medical Practice: Behaviours and Attitudes of Physicians in Soviet Estonia," *Journal of Contemporary Economics* 22 (1996), pp. 33–40.

662 Eesti NSV Statistikakeskvalitsus, *Eesti NSV Rahvamajandus*, p. 220; statistical overview, ERA R-10-43-41, l. 13.

were paid such low wages, it was impossible to find enough qualified teachers. The educational level of teachers (see Table 73) improved from 1950 to 1955; however, it remained low. During the 1950/51 school year, less than a quarter held a degree from a university or a teacher's institute, and many who had finished university had no pedagogical education; nearly six percent of the teachers did not even have a secondary education. Five years later, more than half of the teachers were sent to school with only a secondary education, and nearly four percent did not even have that. Secondary-school teachers had the most education, and primary-school teachers had the least. After the war, substitute teachers were used all over Europe, but not on such a scale as in the Soviet Union. During Estonian independence the prerequisite for teaching at elementary school was a degree from a teacher's seminar, and for teaching at secondary school, it was a university degree. There were undoubtedly some talented pedagogues among the formally unqualified teachers of the 1950s; however, in some places the general level of instruction must have been very low. The quantitative expansion of education could only take place with a severe loss of quality.

Table 73: Teachers and Their Level of Preparation, in Percent

Education	**1950/51**	**1955/56**
Total: Higher education	9.2	14.2
Teacher's training institute	13.9	29.7
Secondary school	71.0	52.2
Without secondary school degree	5.9	3.9
Elementary schools: Higher education	0.4	1.3
Teacher's training institute	4.6	5.9
Secondary school	87.2	88.2
Without secondary school degree	7.8	4.6
Junior high schools: Higher education	7.3	6.5
Teacher's training institute	23.2	54.5

Table 73: Continued

Education	**1950/51**	**1955/56**
Secondary school	64.7	36.5
Without secondary school degree	4.8	2.5
Secondary schools: Higher education	54.9	65.9
Teacher's training institute	21.6	23.8
Secondary school	22.6	10.5
Without secondary school degree	0.9	0.1

Source: Eesti NSV Statistikakeskvalitsus, *Eesti NSV Rahvamajandus*, pp. 235–236.

Just after the war, the number of university students was lower than during the first Soviet year, but the figures increased continuously. By 1955, there were 11,800 students, more than twice as many as before the war.[663] However, part of the increase was due to distance-learning students, who did not always receive adequate training. The number of people employed in research also grew (see Table 74). Yet like the teachers, the vast majority of those classified as "scientists" had inadequate credentials. For the planners, the quantity of those employed in research was more important than their quality. At the end of the 1940s, only one in four researchers held any academic degree, and in the mid-1950s, it was only one in three. Others possessed only a university diploma, or not even that. Naturally, outstanding results could not be expected from such researchers. Even after the death of Stalin, Estonian science was far below its prewar level.

Table 74: Employed and Graduated in Research

Year	**Employed**	**Candidates of Science**	**Doctors of Science**
1940	544	–	–
1947	1,100	188	68

663 Eesti NSV Statistikakeskvalitsus, *Eesti NSV Rahvamajandus*, p. 251.

Table 74: Continued

Year	Employed	Candidates of Science	Doctors of Science
1950	1,221	176	59
1955	1,618	410	56
1956	1,751	462	61

Source: TsSU SSSR, Narodnoe khoziaistvo SSSR v 1956 godu, p. 259; TsSU ESSR, Estonskaia SSR, p. 177.

The real growth of the state apparatus was officially lower than the increase of public services. However, it should be kept in mind that the Soviet state and especially the party apparatus had a clear interest in hiding their dimensions. This was the case with the military and the security organs. In addition, the command economy required far more administrative manpower in industry and agriculture. How some state institutions operated is illustrated by the memories of Eduard (born in 1912), who began work in 1940 with the prosecutor's office: "On the new job I quickly understood why in Russia there was no unemployment, but a shortage of manpower. Namely, those who were employed suffered from unemployment: for me and the others, it was very boring in the procurator's office; there was nothing to do. The work set aside for me was enough to fill one or two hours. The system was still foreign, we did not know it, and there was still no need to go shopping during work hours. And so for eight hours, we sat silently in the office. After settling in, one could spend the time reading or doing crossword puzzles."[664]

In the socialist system, with its networks, personalized power structures, and irregular work rhythms, it made sense for every institution to employ as many people as possible. Such tendencies can also be found at state institutions and administrations in a market economy; however, the soft budget constraints in a command economy intensified those tendencies. At the same time, a large apparatus could potentially increase the prestige of the head, facilitate various tasks, and make the work of the other employees easier. Under Stalin, more of the workforce shifted away from the farm but ended up in the office, rather than in the world of "material production." This naturally impeded increases in productivity and economic growth.

664 KM-EKLA 350-221, l. 88–89.

Craftsmen were brought together in cooperatives. In the postwar years, they often formed a place of hidden self-employment. Minister of Trade Hansen stated in 1946: "In the cooperatives there are as many fictitious as regular members working practically only on their own accord and only rarely for the cooperatives. They do not fulfill the norms but receive ration cards. When checks are conducted, violations of the rules can be found in nearly every cooperative."[665] Another report from 1946 stated that services needed special attention. Only 10–20 percent of the shoe-repairing target was met; prices were not properly indicated, and profits were not earned. The work morale among cobblers in cooperatives was low; often they simply left their place of work to take a stroll. Getting shoes repaired took two to three months.[666] Since the *artel's* did not function efficiently, private crafts thrived for the last time and earned profits.[667] Over time, the *artel's* were consolidated into industrial cooperatives and, in the mid-1950s, used only a small share of their time to customer services.[668] Because of the lack of customer-oriented services, until the end of the Soviet period they remained a place for moonlighting and off-the-books work.

The development of the retail trade network reflects the situation of trade. It grew continuously after the war; however, it remained far below the level of the period of independence (see Table 75). This development started as early as the first Soviet year, when private retail trade still played an important role. After the war the shops were not only empty but also difficult to reach, especially in rural regions. In 1950, the supply situation was still a far cry from what it had been in the era of independence.

---

665 Meeting with Karotamm on the question of ration cards, October 18, 1946, ERA 1-4-377, l. 4.

666 B. Titov to Chairman Perov, July 3, 1946, results of a check of 15 enterprises in Pärnu, Viljandi, Sindi, and Mõisaküla, RGASPI f. 598, o. 1, d. 10, l. 93.

667 Tailors allegedly took 800 to 1,000 rubles for sewing a suit, while the quality of products obtained from state retail was inadequate. Meeting of leading party workers, January 12–15, 1946, ERAF 1-4-370, l. 177.

668 Kaelas, *Das sowjetisch besetzte Estland*, p. 55.

Table 75: The Network of Retail Trade, 1937–1948

	1937	January 1, 1941 private/ state owned	January 1, 1945	January 1, 1946	January 1, 1947	August 1, 1948
Shops	7,460	3,790/1,819	1,190	1,305	1,476	2,124
Kiosks	–	1,266/–	27	90	177	574
Gastronomy	514	194/80	107	244	327	466
Total	7,974 (without kiosks)	7,149	1,324	1,639	1,980	3,164

Source: Report of the Ministry of Trade of the ESSR, October 9, 1948, ERAF 1-47-30, l. 64–65.

Private retail stores were nationalized starting in 1940; however, co-operative retail trade continued, at least in name. This was restructured in 1941 according to the Soviet model; a first wave of purges occurred then, and there was a second wave in 1945. A decisive motivation for joining a consumer co-operative was the opportunity to have preferred access to goods in short supply and to be able to buy on credit. Important decisions were no longer made by general meetings, and the profit distribution became unimportant to the shareholders.[669]

After the end of combat, trade in private shops was allowed for a short time, and not only on the markets. This was a special regulation of the Council of People's Commissars of the USSR for the western regions of the country. They simply recognized reality, since under German occupation, private shops had been reopened, and without them, the supply of the population with goods would have been far more difficult. There were 550 private traders in Estonia in 1945, 308 of which were located in Tallinn. Additionally, non-licensed retailers did operate their businesses. Profits were sometimes quite high. Food retailer Martin Roosileht earned 126,000 rubles in three months and had to pay 95,760 rubles in taxes; stationer Olga Allas earned 84,150 rubles and had to pay 58,161 rubles in taxes.[670] Considering the confiscatory tax rate and the state's complaints about

669 Arnolds P. Aizsilnieks, "Sovietization of Consumers' Cooperation in the Baltic States," *Journal of Baltic Studies* 5 (1974), pp. 40–50.

670 Report of the People's Commissariat of Finance, April 16, 1945, ERAF 1-50-7, l. 7.

the lack of tax inspectors, it seems realistic to conclude that the real profits were much larger. However, the era of private retail shops soon ended with nationalization. Similar profits were realized on the black market, as indicated by recurring reports on embezzlement and profiteering, even in the field of real estate.

Many former traders remained in trade and continued to work in state retail trade, often in managerial positions.[671] The party mistrusted them but lacked the qualified personnel to replace them. For the party, these traders made ideal scapegoats for the shortages caused by the command economy and the ubiquitous corruption. In state shops, the impolite service found in a seller's market appeared very quickly. Even the head of the Planning Committee complained in 1946 that Soviet sales staff typically replied to customer questions by saying "No," "I don't know," or "We don't have it" and that they obviously took no interest in service. He praised the competent sales clerks of the "bourgeois period" and blamed the problems on sabotage and ignorance.[672] The communists never acknowledged that the problems originated from the system. Minister of Security Kumm went one step further: he noted that the Ministry of Trade employed many people from the former political system, and he blamed them for the problems. According to him, in state shops it was not possible to buy anything without paying a bribe, and everywhere were black marketeers.[673] The preferred bribes were vodka and tobacco.[674]

To help with the ubiquitous shortages, many enterprises sent their own purchasing appointees out to find goods. Operating in a gray zone, these purchasers were joined by many fraudsters and "speculators." The appointees fulfilled similar tasks in trade as the *tolkachi* described by Joseph Berliner did in industry. The party instructor from Abja reported in 1946: "Recently there were 10 such specialists in the village; one even drove up by car to the chairman of the village soviet. As a result, one member of the middle peasantry slaughtered his breeding bull and sold him to the speculator. Another peasant slaughtered a milk cow without informing the executive committee. Those people buy everything, butter, meat, eggs, and we look at the Five-Year Plan for cattle breeding and say how the fulfillment of the plan is progressing. In the stable of the kulaks who own six or seven cows, there is not a single young calf; all are large calves. This is

671 See meeting of the CC Bureau of the ECP, June 7, 1945, ERAF 1-4-189, l. 33.

672 Twelfth Plenum of the CC of the ECP, August 2–3, 1946, ERAF 1-4-256, l. 67, 69.

673 Ibid., l. 167–168.

674 Sazonov on the meeting of leading party workers, January 12–15, 1946, ERAF 1-4-370, l. 178.

what happens when there are so many appointees and they buy everything. They speculate and have no set prices. I asked one of them—he had only a letter signed by the director of a food processing facility. Another one we sent to the *militsiia*. He came back sticking his tongue out at us."[675]

In its propaganda, the regime demonized "speculators." However, for many people, petty trade was the only way to survive. This was the case for the hunger refugees from Russia in 1946/47 and for people unable to find a job because their background was, from the state's point of view, politically suspect. Tuuli Jaik (born in 1910), for example, was married to the son of a merchant who had served as an officer in the German army. Because of this, she could not get regular employment and had to commute between Tartu, Elva, and Tallinn to sell, at a small profit, products for daily use that were in short supply, like matches and candles. They were available only under the counter or through contacts. She did this until 1950, and then she sold newspapers for her niece. Finally, in 1951 she joined a cooperative of disabled people to work there, because she suffered from anemia caused by long years of malnutrition.[676] Her activities as a petty trader could have put her in jail.

At the time of the March deportation in 1949, the journal for children and youths, *Pioneer*, presented the mass deportation under the headline "These Are the Enemies of the People" in a way that children could understand. Serving as an image of the enemy, along with kulaks and a Christian believer, was a "speculator" who was punished with seven years of imprisonment for trading in yeast. Yeast was important, since most people in the countryside bake their bread at home. The article closes with the words: "We do not need those people among us. In our country, everyone is working and contributing to the well-being of the people. The court made a justified decision: the speculator Helmi Kivistik is being punished with seven years of imprisonment. This punishment will end her appetite to speculate in yeast."[677] In reality, as in this story for children, the petty traders were mostly women.

The state's great interest in trade is explained less by ideology and more by the possibility to absorb purchasing power and to generate profits. The balance plan for the Ministry of Meat and Dairy Industry of the ESSR for 1950 foresaw total revenues of 229 million rubles, mostly by selling food. One hundred seven million rubles alone were to be transferred to the state budget as turnover tax.[678] The

675 Meeting of party organizers of the parishes, August 9–11, 1946, ERAF 1-4-374, l. 374.

676 "Tuuli Jaik," in Rutt Hinrikus (ed.), *Eesti Rava Elulood I* (Tallinn, 2000), pp. 53–54.

677 *Pioneer*, March 1949.

678 Balance plan of the ministry, ERA R-4-13-20, l. 9–10.

largest individual items of the Estonian Ministry of Trade in 1949 and 1950 were bread and vodka,[679] so vodka generated the most profit by far. In other words, the most important speculator during the Stalinist era was the state, and not only in the framework of commercial stores.

Another way to acquire scarce goods and services was through personal contacts. Practically everyone was able to offer scarce goods of one kind or another. They were exchanged within reciprocal networks, and often not for money. This phenomenon, known in Russian as *blat'*, is described by Alena Ledeneva.[680] This happened in Estonia as well. Aino, born in 1921, remembers the 1950s: "From time to time wages increased, purchasing power grew, and many goods were scarce because of this. This encouraged the exchange of goods for services. Shortages increased, and some of the better and more expensive goods could only be received by those who offered the best services in return."[681]

By the 1950s, the difference between Estonia's service sector and that of the "old" Soviet republics no longer lay in the mechanisms and structure. It lay only in the fact that the supplies in Estonia were sometimes a bit larger and of higher quality. The life stories of immigrants are proof of this, as was the overall image of the Baltic republics as a "Soviet West."

Due to the limitations of the sources, it is extremely difficult to estimate the economic performance of the tertiary sector. There is every indication that productivity per worker declined. There was a great deal of marginal employment, hidden unemployment, and an unproductive bureaucracy. If we estimate that productivity declined by one-fifth per employee and take into account the strong expansion of the sector, then the real economic performance of the sector from 1938 to 1955 might have increased by one-third. This rough estimate seems realistic, especially when it is correlated to CIA data.

---

679 Balance plan of 1950, ERA R-4-13-15, l. 10.

680 Alena V. Ledeneva, "Between Gift and Commodity: the Phenomenon of *Blat'*," *Cambridge Anthropology* 8 (1996), pp. 43–66; Alena V. Ledeneva, *Russia's Economy of Favours: Blat, Networking and Informal Exchange* (Cambridge, 1998).

681 ERM-KV 984, l. 344.

8 Conclusion

The Stalinist reconstruction of the Estonian economy was, along with the policy of state terror and repressions and the mass flight in 1944, responsible for population losses and an unfavorable demographic structure, especially in the countryside. The introduction of the command economy caused a drastic decline in the standard of living. Apart from the structural and organizational shortcomings of the Stalinist economy, the low real incomes took away any incentive to engage in more intensive work. This does not mean that the population did not invest a great deal of time in physically intensive labor. However, there was a lack of motivation and incentive to increase efficiency and productivity, especially in state-run sectors.

The performance of agriculture decreased the most of all sectors, both per capita and in absolute terms. The forced collectivization led to a further decline, and the lowest point was reached in the third year after collectivization, which impeded postwar reconstruction. The alleged huge industrialization turned out to be a fabrication of the party and statisticians; the output level in the mid-1950s might not even have matched that before the war. In a Soviet comparison of 25 industrial regions, Estonia ranked only 16th in output per worker.[682] Only the service sector increased employment and output, and even in this case, per capita performance declined in comparison to the prewar period. The needs of the population were mostly ignored.

The transition to the command economy caused remarkable structural changes. However, the labor force headed from farms to offices rather than to factories. Additionally, soft budget constraints allowed for a huge misallocation of resources and widespread waste. Later on, this kept inefficient enterprises and branches operating. The Soviet tendencies toward autarky, in combination with the lack of incentives for innovation, increased technological backwardness; the dismantling of capital stock in Germany and Central Europe helped for only a brief time. The real modernization and industrialization of the USSR occurred only after the death of Stalin. The principal-agent problem intrinsic to a command economy, an inefficient bureaucracy, turf wars, the black market, corruption, and widespread theft all impeded development. During the process of transition, the state plundered the citizens and, with the methods of "primitive socialist accumulation," tried to direct resources

682 Kazuhiro Kumo, "Soviet Industrial Location: A Re-Examination," *Europe-Asia Studies* 56 (2004), p. 608.

from agriculture to industry. The structure of prices and incomes was intended to support the state's economic policy, but this was not always achieved and sometimes led to unintended consequences.

The importance of private economic activities should not be ignored. Until the forced collectivization, private property dominated agriculture, which back then was the largest sector of the economy. Later, the output of gardens and private plots was officially valued higher than that of kolkhozes and sovkhozes. If we include private economic activities like garden plots, the markets, or the shadow economy, in 1955 up to one-third of economic performance might have originated from the private sector.

How could total economic performance over time be roughly estimated? One way would be to look at the consumption of the population. The best-known and, until now, most widely accepted estimate of Soviet national income under Stalinism was constructed by a team of researchers headed by Abram Bergson. The estimate of the distribution of the final consumption of national income (see Table 76) shows why the real incomes in Stalin's USSR were so low. While in the 1920s, during the New Economic Policy, nearly 80 percent of national income was consumed by private households, in the 1940s and 1950s, this share fell to less than one-half in favor of an investment rate that was extraordinarily high for that era and large state expenditures, largely on the military and arms. One can understand the military expenses made during the war, because the Soviet Union was fighting for its survival. However, the Soviet consumer paid the price for Stalin's dream of great-power status and industrialization with poor and, at times, miserable living conditions.

Table 76: Estimate of the Final Consumption of the Soviet National Income, 1940–1955

Year	Private consumption	Gross investment	Other/state consumption
1928	79.5	12.5	8
1940	49.4	19.1	31.5
1944	31.8	13.1	55
1950	45.7	26.9	27.4
1955	48.0	28.1	23.9

Source: Bergson, The Real National Income, p. 277.

Unfortunately, no data are available on the final use of the Estonian national income before Sovietization. However, a scale of private consumption of 75 to 80 percent of national income might have been similar to other comparable market economies. If the trade balance of the Estonian SSR were balanced from the immediate postwar period until the 1950s, then the standard of living would allow us to draw conclusions on the economic performance of the republic. In comparison to the late 1930s, the real incomes of the population in 1955 were about one-third in agriculture, one-half in industry, and on the average roughly 40 percent. If the share of private consumption dropped from 75–80 percent to the 48 percent calculated by Bergson, then Estonian national income in 1955 was still one-third lower than before the war. If the Estonian SSR generated an export surplus not compensated by imports or money, then the level of economic development was higher. This "export" could also cover the costs of Soviet troops stationed in Estonia, since they were not accounted for in the official Estonian statistics.

Another way to reach a rough estimate would be by adding the performance of different sectors. For this, the prewar period serves as a point of reference, and the Soviet statistics have to be included. Jaak Valge has made the most reliable calculations of the Estonian GDP in 1938 (see Table 77). Estonia was an overwhelmingly agrarian country with a growing industrial and service sector. Such precise calculations cannot be made for the Soviet period.

Table 77: Distribution of GDP and Workforce in Different Sectors, 1938

Agriculture and Forestry		**Industry**		**Service Sector**		**Total in million kroons**
Million kroons	**Employed in percent**	**Million kroons**	**Employed**	**Million kroons**	**Employed**	
250.1	55.8	130.3	19.8	154.9	24.4	535.3

Source: Valge, "Uue majanduse lätteil," pp. 2451, 2718.

During economic restructuring after the death of Stalin, attempts were made to place economic statistics on a more solid foundation. Thus, for 1955, the national income of the Estonian SSR was calculated (see Table 78). The numbers cover gross and net production. Gross production refers to the added products of an entire sector at plan prices; net production deducts the costs. During the introduction of the planned economy, unchanged, fixed prices from 1926/27 were used, yet—as mentioned above—they were subject to inflation, too. At the beginning of the 1950s, the authorities experimented with changing current plan prices annually. Based on the index figures, the current plan prices for industrial products in 1955 were already much higher than the unchanged, fixed prices of 1926/27. Another problem was the weighting of plan prices. Industrial products were assigned much more value than agricultural products or services.

Of special interest is the distribution of net production in 1955. Thirty-two percent came from agriculture, of which two-thirds were from private plots and gardens, 43 percent from industry, and 25 percent from services. Since industrial goods were overvalued and other products and services were undervalued, in reality, the performance of all three sectors might have been quite similar in scale. In other words, not until sometime in the mid-1950s did industrial output exceed agricultural output, and services were at roughly the same level as the other two sectors. In light of the severe decline of agricultural production, which was acknowledged even in published Soviet statistics and in the strictly censored Soviet press, the proclaimed industrial growth is a fantasy. In reality, agricultural output decreased even more than was officially indicated (see Chapter 5).

Notably, industrial employment remained nearly constant compared to 1938, and agricultural employment decreased yet stayed the largest sector of employment, while the service sector hired more and more workers. When we compare employment to net production, it becomes clear that the plan prices were weighted incorrectly. According to official data, for services, per capita net output was just 30 percent of that of industry, and for agriculture, it was just 36 percent of that of industry.

Table 78: Distribution of Gross and Net Production in Different Sectors in 1955 in Million Rubles and in Consecutive Plan Prices of 1955

Sector	Gross production	Net production	Estimated distribution of workforce in percent
Agriculture	2,675	1,473	41
Industry	6,532	1,993	20
Other	1,907	1,157	39
Total	11,114	4,623	100

Net production (*chistaia produktsiia*) = gross production (*valovaia produktsiia*) less costs.

Source: Calculation of the national income of the ESSR for 1955, ERA R-10-19-1, l. 3; estimate of the distribution of workforce based on ERA R-1-5-406, l. 5–6.

By taking into account both tables and the estimates offered in previous chapters for different sectors, we might be able to make a very rough assessment of the economic performance of the Estonian SSR. Agrarian output declined to 40 percent of its initial level, industrial production did not fully recover by 1955, and only the service sector expanded by one-third, yet with a decreased productivity per capita. This very rough estimate indicates that economic performance shrank by about one-fifth or one-fourth from the prewar period.

It might be argued that even if the command economy did not raise the performance per worker, the mobilization of parts of the population not previously employed—mainly women—led to extensive growth. It is definitely the case that economic performance also depends on the scale of employment. If segments of the population not previously employed enter the labor force, the economy might grow without becoming more efficient. After Estonia's large population losses until 1945, the large-scale immigration and return in-migration led to economic growth. However, the framework of the prewar period should not be ignored. The census of 1934 provides a picture of the employment structure and the size of the labor force. According to published data, 359,000 men and 306,400 women were employed, or 68 percent of all males and 51.3 percent of all females of every age. Thus the workforce numbered 666,000.[683] The statistics for the distribution of labor reserves for 1955 state that 356,000 people worked in state or cooperative institutions, 13,300 in *artel*'s, 154,400 on the kolkhoz, and 900 as independent farmers and craftsmen.[684]

This would imply that the size of the workforce from 1934 to 1955 declined by 140,000, while the total population was roughly the same size. However, the statistics for the distribution of workforce did not cover employees of security services, soldiers, and prisoners, and it mentions 139,000 people of working age as working in the household or in the "private economy."[685] "Private economy" in this context meant mostly women working only on private plots, but also those working as petty traders, clandestine workers, or day laborers. In 1955, there was virtually no one of working age who was not working or studying, with the exception of individual housewives married to members of the elite. The same was actually valid for 1934. Internal documents of the 1934 census list namely helping family members, especially on farms. According to this, 70.7 percent of

683 Kaur, *Wirtschaftsstruktur*, p. 18.

684 ERA R-1-5-406, l. 5–6.

685 In the Russian original: "Trudosposobnoe naselenie zaniatoe v domashnem i lichnom khoziaistve" (ibid., l. 6).

females and 71 percent of males were working[686]—nearly 800,000 people altogether. In both years of comparison, a large share of the working-age population was thus in marginal employment or helping family members.

The command economy could not increase the size of the workforce, because it was already at the maximum level in the 1930s. Given that in 1955, more people were studying or participated in other sorts of training or education and more men served in the military, then in reality, the workforce shrank. Even when forced laborers of Soviet camps are not included in the statistics, the available workforce in 1955 was approximately 40,000 less than it had been two decades earlier, and a significant share was in marginal employment. There was no way to expand employment enough to generate extensive growth. In addition, there was a huge loss of human capital in the 1940s, which could not be quickly compensated for by low-skilled immigrants from the "old" republics or by the Stalinist expansion of education. Given the low level of development of Soviet technology, the negative results of the Stalinist restructuring of the economy and the war meant that the economy could not recover quickly.

All in all, the transition to the command economy appeared to be a very painful process that, during the Stalinist era, involved widespread violence. Even 10 years after the end of the war, the prewar level of economic development could not be reached. In other Sovietized and annexed territories like Latvia, Lithuania, or the former eastern Poland, we can presume that the transformation process proceeded in a similar way.

Furthermore, also in the context of the "old" Soviet republics, the example of Estonia might provide food for thought. If a Soviet republic such as Estonia, which suffered relatively modest war damage, required so long for its postwar recovery, then postwar reconstruction in more seriously affected territories like Ukraine would have involved far greater difficulties. Though it was less developed than Western Europe, Estonia was more developed before the war than the Soviet Union was and had benefited from the fact that it did not have to participate in the Soviet experiment until 1940. Though Estonia and Latvia appeared to be model Soviet republics in economic terms starting in the late 1950s, this actually indicated the failure of the Soviet model. For both countries owed their relatively high level of development to their short period of independence and the favorable conditions of the late Russian Empire and not Soviet modernization.

---

686 Evaluation of the census of 1934, ERA R-10-1-29, l. 38. An article in the newspaper *Postimees* (Postman) of May 16, 1942, mentions that before the war, Estonia's employment rate was 10 percent higher than Germany's and 17 percent higher than Italy's.

Given the proof of substantial manipulation of statistics and their methodical shortcomings demonstrated in this case study, the question arises as to how reliable the existing data is for the Stalin-era Soviet Union. Was Soviet agriculture able to recover quickly from collectivization, or were the statistics simply inflated by adding nonexistent cultivated land? In Estonia the latter was the case, and politicians knew that. Which estimate of industrial growth is to be believed? In Estonia, Stalinist industrialization was a fantasy in any case. Is it possible to reconstruct the development of Soviet GDP in a sound way, or do we have to rely on very rough estimates?

Martin Klesment's Estimates of the GDP of the Estonian SSR

Martin Klesment has produced an estimate of the per capita GDP of the Estonian SSR since 1950 based on quantitative output indicators.[687] As mentioned above several times, even quantitative Soviet output statistics could be strongly overstated, as in the case of agriculture since 1950.[688] So Klesment's estimates still seem a bit too high. However, his estimates confirm the general findings of this study and draw a similar picture.

Table 79: Per Capita GDP of the Estonian SSR, 1950–1960, in International Dollars of 1990

Year	GDP	Year	GDP
1950	1,674	1956	2,901
1951	1,844	1957	3,074
1952	1,991	1958	3,377
1953	2,110	1959	3,775
1954	2,253	1960	3,949
1955	2,637		

Source: Klesment, Puur, and Valge, *Childbearing and Macro-Economic Trends in Estonia*, p. 44.

687 This is a multi-author work, but the GDP estimates were done by Klesment. Klesment, Puur, and Valge, *Childbearing and Macro-Economic Trends in Estonia*, p. 44.
688 According to Klesment, agricultural output grew steadily starting in 1950; in reality, however, it shrank. Ibid., 43.

According to Klesment, the Estonian SSR recovered from the war not by 1950, as the Soviets claimed, but only by 1957. In 1950, only 54 percent of the prewar GDP level had been reached. This means that under Soviet conditions (higher investment rates and larger state consumption), real incomes would have recovered only in the mid-1960s. The miracle 6.7-fold industrial growth claimed under Stalin is absolutely not visible in Klesment's data. So Klesment thinks that this, too, was only a fantasy, and quantitative statistics do not confirm such an increase in output. However, his estimates require an annual GDP growth of between 5 and 17 percent in the 1950s. In my view, the qualitative information in the available sources does not allow for the possibility that such growth rates are realistic. The decline of agriculture, the low level of investment (mainly in buildings and not in technology and equipment), and the composition of the workforce with so many underemployed people simply do not allow for such growth rates.

The Situation from the Perspective of the Theory of Deep Transitions

Since 2019 I have participated in a project looking at deep transitions from the perspective of Estonia. The theoretical framework of the project is laid out in a paper by Johan Schot and Laur Kanger.[689] According to them, the first deep transition started about 250 years ago, laying the foundation for modern industrial society. A second deep transition will be necessary to cope with all the environmental damage brought on by our use of fossil energy. The authors define a deep transition as "a series of connected and sustained fundamental transformations of a wide range of socio-technical systems in a similar direction. Examples of this directionality include a move towards increased labour productivity, mechanization, reliance on fossil fuels, resource-intensity, energy-intensity, and reliance on global value chains."[690]

The Stalinist reconstruction of Estonia's economy definitely led to a slower pace of development. Because it was a non-market economy, certain inappropriate developments, like the growth of the oil shale sector, were even enhanced, even

689 Johan Schot and Laur Kanger, "Deep Transitions: Emergence, Acceleration, Stabilization and Directionality," *Research Policy* 47 (2018), pp. 1045–1059; Johan Schot, "Confronting the Second Deep Transition through the Historical Imagination," *Technology and Culture* 57 (2016), pp. 445–456.

690 Schot and Kanger, "Deep Transitions," p. 1045.

if this seemed to be an example of path dependence. One might argue that the Soviet economy followed the general lines of the development of contemporary modern industrial societies. However, it is important to note that the command economy was an aberration of the "normal" path of development, creating even more havoc for the environment and society than modern capitalism. Thus the case of Soviet Estonia under Stalinism does not fit so well into Schot and Kanger's theoretical frame. However, the theory is definitely still of value when applied to a non-capitalist society.

In energy, transport, and communications—the three sectors explored here—under Stalinism, the previously existing social-technical systems continued more or less as under capitalism. There were institutional changes such as the nationalizations, but the overall framework persisted. Concerning energy, development accelerated based on the prewar ideas of the Soviet leadership from 1940/41, while in transport and communications, development was slower due to the dire economic situation.

Alternative Scenarios of Development

Generally speaking, one should be skeptical of counterfactual history, because often it is not much more than speculation. Yet in certain cases it offers interesting food for thought.[691] Concerning the economic development of Estonia and the Stalinist reconstruction, it might indeed be worthwhile to ponder what might have been. It should be clear that on economic questions, the main decisions were made in Moscow, and the political leadership in Tallinn had very little room for decision-making. To evaluate the Stalinist reconstruction, counterfactual history can be useful.

Alternatives in the Soviet Framework

First of all, we need to ask whether Moscow might have chosen a different path for Estonia. The development of the Estonian economy proceeded according to the Soviet model; any other path would have required independence and the status of a people's republic. However, the Baltic republics possessed a special economic status until the beginning of the 1950s. The leadership of the republic had far more leeway in economic questions in the first Soviet year than it did

---

691 See, for example, Niall Ferguson (ed.), *Virtual History: Alternatives and Counterfactuals* (London, Basingstoke, and Oxford, 1997).

later on. Private retail trade and private trades were nationalized after the war or hid in the shadow economy; only then were Soviet prices introduced on all levels, apart from the markets. Private farms dominated agriculture until forced collectivization and disappeared only in the mid-1950s. In early 1947, Andrei Zhdanov said to Nikolai Karotamm that the fate of socialism did not depend on the collectivization of the Estonian peasantry.[692]

The decline of agricultural output was caused to a large extent by the low state procurement prices. Higher prices would have decreased state revenues and thus led to less investment in heavy industry; yet at the same time, they would have represented important incentives for agriculture. As a direct result, food production would have decreased less and thus indirectly improved food supplies for the population. Hunger and malnutrition in the 1940s and poor nutrition in the 1950s was an important cause of low work discipline and productivity. Higher agricultural prices or even market prices would have meant a better economic performance.

Collectivization undoubtedly led to a further decline of agricultural output and decreased the per capita output in this sector tremendously. Actually, collectivization was a large-scale waste of resources. In combination with low procurement prices paid by the state, not only did the peasants' standard of living decline, but it also minimized any motivation to work on the kolkhoz. This is widely accepted in research, yet it is argued that the catastrophe in agriculture resulted in a rural exodus that brought many new workers into industry. This led indirectly to economic growth, because industrial labor was more productive than the collectivized peasants.[693] However, the demographic data in Chapter 3 proves that the rural exodus after collectivization in Estonia was less dramatic than one might expect. New workers for industry were often immigrants, who arrived in larger numbers before collectivization than afterward. A non-collectivized agriculture would also have seen workers leave for factories as a result of increasing productivity and the higher standard of living in towns; perhaps the exodus would simply have been slower. However, agricultural output would not have contracted so much, and the standard of living would have risen faster.

After the war, the regime faced the choice of whether to invest more in light industry or heavy industry. Robert C. Allen argues that the extraordinary

---

692 Elena Zubkova, "Estland unter sowjetischer Herrschaft, 1944–1953: Die Moskauer Perspektive," in Mertelsmann (ed.), *Vom Hitler-Stalin-Pakt*, p. 273.

693 Allen, *From Farm to Factory*, pp. 183–186.

investment in heavy industry in the 1930s was sound, and he supports soft budget constraints.[694] However, in the case of Estonia, there was a huge misallocation of scarce capital in the oil shale industry, which probably would not have been competitive under market conditions. Moreover, investment in heavy industry needed more time to show results. Had there been an accelerated investment in light industry in Estonia, not only could it have raised the standard of living and thus work morale more quickly, but Estonian industry could have delivered scarce consumer goods to other regions, like Leningrad. The consequences of war might have been overcome more quickly.

In the Soviet framework, too, there were alternatives to the path of economic development that Stalin actually took. Later on, Khrushchev and Brezhnev pushed through alternatives to Stalin's ruthless economic policy. As for the likely effects of capitalist elements in the economy, alternatives to the planned economy, increased foreign trade, and much smaller defense expenses, we cannot consider them here.

The Finnish Way

It is worth reflecting on what what might have happened if Estonia's independence had been restored according to the Finnish model. After the war, Finland managed to preserve its democracy and market economy by compromising a degree of its sovereignty. Aware of its vulnerability to its powerful neighbor, it prioritized good relations with Moscow, accepting Soviet influence on its foreign relations and even some of its domestic affairs. Officially Finland belonged to the non-aligned states, but in practice the country had special relations with the USSR.[695]

In this scenario, Estonia would still have gone through the experience of Soviet and Nazi occupation and suffered war damage. However, the population losses would have been smaller, since years of Stalinist terror and postwar malnutrition would not have happened, and many refugees would have returned. Because postwar Europe lacked food and other goods, Estonia would have returned quickly to its prewar position as a net food exporter. Due to international trade, the producers would have received relatively high prices for agrarian goods, expanded production, and imported fertilizer and machinery. There would have

694 Ibid., pp. 160–165.

695 See Ruth Büttner, *Sowjetisierung oder Selbständigkeit? Die sowjetische Finnlandpolitik 1943–1948* (Hamburg, 2001).

been less investment in heavy industry and more in light industry. Undoubtedly, the prewar level of economic performance would have been restored by the first half of the 1950s in Estonia, as it was in Western Europe, along with a substantially higher standard of living and a faster rebuilding of destroyed living space. Whether Estonia's government would have been democratic or authoritarian is of secondary importance in this scenario. Estonia might have chosen a path similar to that of Finland (though probably not quite as successful), especially since international trade would have helped modernize the economy and improve its competitiveness. It is possible that initially, the importance of agriculture would have decreased more slowly. However, by the 1960s, the agrarian sector in our imagined independent Estonia would have employed fewer people than in the actual Soviet Estonia, given the importance of private plots and gardens for supplying the population with basic goods under Soviet conditions. Some parameters might not have changed as quickly at the beginning as they did in reality, such as the degree of urbanization. However, independence based on the Finnish model would definitely have been a better path for the economy than the Stalinist reconstruction.

Neutrality and Independence

If Estonia had not become a pawn in the Hitler-Stalin Pact but had remained independent and neutral in the war, its large population losses would not have happened. Whether the authoritarian regime of Konstantin Päts would have developed like Salazar's Portugal or returned after the war to democracy remains an open question.

In an unoccupied Estonia, it is possible that economic performance would have slightly declined during the war, due to limitations in trade. However, after World War II, under market-economy conditions, resurgent demand, the Marshall Plan, and the boom caused by the Korean War would have quickly led to economic growth and an increasing standard of living. The tempo of development would have depended essentially on Estonia's ability to solve problems of the prewar period, such as subsidies for the oil shale industry, corrupt economic structures symbolized by the economic activities of Päts and general Laidoner, the high degree of state intervention and regulations, and inefficient institutions. If this had happened quickly, Estonia might have been able, due to its human capital, to reach the top rung of developed nations, as Finland did.

Finally

After the above look at counterfactual scenarios, it should be stated that the Stalinist restructuring and the command economy were definitely the worst path of economic development that Estonia could have taken. If we compare Estonia's GDP with that of other European countries for 1938 and for today, the result is sobering. Despite the positive development of the last 28 years, the long-term growth in Estonia was small and compared to many other states that preserved their market economies, Estonia's position actually became worse.[696] The main reason was the path of development prescribed by the Stalinist restructuring. While Western Europe experienced a "golden age of capitalism" from 1950 to 1973, Estonia was dominated by an inefficient economic system that, by the late 1980s, was stumbling toward collapse. The suppression of consumption for the sake of often meaningless investment, along with the forced collectivization, terror, and dictatorship, led to a dead end. From the perspective of the population, the economic policy of Stalin's successors in the Kremlin was an improvement, since those leaders made more efforts to ensure the people a minimum standard of living. However, these policies also failed.

In a paper, Marina Grondona constructs two ideal cases of value systems: one supports economic development, while the other impedes it. Many of those impediments can be found not only in developing countries but also in socialist command economies.[697] The surprising thing about the Soviet economic system was not its eventual collapse but its longevity. Despite the tight corset in which Stalin put the Soviet command economy and the intrinsic deficits, the system proved to be adaptable and endured for a long time.

---

696 Valge, "Uue majanduse lätteil," pp. 2726–2729.

697 See Marina Grondona, "A Cultural Typology of Economic Development," in Laurence E. Harrison and Samuel P. Huntington (eds.), *Culture Matters: How Values Shape Human Progress* (New York, 2000), pp. 44–55.

Bibliography

Primary Sources

Archives

Estonian Literary Museum: Estonian Archive of Cultural History—Eesti Kirjandusmuuseum—Eesti Kultuurilooline Arhiiv (KM-EKLA).

Estonian National Archives—Rahvusarhiiv (RA):

- Branch of Estonian State Archives—Eesti Riigiarhiivi Filiaal (ERAF);

373 - Estonian State Archives—Eesti Riigiarhiiv (ERA).

Estonian National Museum: Archive of the Replies of the Correspondents of the Museum—Eesti Rahva Muuseum—Korrespondentide vastuste arhiiv (ERM-KV).

Russian State Archive of Economics—Rossiiskii gosudarstvennyi arkhiv ekonomiki (RGAE).

Russian State Archive of Socio-Political History—Rossiiskii gosudarstvennyi arkhiv sotsial'no-politicheskoi istorii (RGASPI).

State Archives of the Russian Federation—Gosudarstvennyi arkhiv Rossiiskoi Federatsii (GARF).

Newspapers and Journals

Eesti Kommunist
Eesti Statistika
ENSV Teataja
Pioneer
Postimees
Rahva Hääl
Riigi Teataja
Sirp ja Vasar

Interviews

Interview projects of the Estonian National Museum (Jaanus Plaat) conducted in Narva (August, 2003) and at Lake Peipus (July, 2004 and July, 2005).

Interview project of the Museum of Coastal Swedes (Alar Schönberg) conducted at the Estonian Western coast (2001–2002).

Other Primary Sources and Document Publications

Allik, Hendrik. "Eesti töölisklassi elatustase kodanlikul ajal ja praegu," *Eesti Kommunist* no. 10 (1956).

Angelus, Oskar. *Tuhande valitseja maa: Mälestusi Saksa okupatsiooni ajast 1941-1944* (Stockholm, 1956).

Bol'shaia Sovetskaia Entsiklopediia, vol. 40 (Moscow, 1957).

Brandt, Eduard. *Estonskaia SSR: Razvitie ekonomiki* (Tallinn, 1960).

Brutus, L. "Eesti NSV sotsialistlikust industrialiseerimisest," in *Nõukogude Eesti majandus 1940–1960*, pp. 15–64.

Czollek, Roswitha. *Faschismus und Okkupation: Wirtschaftspolitische Zielsetzung und Praxis des faschistischen deutschen Besatzungsregimes in den baltischen Sowjetrepubliken während des zweiten Weltkrieges* (Berlin, 1974).

Eesti arvudes 1920–1935 (Tallinn, 1937).

Eesti NSV Rahvamajandus (Tallinn, 1957).

Eesti Nõukogude Entsüklopeedia, vol. 2 (Tallinn, 1987).

Eesti riik ja rahvas teises maailmasõjas, 10 vols. (Stockholm, 1954–1962).

Estonskaia SSR za gody sovetskoi vlasti (Tallinn, 1967).

Horm, Arvo. *Eesti elatusstandard* (Tartu, 1940).

Kaganovitš, I. "Materiaalse ja tehnilise baasi arenemine ja tööviljakuse tõus Eesti NSV põlevkivi kaevandavas tööstuses," *Nõukogude Eesti majandus*, pp. 229–249.

Kleist, Peter. *Zwischen Hitler und Stalin 1939–1945* (Bonn, 1950).

Kuuli, Olaf. *Revolutsioon Eestis 1940* (Tallinn, 1980).

Kõll, G.J.K. "Eesti pangaduse ja rahanduse likvideerimine," *Eesti riik ja rahvas teises maailmasõjas*, 3, pp. 129–138.

Laasi, Evald. *Eesti kommunistlik partei ellu viimas V. I. Lenini kooperatsiooni plaani 1944–1950* (Tallinn, 1980).

Leede, E. *Bor'ba partiinich organizatsii Estonskoj SSR za povyshenie proizvodel-tel'nosti truda v promyshlennosti v gody chetvertoi piatiletki* (Tallinn, 1962).

Lepp, A. "Lõpetanute arv õppeasutustes," *Eesti Statistika* (1940), pp. 217–234.

Maasing, Richard et al. (eds.). *Eesti saatusaastad, 1945–1960*, 6 vols. (Stockholm, 1963–1972).

Mäe, Hjalmar. *Kuidas kõik teostus: Minu mälestusi* (Stockholm, 1993).

Mägi, Arvo. "Mis meelde jäänud," *Akadeemia* 9 (1997), pp. 438–439.

Mothander, Carl. *Parunid, eestlased ja enamlased* (Tartu, 2nd edition, 1998).

Narodnoe khoziaistvo SSSR v 1956 godu (Moscow, 1957).

Narodnoe khoziaistvo SSSR za 60 let (Moscow, 1977).

Nurk, H. "Eesti majandus punasel aastal," in *Eesti riik ja rahvas teises maailmasõjas*, vol. 3, p. 108–129.

Nõu, J. "Hoop Eesti põllumajandusele," in *Eesti riik ja rahvas teises maailmasõjas*, vol. 3, pp. 85–98.

Nõukogude Eesti majandus 1940–1960 (Tallinn, 1960).

Pullat, Raimo (ed.). *Istoriia rabochego klassa Sovetskoi Estonii* (Tallinn, 1985).

Purre, Arnold. "Ehitustegevus ja korteriolud," in *Eesti saatusaastad, 1945–1960*, vol. 5 (Stockholm, 1968), pp. 43–71.

Raud, V. "Majanduselust Eestis," in *Eesti riik ja rahvas teises maailmasõjas*, vol. 1 (Stockholm, 1954), pp. 116–131.

Retours d'URSS: Les prisonniers de guerre et les internés français dans les archives soviétiques 1945–1951 (Paris, 2001).

Riigi Statistika Keskbüroo. *I majandusloendus Eestis: Büdžetiuurimus*, booklet 4 (Tallinn, 1940).

———. *I majandusloendus Eestis: Tööstus*, booklet 1 (Tallinn, 1939).

Roos, Jaan. *Läbi punase öö* I (Tartu, 1997).

---. *Läbi punase öö* II (Tartu, 2000).

---. *Läbi punase öö* III (Tartu, 2001).

Rubin, M. "Varumishinnad ja kolhooside rahalised sissetulekud Eesti NSV-s aastail 1950–1960," *Eesti NSV Teaduste Akadeemia Toimetised: Ühiskonnateadused* 30 (1981), pp. 350–361.

Ruus, Vilmar. *Sotsialistlikud ümberkorraldused Eestis 1940–1941* (Tallinn, 1980).

Statistisches Jahrbuch für das Deutsche Reich 1938 (Berlin, 1938).

Sõrmus, R. "Palgaolud tööstuses," *Eesti Statistika* 1940.

TsSU SSSR (ed.), *Narodnoe khoziaistvo SSSR 1922–1972 gg.* (Moscow, 1972).

"Tuuli Jaik," in Rutt Hinrikus (ed.), *Eesti Rava Elulood I* (Tallinn, 2000), pp. 46–56.

Veimer, Arnold. *Kompleksnoe razvitie i spetsializatsija promyshlennosti Estonskogo Ekonomicheskogo Administrativnogo Raiona* (Tallinn, 1961).

Vint, E. "Põllumajanduse areng Nõukogude Eestis," *Nõukogude Eesti majandus 1940–1960*, pp. 65–125.

Walter, E. *Estland, Lettland und Litauen: Das Gesicht der baltischen Staaten* (Berlin, 1939).

Zubkova, Elena (ed.). *Sovetskaia model' ekonomiki: Soiuznyi tsentr i respubliki Pribaltiki 1953 g.—mart 1965 g.* (Moscow, 2015).

Zubkova, Elena et al. (eds.). *Sovetskaia zhizn' 1945–1953* (Moscow, 2003).

25 aastat Nõukogude Eesti (Tallinn, 1965).

Secondary Literature

Aizsilnieks, Arnolds P. "Sovietization of Consumers' Cooperation in the Baltic States," *Journal of Baltic Studies* 5 (1974), pp. 40–50.

Allen, Robert C. *Farm to Factory: A Reinterpretation of the Soviet Industrial Revolution* (Princeton, 2003).

Andrle, Vladimir. *Managerial Power in the Soviet Union* (Westmead, 1976).

——. *Workers in Stalin's Russia: Industrialization and Social Change in a Planned Economy* (New York, 1988).

Angelus, Oskar. "Wirtschaftsfragen im deutschbesetzten Estland 1941–1944," *Acta Baltica* 16 (1976), pp. 147–171.

Ant, Jüri. *Eesti 1939–1941: Rahvast, valitsemist, saatusest* (Tallinn, 1999).

Apor, Balázs, Apor, Péter, and Rees, E.A. (eds.). *The Sovietization of Eastern Europe: New Perspectives on the Postwar Period* (Washington, DC, 2008).

Arnold, Klaus Jochen. *Die Wehrmacht und die Besatzungspolitik in den besetzten Gebieten der Sowjetunion: Kriegführung und Radikalisierung im "Unternehmen Barbarossa"* (Berlin, 2005).

Åslund, Anders. *Building Capitalism: The Transformation of the Former Soviet Bloc* (Cambridge, 2002).

——. *How Capitalism Was Built: The Transformation of Central and Eastern Europe, Russia, and Central Asia* (Cambridge, 2007).

Barber, John D. and Davies, R.W. "Employment and Industrial Labour," in Davies, Harrison, and Wheatcroft (eds.). *The Economic Transformation*, pp. 81–105.

Barber, John and Harrison, Mark (eds.). *The Soviet Defence-Industry Complex from Stalin to Khrushchev* (London and New York, 2000).

Barr, Donald A. "The Ethics of Soviet Medical Practice: Behaviours and Attitudes of Physicians in Soviet Estonia," *Journal of Contemporary Economics* 22 (1996), pp. 33–40.

Bergson, Abram. *The Real National Income of Soviet Russia since 1928* (Cambridge, MA, 1961).

Berliner, Joseph S. *Factory and Manager in the USSR* (Cambridge, MA, 1957).

——. "The Contribution of the Soviet Archives," in Gregory (ed.). *Behind the Façade*, pp. 1–10.

Beyrau, Dietrich. "Nationalsozialistisches Regime und Stalin-System: Ein riskanter Vergleich," *Osteuropa* 50 (2000), pp. 709–720.

Birke, Ernst and Neumann, Rudolf (eds.), *Die Sowjetisierung Ost-Mitteleuropas, 1945–1957: Untersuchungen zu ihrem Ablauf in den einzelnen Ländern*, vol. 1 (Frankfurt and Berlin, 1959).

Birn, Ruth Bettina. *Die Sicherheitspolizei in Estland, 1941–1944: Eine Studie zur Kollaboration im Osten* (Paderborn, 2006).

Bonwetsch, Bernd. "Sowjetunion—Triumph im Elend," in Herbert, Ulrich and Schildt, Axel (eds.), *Kriegsende in Europa* (Essen, 1998), pp. 52–88.

Brüggemann, Karsten. "Der Wiederaufbau Narvas nach 1944 und die Utopie der 'sozialistischen Stadt,'" in Brüggemann, Karsten (ed.). *Narva und die Ostseeregion* (Narva, 2004), pp. 81–103.

Brüggemann, Karsten, Tuchtenhagen, Ralph, and Wilhelmi, Anja (eds.). *Das Baltikum. Geschichte einer europäischen Region*, vol. 3: *Die Staaten Estland, Lettland und Litauen* (Stuttgart, 2020).

Buckley, Cynthia. "The Myth of Managed Migration: Migration Control and Market in the Soviet Period," *Slavic Review* 54 (1995), pp. 896–916.

Burton, Chris. "Minzdrav, Soviet Doctors, and the Policing of Reproduction in the Late Stalinist Years," *Russian History* 27 (2000), pp. 197–221.

Büttner, Ruth. *Sowjetisierung oder Selbständigkeit? Die sowjetische Finnlandpolitik 1943–1948* (Hamburg, 2001).

Carr, E.H. and Davies, R.W. *Foundations of a Planned Economy, 1926–1929*, vol. 1 (London, 1969).

Central Statistical Bureau of Latvia, *The Baltic States before the Second World War: Brief Collection of Statistical Data* (Riga, 2002).

Chapman, Janet G. *Real Wages in Soviet Russia since 1928* (Cambridge, MA, 1963).

Chlevnjuk, Oleg. "Die sowjetische Wirtschaftspolitik im Spätstalinismus und die 'Affäre Gosplan,'" *Osteuropa* 50 (2000), pp. 1031–1047.

Davies, R.W. (ed.), *From Tsarism to the New Economic Policy: Continuity and Change in the Economy of the USSR* (London, 1990).

Davies, R.W., Harrison, Mark, and Wheatcroft, S.G. (eds.), *The Economic Transformation of the Soviet Union, 1913–1945* (Cambridge, 1994).

Dieckmann, Christoph. "Deutsche und litauische Interessen: Grundlinien der Besatzungspolitik in Litauen 1941 bis 1944," in Bartusevičius, Vincas, Tauber, Joachim, and Wette, Wolfram (eds.), *Holocaust in Litauen: Krieg, Judenmorde und Kollaboration im Jahre 1941* (Cologne, 2003), p. 63–76.

Domansky, Elisabeth and Welzer, Harald. "Die allmähliche Tradierung von Geschichte," in Domansky, Elisabeth and Welzer, Harald (eds.). *Eine offene Geschichte* (Tübingen, 1999), pp. 7–25.

Dunmore, Timothy. *The Stalinist Command Economy: The Soviet State Apparatus and Economic Policy 1945–53* (London, 1980).

Duskin, J. Eric. *Stalinist Reconstruction and the Confirmation of a New Elite, 1945–1953* (New York, 2001).

Ellmann, Michael. "The 1947 Soviet Famine and the Entitlement Approach to Famines," *Cambridge Journal of Economics* 24 (2000), pp. 603–630.

Feest, David. "Terror und Gewalt auf dem estnischen Dorf," *Osteuropa* 50 (2000), pp. 656–671.

——. *Zwangskollektivierung im Baltikum: Die Sowjetisierung des estnischen Dorfes 1944–1953* (Cologne, 2007).

Ferguson, Niall (ed.). *Virtual History: Alternatives and Counterfactuals* (London, Basingstoke, and Oxford, 1997).

Field, Mark G. *Doctor and Patient in Soviet Russia* (Cambridge, MA, 1957).

Filtzer, Donald. *Soviet Workers and Stalinist Industrialization: The Formation of Modern Soviet Production Relations, 1928–1941* (London, 1986).

——. "The Standard of Living of Soviet Industrial Workers in the Immediate Postwar Period, 1945–1948," *Europe-Asia Studies* 51 (1999), pp. 1013–1038.

——. *Soviet Workers and Late Stalinism: Labour and the Restoration of the Stalinist System after World War II* (Cambridge, 2002).

——. "Wirtschaft und Gesellschaft der Nachkriegszeit," in Plaggenborg, Stefan (ed.). *Handbuch der Geschichte, Russlands*, vol. 5, part 1 (Stuttgart, 2002), pp. 78–130.

——. *The Hazards of Urban Life in Late Stalinist Russia: Health, Hygiene, and Living Standards, 1943–1953* (Cambridge, 2010).

Fitzpatrick, Sheila. *On Stalin's Team: The Years of Living Dangerously in Soviet Politics* (Princeton, 2015).

——. *Stalin's Peasants: Resistance and Survival in the Russian Village after Collectivization* (New York and Oxford, 1994)

Frank, Odile and Gacic Dobo, Marta. "Historical Records, Mortality Decline and Changing Causes of Death: Estonia and Uruguay in the Twentieth Century," *World Health Statistics Quarterly* 51 (1998), pp. 145–173.

Gaddy, Clifford G. and Ickes, Barry W. *Russia's Virtual Economy* (Washington, DC, 2002).

Ganson, Nicholas. *The Soviet Famine of 1946–1947 in Global and Historical Perspective* (Houndsmills, 2009).

Gestwa, Klaus. "Herrschaft und Technik in der spät- und poststalinistischen Sowjetunion: Machtverhältnisse auf den 'Großbaustellen des Kommunismus,' 1948–1964," *Osteuropa* 51 (2001), pp. 171–197.

——. "Reflektierte Archivarbeit—der 'Königsweg' osteuropäischer Zeitgeschichte," *Osteuropa* 50 (2000), pp. 549–561.

Getty, J. Arch. *Practicing Stalinism: Bolsheviks, Boyars, and the Persistence of Tradition* (New Haven, 2013).

Gilly, Seraina. *Der Nationalstaat im Wandel: Estland im 20. Jahrhundert* (Bern, 2002).

Gorlizki, Yoram and Khlevniuk, Oleg. *Cold Peace: Stalin and the Soviet Ruling Circle, 1945–1953* (Oxford, 2004).

Graziosi, Andres. "The New Soviet Archival Sources: Hypotheses for a Critical Assessment," *Cahiers du monde Russe* 40 (1999), pp. 13–64.

Gregory, Paul R. *Before Command: An Economic History of Russia from Emancipation to the First Five-Year Plan* (Princeton, 1994).

——. (ed.). *Behind the Façade of Stalin's Command Economy* (Stanford, 2001).

---. *The Political Economy of Stalinism: Evidence from the Soviet Secret Archives* (Cambridge, 2004).

——. "The Political Economy of Stalinism: A Bergson Retrospective," *Comparative Economic Studies* 47 (2005), pp. 402–417.

---. "The Dictator's Orders," in Gregory (ed.), *Behind the Façade*, pp. 11–33.

Gregory, Paul R. and Lazarev, Valery (eds.). *The Economics of Forced Labor: The Soviet Gulag* (Stanford, 2003).

Grondona, Marina. "A Cultural Typology of Economic Development," in Harrison, Laurence E. and Huntington, Samuel P. (eds.). *Culture Matters: How Values Shape Human Progress* (New York, 2000), pp. 44–55.

Gross, Jan T. *Revolution from Abroad: The Soviet Conquest of Poland's Western Ukraine and Western Belorussia* (Princeton, 1988).

Guseinov, Rifat. *Istoriia Ekonomiki Rossii* (Moscow, 1999).

Harrison, Mark. *Soviet Planning in Peace and War 1938–1945* (Cambridge, 1985).

——. *Accounting for War: Soviet Production, Employment, and the Defence Burden, 1940–1945* (Cambridge, 1996).

—— (ed.). *The Economics of World War II: Six Great Powers in International Comparison* (Cambridge, 1998).

——. "Prices, Planners, and Producers: An Agency Problem in Soviet Industry, 1928–1950," *Journal of Economic History* 58 (1998), pp. 1032–1062.

——. "Soviet Industrial Production, 1928 to 1955: Real Growth and Hidden Inflation," *Journal of Contemporary Economics* 28 (2000), pp. 134–155.

——. (ed.). *Guns and Rubles: The Defense Industry in the Stalinist State* (New Haven, 2008).

——. "Forging Success: Soviet Managers and Accounting Fraud, 1943 to 1962," *Journal of Comparative Economics* 39 (2011), pp. 43–64.

——. *One Day We Will Live Without Fear: Everyday Lives Under the Soviet Police State* (Stanford, 2016).

---. "Wartime Mobilization: A German Comparison," in Barber and Harrison (eds.). *The Soviet Defense-Industry Complex*, pp. 99–117.

---. "The Soviet Union: The Defeated Victor," in Harrison (ed.), *The Economics of World War II*, pp. 268–301.

Heinzen, James. *The Art of the Bribe: Corruption under Stalin, 1943–1953* (New Haven and London, 2016).

Hessler, Julie. *A Social History of Soviet Trade: Trade Policy, Retail Practices, and Consumption, 1917–1953* (Princeton and Oxford, 2004).

——. "Postwar Normalisation and Its Limits in the USSR: The Case of Trade," *Europe-Asia Studies* 53 (2001), pp. 445–471.

Hiio, Toomas. "Ein kurzer Überblick über Truppenverbände und Kampfhandlungen 1939–1941," in Mertelsmann (ed.). *Vom Hitler-Stalin-Pakt*, pp. 67–95.

Hiio, Toomas, Maripuu, Meelis, and Paavle, Indrek (eds.). *Estonia 1940–1945: Reports of the Estonian International Commission for the Investigation of Crimes Against Humanity* (Tallinn, 2006).

——. *Estonia since 1944: Reports of the Estonian International Commission for the Investigation of Crimes Against Humanity* (Tallinn, 2009).

Hiio, Toomas and Saueauk, Meelis (eds.). *Sovietisation and Violence: The Case of Estonia* (Tartu, 2018).

Hoffmann, Dierk. *Aufbau und Krise der Planwirtschaft: Die Arbeitskräftelenkung in der SBZ/DDR 1945 bis 1963* (Munich, 2002).

Holmberg, Rurik. *Survival of the Unfit: Path Dependence and the Estonian Oil Shale Industry* (Linköping, 2008).

Hosking, Geoffrey. *Russia and the Russians: From Earliest Times to 2001* (London, 2002).

Hunter, Holland and Szyrmer, Janusz M. *Faulty Foundations: Soviet Economic Politics, 1928–1940* (Princeton, 1992).

Igolkin, A.A. and Sokolov, A.K. "Neftianoi shturm i ego posledstviia," *Ekonomicheskaia istoriia: Ezhegodnik* 2006, pp. 385–438.

IMF Country Report No. 07/256. *Republic of Estonia: Selected Issues* (Washington, DC, 2007).

Isberg, Alvin. *Zu den Bedingungen des Befreiers: Kollaboration und Freiheitsstreben in dem von Deutschland besetzten Estland 1941 bis 1944* (Stockholm, 1992).

Isupov, Vladimir A. *Demograficheskie katastrofy i krizisy v Rossii v pervoi polovine XX veka* (Novosibirsk, 2000).

Ivanova, G.M. *GULAG v sisteme totalitarnogo gosudarstva* (Moscow, 1997).

Ivnitskii, N. A. *Kollektivizatsiia i raskulachivanie (nachalo 30-kh godov)* (Moscow, 1996).

Järvesoo, Elmar. "Die Wirtschaft Estlands und deren strukturelle Veränderungen," *Acta Baltica* 9 (1969), pp. 9–45.

---. "Privatunternehmen in der sowjetestnischen Landwirtschaft," *Acta Baltica* 14 (1976), pp. 124–146.

Johansson, Anders, Kangeris, Kārlis, Loit, Aleksander, and Nordlund, Sven (eds.). *Emancipation and Interdependence: The Baltic States as New Entities in the International Economy, 1918–1940* (Uppsala, 1994).

Jones, Jeffrey W. "'People Without a Define Occupation': The Illegal Economy and 'Speculators' in Rostov-on-the-Don, 1943–48," in Raleigh, Donald J. (ed.). *Provincial Landscapes: Local Dimensions of Soviet Power, 1917–1953* (Pittsburgh, 2001), pp. 236–254.

Kaasik, Peeter. *Nõukogude Liidu sõjavangidepoliitika teise maailmasõja ajal ja sõjajärgsetel aastatel: Sõjavangide kinnipidamissüsteem Eesti näitel ja hinnang sõjavangide kohtlemisele rahvusvahelise õiguse järgi* (Tallinn, 2012).

Kaelas, Aleksander. *Das sowjetisch besetzte Estland* (Stockholm, 1958).

Kala, Kulno. "Eesti rahvuslikust koosseisust pärast Teist maailmasõda," *Akadeemia* 4 (1992).

Kala, Kulno and Juursoo, Raul. "Nõukogude Eesti töölisklass 1940–1960," *Eesti NSV Teaduste Akadeemia Toimetised: Ühiskonnateadused* 38 (1989), pp. 131–140, 249–259.

Kahk, Juhan (ed.). *World War II and Soviet Occupation in Estonia: A Damages Report* (Tallinn, 1991).

Kahk, Juhan and Tarvel, Enn. *An Economic History of the Baltic Countries* (Stockholm, 1997).

Karcz, Jerzy F. *The Economics of Communist Agriculture* (Bloomington, 1979).

Katasonov, Valentin. *Ekonomika Stalina* (Moscow, 2016).

Kaur, Uno. *Wirtschaftsstruktur und Wirtschaftspolitik des Freistaates Estland 1918–1940* (Bonn, 1962).

Khanin, G.I. *Ekonomicheskaia istoriia Rossii v noveishee vremia: Ekonomika SSR v kontse 1930-kh gg.–1987* (Novosibirsk, 2008).

Klesment, Martin. "The Estonian Economy under Soviet Rule: A Historiographic Overview," *Journal of Baltic Studies* 40 (2009), pp. 245–264.

Klesment, Martin, Puur, Allan, and Valge, Jaak. *Childbearing and Macro-Economic Trends in Estonia in the XX Century* (Tallinn, 2010).

Kroener, Bernhard R., Müller, Rolf Dieter, and Umbreit, Hans.*Organisation und Mobilisierung des deutschen Machtbereichs: Kriegsverwaltung, Wirtschaft und personelle Ressourcen*, first part, 1939–1941 (Stuttgart, 1988); second part, 1942–1944/45 (Stuttgart, 1999).

Kuddo, Arvo, Kirch, Aksel, and Kirch, Marika. "Demographic Processes in Estonia," in Kahk (ed.), *World War II*, pp. 42–47.

Kukk, Kalev. "Economic Damage," in Salo, Vello (ed.). *The White Book: Losses Inflicted on the Estonian Nation by Occupation Regimes 1940–1991* (Tallinn, 2005), pp. 141–174.

---. "Industry," in Kahk, *World War II*, pp. 63–67.

Kulu, Hill. *Eestlaste tagasiränne 1940–1989* (Tartu, 1997).

Kumo, Kazuhiro. "Soviet Industrial Location: A Re-Examination," *Europe-Asia Studies* 56 (2004), pp. 595–613.

Kütt, Alexander. "Die Wirtschaft Sowjetestlands," *Acta Baltica* 2 (1962), pp. 107–128.

Kuuli, Olaf. *Sotsialistid ja kommunistid Eestis 1917–1991* (Tallinn, 1999).

Kuusik, Argo. "Die deutsche Vernichtungspolitik in Estland 1941–1944," in Mertelsmann (ed.), *Vom Hitler-Stalin-Pakt*, pp. 130–150.

Kõll, Anu Mai. *Peasants on the World Market: Agricultural Experience of Independent Estonia 1919–1939* (Stockholm, 1994).

——. "Economy and Ethnicity in the Hands of the State: Economic Change and the National Question in Twentieth-Century Estonia," in Teichova, Alice, Matis, Herbert, and Pátek, Jaroslav (eds.). *Economic Change and the National Question in Twentieth-Century Europe* (Cambridge, 2000), pp. 357–381.

——. (ed.). *The Baltic Countries under Occupation: Soviet and Nazi Rule 1939–1991* (Stockholm, 2003).

——. *The Village and the Class War: Anti-Kulak Campaign in Estonia* (Budapest, 2013).

——. "Tender Wolves: Identification and Persecution of Kulaks in Viljandimaa, 1940–1949," in Mertelsmann (ed.). *The Sovietization of the Baltic States*, pp. 127–149.

Kõll, Anu Mai and Valge, Jaak. *Economic Nationalism and Industrial Growth: State and Industry in Estonia 1934–39* (Stockholm, 1998).

Kõre, Jüri, Ainsaar, Mare, and Hendrikson, Magnus. "Eluasemepoliitika Eestis 1918–1995," *Akadeemia* 8 (1996), pp. 2133–2163.

Laar, Mart. *War in the Woods: Estonia's Struggle for Survival* (Washington, DC, 1992).

——. "Eesti ja kommunism," in Stéphane Courtois et al. (eds.). *Kommunismi must raamat: Kuriteod. Terror. Repressionid* (Tallinn, 2000), pp. 823–894.

Ledeneva, Alena V. "Between Gift and Commodity: The Phenomenon of *Blat*'," *Cambridge Anthropology* 8 (1996), pp. 43–66.

——. *Russia's Economy of Favours: Blat, Networking and Informal Exchange* (Cambridge, 1998).

Lemberg, Hans. (ed.). *Sowjetisches Modell und nationale Prägung* (Marburg, 1991).

Lemke, Michael. (ed.). *Sowjetisierung oder Eigenständigkeit in der SBZ/DDR (1945–1953)* (Cologne, 1999)

Liivik, Olev, *Eesti NSV Ministrite Nõukogu institutsionaalne areng ja kaadrid 1940–1953* (Tartu, 2014).

——. "EKP Kekskomitee rahvamajanduse valitsemisel," in Tarvel (ed.), *Eestimaa Kommunistliku Partei Keskkomitee*, pp. 209–241.

—— and Tammela, Hiljar (eds.), *Uuemaid aspekte märtsiküüditamise uurimisest* (Tallinn, 2009).

Lillak, Rein. *Eesti põllumajanduse ajalugu* (Tartu, 2003).

Maddison, Angus."Measuring the Performance of a Communist Command Economy: An Assessment of the CIA Estimates for the U.S.S.R.," *Review of Income and Wealth* 44 (1998), pp. 307–323.

——. *The World Economy: A Millenial Perspective* (Paris, 2001).

Maier, Konrad. "Estland in der Zwischenkriegszeit: Die 'Ära des Schweigens,'" in Mertelsmann (ed.). *Vom Hitler-Stalin-Pakt*, pp. 10–30.

Maremäe, Ello. "Sillamäe uraanitehaste asutamine ja töö aastatel 1946–1952 (1973): Eesti düktüoneemakilda kasutamine," *Akadeemia* 12 (2000), pp. 476–512.

Maripuu, Meelis. (ed.). *Sõja ja rahu vahel: Eesti julgeolekupoliitiline olukord sõja alguseni*, vol. 2 (Tallinn, 2010).

——. *Omavalitsuseta omavalitsused: halduskorraldus Eestis Saksa okupatsiooni ajal 1941–1944* (Tartu, 2012).

Maripuu, Meelis and Paavle, Indrek. "Die deutsche Zivilverwaltung in Estland und die estnische Selbstverwaltung," in Mertelsmann (ed.), *Vom Hitler-Stalin-Pakt*, pp. 96–129.

Markevich, Andrei. "Byla li sovetskaia ėkonomika planovoi? Praktika planirovaniia v narkomatakh v 1930-gg," *Ekonomicheskaia istoriia. Ezhegodnik* (2003), pp. 20–54.

——. "Soviet Planning Archives: The Files That Bergson Could Not See," *Comparative Economic Studies* 47 (2005), pp. 364–386.

——. "How Much Control Is Enough? Monitoring and Enforcement under Stalin," *Europe-Asia Studies* 63 (2011), pp. 1449–1468.

Martin, Terry. *The Affirmative Action Empire: Nations and Nationalism in the Soviet Union, 1923–1939* (Ithaca and London, 2001).

Merl, Stephan. *Bauern unter Stalin: Die Formierung des sowjetischen Kolchossystems* (Berlin, 1990).

——. *Sozialer Aufstieg im sowjetischen Kolchossystem der 30er Jahre?* (Berlin, 1990).

Mertelsmann, Marju and Mertelsmann, Olaf. *Landreform in Estland 1919: Die Reaktion von Esten und Deutschbalten* (Hamburg, 2012).

Mertelsmann, Olaf. "Did Estonian Industry Really Grow So Fast after the War? Soviet Statistics and a More Realistic Approach," *The Soviet Occupation Regime in the Baltic States 1944–1959* (Riga, 2003), pp. 232–242.

--- (ed.). *The Sovietization of the Baltic States, 1940–1956* (Tartu, 2003).

——. "Estonian Moonshine in the 1940s," *Humanitāro Zinātņu Vēstnesis* (2004), no. 6, pp. 86–95.

---. "How the Russians Turned into the Image of the 'National Enemy' of the Estonians," *Pro Ethnologia* (2005), no. 19, pp. 43–58.

--- (ed.), *Vom Hitler-Stalin-Pakt bis zu Stalins Tod: Estland 1939–1953* (Hamburg, 2005).

---. *Der stalinistische Umbau in Estland: Von der Markt- zur Kommandowirtschaft* (Hamburg, 2006).

---. "Die Arbeiter des estnischen Ölschieferbeckens—eine Industrieregion des Stalinismus," *Mitteilungsblatt des Instituts für soziale Bewegungen* (2007), no. 37, pp. 113–131.

---. "Mehrdimensionale Arbeitswelten als Überlebensstrategie während der stalinistischen Industrialisierung am Beispiel Estlands," in Schmidt, Burghart and Hogeforster, Jürgen (eds.). *Mehrdimensionale Arbeitswelten im baltischen Raum* (Hamburg, 2007), pp. 94–106

---. "Living on a Stalinist Kolkhoz: Peasant Survival Strategies in Estonia," *Humanitāro Zinātņu Vēstnesis* (2009), no. 15, pp. 83–94.

---. "Searching for Reasons of the Forced Collectivization in the Baltic Republics," in Ērglis, Dzintars (ed.). *Occupation Regime in the Baltic States 1940–1991* (Riga, 2009), pp. 634–640.

---. "The Cost of Transition from Market to Command Economy: The Case of Estonia," *Revista Română pentru Studii Baltice și Nordice* 1 (2009), pp. 8–31.

---. "Transition to Command Economy and Economic Exploitation: The Experience of Estonia 1940–1941," in Ērglis, Dzintars (ed.). *History of the Baltic Region of the 1940s–1980s* (Riga, 2009), pp. 349–375.

---. "Keskmine oodatav eluiga stalinismiaegses Eestis," *Ajalooline Ajakiri* (2010), no. 1, pp. 105–110.

---. "Poslevoennoe vosstanovlenie v pribalttiiskikh respublikakh na primere Estonii," in Fieseler, Beate and Moine, Nathalie (eds.). *Pobeditely i pobezhdennye: Ot voiny k miru: SSSR, Frantsiia, Velikobritanniia, SShA* (1941–1950) (Moscow, 2010), pp. 213–226.

——. "Creating Malnutrition in an Agricultural Surplus Area: Stalinist Food Policy in Newly Acquired Territory," in Middel, Matthias l and Wemheuer, Feliks (eds.). *Hunger and Scarcity under State-Socialism* (Leipzig, 2012), pp. 225–251.

---. "Das 'kleinere Übel'? Das Generalkommissariat Estland im estnischen Vergangenheitsdiskurs," in Lehmann, Sebastian, Bohn, Rainer, and Danker, Uwe (eds.). *Reichskommissariat Ostland: Tatort und Erinnerungsort* (Paderborn, 2012), pp. 349–366.

--- (ed.). *The Baltic States under Stalinist Rule* (Cologne, 2016).

---. "Die Herausbildung des Sonderstatus der Nordostregion innerhalb der Estnischen SSR," in Brüggemann (ed.). *Narva und die Ostseergion*, pp. 105–121.

---. "The Economic Impact of the Early Cold War on the Estonian SSR," in Tannberg (ed.). *Behind the Iron Curtain*, pp. 119–137.

---. "Was There a Stalinist Industrialization in the Baltic Republics? Estonia—An Example," in Mertelsmann (ed.), *The Sovietization*, pp. 151–170.

Mertelsmann, Olaf and Rahi-Tamm, Aigi. "Cleansing and Compromise: The Estonian SSR in 1944–1945," *Cahiers du Monde Russe* 49 (2008), pp. 319–340.

——. "Soviet Mass Violence in Estonia Revisited", *Journal of Genocide Research* 11 (2009), pp. 307–322.

Mises, Ludwig von. *Die Gemeinwirtschaft: Untersuchungen über den Sozialismus* (Jena, 1922).

Misiunas, Romuald and Taagepera, Rein. *The Baltic States: Years of Dependence 1940–1990* (London, 1993).

Moskoff, William. *The Bread of Affliction: The Food Supply in the USSR During World War II* (Cambridge, 1990).

Mrowczynski, Rafael. "Gordische Knoten: Verwaltungshierarchien und Netzwerke in der UdSSR," *Osteuropa* 55 (2005), no. 10, pp. 31–46.

Myllyniemi, Seppo. *Die Neuordnung der baltischen Länder 1941–1944: Zum nationalsozialistischen Inhalt der deutschen Besatzungspolitik* (Helsinki, 1973).

North, Douglass C. *Institutions, Institutional Change and Economic Performance* (Cambridge, 1990), pp. 32–33.

Nove, Alec. *Das sowjetische Wirtschaftssystem* (Baden-Baden, 1980).

——. *An Economic History of the USSR 1917–1991* (London, 1992).

Nutter, Warren G. *Growth of Industrial Production in the Soviet Union* (Princeton, 1962).

Osokina, Elena. "Tsena 'bol'shogo skachka,'" in Afanas'ev, Iurii (ed.). *Sovetskoe Obshchestvo: Vozniknovenie, razvite, istoricheskii final*, vol. 1 (Moscow, 1997), pp. 205–243.

---. *Za fassadom "stalinskogo izobiliia": Raspredelenie i rynok v snabzhenii naseleniia v gody industrializatsii 1927–1941* (Moscow, 1998).

Õispuu, Leo (ed.). *Nõukogude Okupatsioonivõimu poliitilised arreteerimised Eestis*, vol. 2 (Tallinn, 1998).

Paavle, Indrek. "Grain and Eggs in the Service of the Regime: Coercive Procurement in Estonian Villages in the 1940s," in Hiio and Saueauk (eds.), *Sovietisation and Violence*, pp. 235–253

Pajur, Ago and Tannberg, Tõnu (eds.). *Eesti ajalugu VI: Vabadussõjast taasiseseisvumiseni* (Tartu, 2005).

Parming, Tönu and Järvesoo, Elmar (eds.), *A Case Study of a Soviet Republic: The Estonian SSR* (Boulder CO, 1978).

Penter, Tanja. *Kohle für Stalin und Hitler: Arbeiten und Leben im Donbass 1929 bis 1953* (Essen, 2010).

Pihlamägi, Maie. Maie Pihlamägi. "Eesti tööstus murrangulisel 1940–1941. aastal: turumajanduselt plaanimajandusele," *Acta Historica Tallinnensia* 1 (1997), pp. 152–172.

---. *Eesti industrialiseerimine 1870–1940* (Tallinn, 1999).

---. *Väikeriik maailmaturul: Eesti väliskaubandus 1918–1940* (Tallinn, 2004).

---. "Esimene nõukogude aasta Eesti majanduses: 1940–1941," *Acta Historica Tallinnensia* 9 (2005), pp. 187–209.

---. "Industry of the Estonian SSR in the Light of the First Post-War Five-Year Plan (1946–1950)," *Acta Historica Tallinnensia* 15 (2010), pp. 1–18.

——. "Die Sowjetisierung der Industrie Estlands unter dem ersten Fünfjahresplan (1946–1950)," in Iber, Walter M. and Ruggenthaler, Peter (eds.). *Stalins Wirtschaftspolitik an der sowjetischen Peripherie: Ein Überblick auf der Basis sowjetischer und osteuropäischer Quellen* (Innsbruck-Vienna-Bozen, 2011), pp. 211—241.

Pikhoia, Rudol'f G. *Sovetskii Soius: Istoriia vlasti 1945–1991* (Novosibirsk, 2000).

Pipes, Richard. *Die Russische Revolution*, vol. 2 (Berlin, 1992).

Polian, Pavel. *Zhertvy dvuch diktatur: Ostarbeitery i voennoplennye v Tret'em Reikhe i ikh repatriatsiia* (Moscow, 1996).

Popov, Vassilii P. *Ekonomicheskaia politika sovetskogo gosudarstvo 1946–1953 gg.* (Moscow-Tambov, 2000).

Purre, Arnold. *Soviet Farming Failure Hits Estonia* (Stockholm, 1964).

——. "Estlands Industrie unter sowjetischer Herrschaft," *Acta Baltica* 9 (1969), pp. 47–80.

Rahi, Aigi. *1949. aasta märtsiküüditamine Tartu linnas ja maakonnas* (Tartu, 1998).

Rahi-Tamm, Aigi. "Deportation und Verfolgung in Estland 1940–1953," in Mertelsmann (ed.), *Vom Hitler-Stalin-Pakt*, pp. 211–237.

——. *Teise maailmasõja järgsed massirepressioonid Eestis: allikad ja uurimisseis* (Tartu, 2004).

Rauch, Georg von. *Geschichte der baltischen Staaten* (Stuttgart, 1970).

Raun, Toivo U. *Estonia and the Estonians* (Stanford, 2001).

Reinvelt, Riina. *Ingeri elud ja lood: Kultuurianalüütiline eluloouurimus* (Tartu, 2002).

Ritschl, Albrecht. *Quantitative Wirtschaftsgeschichte der DDR* (Berlin, 1995).

Roesler, Joerg. *Die Herausbildung der sozialistischen Planwirtschaft in der DDR* (Berlin, 1978).

Ruchniewicz, Małgorzata. *Das Ende der Bauernwelt: Die Sowjetisierung des westweißrussischen Dorfes 1944–1953* (Göttingen, 2015).

Ruusmann, Ants. "Eesti agraarajaloo allikad aastail 1945–1950: Kasutatavus uurimustes," in Enn Tarvel (ed.), *Ajaloolise tõe otsinguil* (Tallinn, 1999), pp. 73–87.

Salo, Vello (ed.). *The White Book: Losses Inflicted on the Estonian Nation by Occupation Regimes 1940–1991* (Tallinn, 2005).

Saueauk, Meelis. *Propaganda ja terror: Nõukogude julgeolekuorganid ja Eestimaa Kommunistlik Partei Eesti sovetiseerimisel 1944–1953* (Tallinn, 2015).

Schot, Johan. "Confronting the Second Deep Transition through the Historical Imagination," *Technology and Culture* 57 (2016), pp. 445–456.

Schot, Johan and Kanger, Laur. "Deep Transitions: Emergence, Acceleration, Stabilization and Directionality," *Research Policy* 47 (2018), pp. 1045–1059.

Seckendorf, Martin. "Deutsche Baltikumskonzeption 1941–1944 im Spiegel von Dokumenten der zivilen Okkupationsverwaltung. Eine Dokumentation," *1999* 16 (2001), pp. 140–172.

Simonov, Nikolai S. *Voenno-promyshlennyi kompleks SSSR v 20–50-e gody* (Moscow, 1996).

Steiner, André. *Von Plan zu Plan: Eine Wirtschaftsgeschichte der DDR* (Munich, 2004).

Stern, Karl. *Mittetariifsete kaubandusmeetmete rakendamine 1930. aastatel Eesti Vabariigi näitel* (Tartu, 2017).

Taagepera, Rein. "Soviet Collectivization of Estonian Agriculture: The Deportation Phase," *Soviet Studies* 32 (1980), pp. 379–397.

---. "Soviet Collectivization of Estonian Agriculture: The Taxation Phase," *Journal of Baltic Studies* 10 (1979), pp. 263–282.

Tammaru, Tiit. *Venelased Eestis: Ränne ja kohanemine* (Tallinn, 1999).

Tannberg, Tõnu. *Sõja ja rahu vahel: Eesti julgeolekupoliitika 1940. aastani*, vol. 1 (Tallinn, 2004).

--- (ed.). *Eesti NSV aastatel 1940–1953: Sovetiseerimise mehhanismid ja tagajärjed Nõukogude Liidu ja Ida-Euroopa arengute kontekstis* (Tartu, 2007).

—— (ed.). *Behind the Iron Curtain: Soviet Estonia in the Era of the Cold War* (Frankfurt, 2015).

--- (ed.). *Nõukogude Eesti külma sõja ajal* (Tartu, 2015).

Tarvel, Enn (ed.). *Eestimaa Kommunistliku Partei Keskkomitee organisatsiooniline struktuur 1940–1991* (Tallinn, 2002).

Tiit, Ene. "Eesti rahvastik ja selle probleemid," *Akadeemia* 5 (1993).

Toivonen, Timo. "Classes, Countries and Consumption Between the World Wars: A Comparison of the Structure of Expenditure in Estonia, Finland and Sweden in the 1920s and 1930s," *Acta Sociologia* 35 (1992), pp. 219–233.

Tomson, Ene. *Eesti majandusajalugu 20. sajandil* (Tartu, 1998).

Tooze, J. Adam. *Statistics and the German State, 1900–1945: The Making of Modern Economic Knowledge* (Cambridge, 2001).

Umbreit, Hans. "Auf dem Weg zur Kontinentalherrschaft," in Kroener, Müller, and Umbreit (eds.), *Organisation und Mobilierung des deutschen Machtbereichs*, first part, pp. 1–345.

——. "Die deutsche Herrschaft in den 'germanischen' Ländern 1942–1945," in Kroener, Müller, and Umbreit (eds), *Organisation und Mobilierung des deutschen Machtbereichs*, second part, p. 1–272.

Vaimann, Toomas and Risthein, Endel. *Eesti energeetika 100 aastat* (Tallinn, 2018).

Valge, Jaak. "Eesti Panga rahakraanide kallal," *Tuna* 5 (2002), no. 3, pp. 28–39.

---. "Riiklik põlevkivitööstuse majandustingimused ja -tulemused 1920. ja 1930. aastatel," *Akadeemia* 7 (1995), pp. 1712–1740, 1929–1949.

---. *Lahtirakendamine: Eesti Vabariigi majanduse stabiliseerimine 1918–1924* (Tallinn, 2003).

---. "Uue majanduse lätteil: Eest sisemajanduse kogutoodang aastatel 1923–1938," *Akadeemia* 15 (2003), pp. 2202–2228, 2443–2486, 2712–2735.

---. "Es ist nicht alles Gold, was glänzt: Das Gold der Bolschewiki in Estland und die Folgen," in Mertelsmann, Olaf (ed.). *Estland und Russland: Aspekte der Beziehungen beider Länder* (Hamburg, 2005).

——. *Breaking away from Russia: Economic Stabilization in Estonia 1918–1924* (Stockholm, 2006).

Verbitskaia, O.M. *Rossiiskoe krest'ianstvo: ot Stalina k Khrushkhevu* (Moscow, 1992).

Viola, Lynne. *Peasant Rebels under Stalin: Collectivization and the Culture of Peasant Resistance* (New York and Oxford, 1996).

Vseviov, David. *Kirde-Eesti urbaanse anomaalia kujunemine ning struktuur pärast Teist maailmasõda* (Tallinn, 2002).

Weiner, Amir. *Making Sense of War: The Second World War and the Fate of the Bolshevik Revolution* (Princeton, 2001).

Weiss, Hellmuth. "Die baltischen Staaten," in Birke and Neumann (eds.). *Die Sowjetisierung Ost-Mitteleuropas*, pp. 21–64.

Weiss-Wendt, Anton. *Murder without Hatred: Estonians and the Holocaust* (Syracuse, 2009).

Wheatcroft, Stephen G. "The Great Leap Upwards," *Slavic Review* 58 (1999), pp. 27–60.

Wheatcroft, S.G. and Davies, R.W. "The Crooked Mirror of Soviet Economic Statistics," in Davies, Harrison, and Wheatcroft (eds.), *The Economic Transformation*, pp. 24–37.

Wischerding, Clemens and Nieberling, Anne. *Die institutionelle Revolution: Eine Einführung in die deutsche Wirtschaftsgeschichte des 19. und 20. Jahrhunderts* (Stuttgart, 2004).

Zaleski, Eugène. *Stalinist Planning for Economic Growth, 1933–1952* (Chapel Hill, 1980).

Zank, Wolfgang. *Wirtschaft und Arbeit in Ostdeutschland 1945–1949: Probleme des Wiederaufbaus in der Sowjetischen Besatzungszone Deutschlands* (Munich, 1987).

Zelenin, E. "Agrarnaja politika N. S. Khrushcheva i sel'skoe khoziaistvo strany," *Otechestvennaia istoriia* 9 (2000), no. 1, pp. 76–93.

Zetterberg, Seppo. *Eesti ajalugu* (Tallinn, 2009).

Zima, V.F. *Golod v SSSR 1946–1947 godov: proiskhodeshchdenie i posledstviia* (Moscow, 1996).

Zubkova, Elena. "Estland unter sowjetischer Herrschaft, 1944–1953: Die Moskauer Perspektive," in Mertelsmann (ed.). *Vom Hitler-Stalin-Pakt*, pp. 266–281.

---. "Kaderpolitik und Säuberungen in der KPdSU (1945–1953)," in Weber, Hermann and Mählert, Ulrich (eds.). *Terror: Stalinistische Parteisäuberungen 1936–1953* (Paderborn, 1998), pp. 187–236.

---. *Russia after the War: Hopes, Illusions and Disappointments, 1945–1957* (Armonk, NY, and London, 1998).

---. "Fenomen 'mestnogo natsionalizma': 'estonskoe delo' 1949–1952 godov v kontekste sovetizatsii Baltii," *Otechestvennaia istoriia* 10 (2001), no. 3, pp. 89–102.

---. *Pribaltika i Kreml' 1940–1953* (Moscow, 2008).

Zunde, Pranas. *Die Landwirtschaft Sowjetlitauen* (Marburg, 1962).

Tartu Historical Studies

Edited by Eero Medijainen and Olaf Mertelsmann

Vol. 1 Olaf Mertelsmann (ed.): Central and Eastern European Media under Dictatorial Rule and in the Early Cold War. 2011.

Vol. 2 Olaf Mertelsmann: Everyday Life in Stalinist Estonia. 2012.

Vol. 3 Olaf Mertelsmann / Kaarel Piirimäe (eds.): The Baltic Sea Region and the Cold War. 2012.

Vol. 4 James S. Corum / Olaf Mertelsmann / Kaarel Piirimäe (eds.): The Second World War and the Baltic States. 2014.

Vol. 5 Tõnu Tannberg (ed.): Behind the Iron Curtain. Soviet Estonia in the Era of the Cold War. 2015.

Vol. 6 Kaarel Piirimäe / Olaf Mertelsmann (eds.): The Baltic States and the End of the Cold War. 2018.

Vol. 7 Olaf Mertelsmann: Stalinist Restructuring in Estonia. From Market to Command Economy. 2024.

www.peterlang.com

www.ingramcontent.com/pod-product-compliance
Ingram Content Group UK Ltd.
Pitfield, Milton Keynes, MK11 3LW, UK
UKHW021009120926
8556IPUK00029B/284

9 783631 919163